Humanizing the Workplace

Humanizing the Workplace

Roy P. Fairfield, editor

P̃ Prometheus Books
Buffalo, New York 14215

Publication of this book was made possible, in part, by a grant
from the Ford Foundation.

Published by Prometheus Books
923 Kensington Avenue, Buffalo, New York 14215

Library of Congress Catalog Card Number 74-84280
ISBN 0-87975-036-7

Printed in the United States of America

°Index

This book is dedicated

to

. . . any person or organization
really working to humanize
work.

Acknowledgments

No one's memory is long enough to plumb the depths of debt for a book such as this, but a few memories are crystal clear.

The authors were most cooperative in responding to all of our requests for further information or clarification.

Colleagues who assisted with substantive issues in one way or another—through discussion, the loan of materials, or suggestions for readings—were Robert Schrank, Otto Krash, Gordon Keller, and John Pool.

Editorial colleagues who did yeoman work in preparing the volume for publication were Paul Kurtz, Cynthia Dwyer, Doris Doyle, Broady Richardson, and Rita Wilson. My gratitude also goes to the production staff, Floyd Wong and Rose Giunta.

It is also important to pay tribute to members of the Union Graduate School supporting staff who helped in so many ways to make the book possible, especially Betty Jo Pool and Debbie Miller. Also a word of appreciation goes to other people at *The Humanist* and the Union Graduate School who put up with my constant discussion of the issues and my hopes pertaining to humanizing work.

Thanks, too, to the Ford Foundation for a travel grant enabling me to reach into some previously unexplored corners of the problem.

And finally, to Maryllyn Rumery Fairfield goes the patience award for tolerating me while I worked on this project.

Contents

Some Specifics

New Directions

Introduction

Roy P. Fairfield

One spring day about 1950, while reading about work and automation, I looked out into the blooming forsythia and fantasized a cyclical view of history: Long ago our ancestors were hunters and fishers, but gradually they put animals to work for them; then they put slaves and other citizens to work; they went on to invent machines to work for them; and finally, at midcentury, it seems that machines are about to produce machines via automation, so that future generations will be able to close the circle and go hunting and fishing again.

One spring day more recently when I told a former colleague and chairman of a major department in a neighboring state university that I was editing a book on humanizing work, he nearly split with sarcastic laughter. "How in hell," he exclaimed, "could you *ever* humanize *my* work?" I chuckled, for we had just spent several hours talking about the hopeless morass that seems to constitute the bureaucracy of the multiversity, as well as the petty politics, the threats to one's job in a constricting educational scene, the tenure hooks on which so many persons hang, in a day when tenure no longer is so sacred, the medieval fiefdoms that departments in major universities seem to be—in short, a kind of Kafkaesque nightmare. My response to my friend was, "Maybe the test of your capacity to humanize *your* work is to know when you can no longer change the conditions, and *get out!*"

But, of course, the vast majority of working men and women in the United States (and the number would be larger in the world context) do not have the luxury of working themselves out of a job or finding another more congenial to their wishes and way of life. And yet, it is my hunch that many, many people do not move from one job to another or "make a difference" in establishing or changing work conditions because they *think* they cannot or they do not know what the alternatives might be—or, they are simply trapped in their own inertia.

Yet few sensitive persons reading in the popular press about automobile assembly lines or the now-famous Lordstown Vega plant near Youngstown, Ohio, or watching a telecast on white-collar work can deny that there is the monumental task of "turning America around" in such a way that the rising tide of absenteeism, dissatisfaction, and alienation from job (and perhaps the larger community too) can be met. Anybody truly concerned about these problems will wish to read such definitive books as Harold L. Sheppard and Neal Q. Herrick's *Where Have All The Robots Gone?* or the controversial Department of Health, Education and Welfare report, *Work in America*. A much more existential view, which is both delightful reading and an insightful reference, can be found in Studs Terkel's *Working*, a monumental compilation of workers' life stories. Terkel does not offer a comprehensive statistical or analytical picture but gives us instead the hopes, struggles, alienations, and conflicts of workers from every strata of life. And there but for the grace of one's own place in space and time goes the neighboring carpenter, one's cousin's daughter, and persons (as types and individuals) with whom one bumps shoulders throughout all life's journey.

In short, there is as much focus on work today for seemingly as many reasons as there are persons. Unfortunately, despite many statistical and empirical analyses to the contrary, a very large proportion of humans perceive work negatively in a country that rushes from one crisis to another, from one complex of crises to ten—all etched in our minds almost instantly by our media. It is not surprising that Studs Terkel opens his book by saying, "This book, being about work, is, by its very nature, about *violence*—to the spirit as well as to the body. It is about ulcers as well as accidents, about shouting matches as well as fistfights, about nervous breakdowns as well as kicking the dog around. It is, above all (or *beneath* all), about *daily humiliations*. To survive the day is triumph enough for the *walking wounded* among the great many of us."[1] [Emphasis added—RPF]

Such negativity, such resignation, such alienation deserve attention. Also, in the context of the American saying, "The difficult we do immediately, the impossible takes a little longer," we may rightly ask, "Who is *doing* what, how, where and when?" This book is devoted to discussing that question, to one degree or another.

In approaching some of the problems the workplace presents in the 1970s, it is all too tempting to resort to a romantic illusion of what work once was, despite the evidence that work, like the poor, "ye have with you always!" It is sometimes argued that once upon a time work was human, when men and women bent themselves to the soil, the potter's wheel, or to the pen or needle with some sense of self-determination. But along came the machine to extend, even as it maimed, the human hand in getting work done. Then men invented the factory to replace the cottage system in organizing work. And the wheels turned faster, until humans were run by machines rather than being their masters.

To complete that line of thinking: It is argued that we are riding the main currents of this historical trend. Human satisfactions have become subordinate to production. Humans have become alienated from their natural heritage, from their neighborhoods (as they repair to factory or office), from their work, and hence from themselves. It is not difficult to trace many of the theories of socialism back to Karl Marx, who built his philosophical structure on the foundation of such alienation. In fact, many views of social reconstruction, whether reformist or radical, are built on the observation that humans are being cut from the very roots that nourish them.

Drawing such swift strokes on an historical canvas has value, but two questions remain: Is this an accurate picture? And for whom? If, as Carl Jung allegedly claimed, 95 percent of all perception is projection, then an artist can paint any picture he or she wishes and there is no disputing the haste or taste with which it is done. If on the other hand one relies upon the social-science researcher for the picture, then the rules are different. The data must be structured in the context of the method chosen to present it. As Studs Terkel's book suggests, any worker may be listened to, since his or her perceptions may fit a larger typology when the worker defines himself or herself in a role such as bookbinder, priest, airline stewardess, or the thousands of other occupations to which humans are heir or aspire. Hence any reader must beware of the assumptions undergirding observation. One person's burdensome work may be another's releasing joy, for the human spirit works in strange ways between euphoria and martyrdom.

In many respects, of course, the problem of work and humanizing the workplace is really the human task of responding creatively to existence in the cosmos. It is the problem of living. And this naturally conjures up a host of questions and a host of answers. If, for instance, one assumes that there is a God and that God put humans on earth to do His work, then how could the believer feel disenchanted with what-

ever God directed a person to do? Minor griping might ensue, but surely reacting violently, as Terkel suggests in his introductory statement,
would be sacrilegious and taboo. Millions upon millions in human
history have lived their lives unquestioningly in precisely that context.
And the world's great literature is full of both the agony and the anguish of that cosmic adjustment.

If, on the other hand, one's culture, whether a small isolated tribe or
a huge nation-state, clearly delineates work as furthering societal ends,
then work may be perceived as constructive and promoting individual
esteem, no matter what pain is involved. Here again, the historical record is crystal clear. Millions upon millions of humans have worked at
some of the most onerous tasks imaginable to perpetuate their
society's values, both tangible and intangible. Today, for instance,
more than a billion of the world's people are devoted to perpetuating
Marxist-Leninist-Maoist values through hard work. Unfortunately, in
the past there were no Harold Sheppards, Neal Herricks, or Studs Ter-
kels to capture the comments of Egyptian slaves hauling stones to the
Great Pyramids or of French peasants doing the same at Chartres; and
only recently have anthropologists begun to give us pictures of what it
is like to grow up in Samoa or to be a pygmy in the African rain for-
est. How powerful are cultural norms was driven home to me one day in
Greece while driving through the Thessaly wheatfields. There in the
one-hundred-degree heat was an old woman, dressed entirely in black,
sitting on a flat, plank drag and being hauled around a tiny threshing
floor by her gray donkey. Directly across the asphalt highway was a
powerful threshing machine, delivering in seconds what it was taking
her hours to accomplish. In my own naive way I turned to a Greek
friend in the car to inquire, "Why doesn't she carry her wheat across
the road and let the thresher do it?" He quickly shot back with a chuckle,
"If she weren't doing that, what would she be doing?" A typical Greek-
male response, but an attitude centuries old in many cultures.

THE DILEMMA OF AFFLUENCE

In many ways, as most contemporary commentary on work suggests,
ours is the dilemma of affluence—the affluence of money, the affluence of knowledge, the affluence of alternatives. In many respects it is
the dilemma of choice, and choosing is hard. While the ex-heroin-ad-
dict on an assembly line may be grateful for his job, and though the
monotony of one life may be better than the monotony of another, the
American value structure in which that ex-addict lives provides him
with the notion that he *can* choose, if he wants to. And even if he
eventually becomes aware that his range of choice is limited, he may

cherish illusions or fantasies of the possible. This is at once the agony and the ecstasy of the American Dream—for persons in all walks of life. And in a society such as ours, where some people (some blacks, Puerto Ricans, Chicanos, poor whites, and Indians) do make it, it is tempting to cherish the illusion that *all* can make it, even though the notion is contradicted by overwhelming statistical evidence. But television's promises are phenomenological, not logical or statistical; imagination is not limited to off-job hours. Give us this day, our daily fantasy. So, is it any wonder that a worker on the assembly line or "manning" an office desk or whatever may be ambivalent about his or her work? If each day is like every other day, is it so surprising that monotony and boredom are standard mind-sets? If one cannot identify with a product or a process in his or her work, if one cannot distinguish one day from another, is one much different from the tubercular hero in Thomas Mann's *Magic Mountain*, who loses his identity with other humans because all time ran into a blur?

As several authors in this anthology suggest, it's the identifying with a product, a process, or a group of persons engaged in a common endeavor (even if it is collecting garbage), as well as the worker's having a sense that somebody cares about what he does, that seems so critical in humanizing workplaces. The tragedy is, we learned that lesson nearly half a century ago at the Hawthorne plant of Western Electric, where a group of women were more satisfied and productive when they were part of an exciting experiment, no matter how little work conditions were altered. It was important that they were participating, not so terribly important what happened. As Ed Walsh points out in his observations about garbagemen, the standard stereotyping about dirty work seems to vanish under the light of evidence that his garbagemen friends found self-esteem, even on that job. And, as M. H. Ross argues so eloquently in discussing coal miners, one must look at the total context in which they have their being and not merely describe as "horrible" the darkness and dirtiness of their jobs—though the unsafe conditions that still exist in many mines *are* horrible.

If it were an inexorable fact that human beings were forever condemned to "lousy" jobs, to eternal monotony, to being cut off from their sister and brother workers (as they are on auto assembly lines), then it would be an act of mercy to employ *Brave New World* conditioning methods so that humans could be "de-person-ized" or freed from the illusion that they can expect more from a job than the job can possibly give. In this eventuality, it might be wise to condition ourselves to accept the values of "Alexander Zuckerkandl," namely, that the object of life is to get through it and that we must get through it without pain or pleasure.[2]

A CLIMATE OF HOPE

But despite monotonous assembly lines, seemingly sterile office atmospheres, the bureaucratic relationships of a "service society," the automaticity of a technocratic world, and a seemingly homogenous consumer society—despite all these trends, there does seem to be hope for humanizing work, in both reformist and radical contexts. Surely, as Alan Gartner and Frank Riessman observe,[3] work conditions are going to be different as we evolve a "service society," where humans will devote more energy to humans rather than to making products; to an exponential degree, changing work patterns, satisfactions, and configurations are going to change expectations and self-concepts. Third Force psychology, wherein a major objective of life is self-actualization, is working its "miraculous" ways. Too, in the context of the service society, as Andre Gorz points out so well, scientific and cultural industries will not be bureaucratized and hence should always serve as a yeast in the work force. Even in a welfare-warfare society, such as America has been for two generations, social-security devices do provide alternatives for some fairly large segments of the population. This is not to suggest that many nonworkers do not become demeaned by this route; nor is it to suggest that many real concerns about such dehumanization should be forgotten. It *is* to suggest that my cousin's boyhood objective in 1930—namely, "to have two six-month vacations per year, with pay"— is closer to realization for many persons today, persons who must find new definitions of work.

WORK AND/OR JOBS?

Thorstein Veblen was an eloquent advocate of the "instinct of workmanship." Everybody presumably had it. Hence, for half a century we have had his observations and concepts as referents. We have also had the concept of craftsmanship, the ideals of the master worker and the masterpiece, the notion of excellence and pride of workmanship. There are still craftsmen, still men and women dedicated to mixing their sweat with their work to produce the perfect house, manuscript, or necklace, still persons who find great joy and self-esteem from "taking pains." Sadly, however, the bureaucratized, industrialized, and urbanized society decreases the probability of humans working for humans' sake. More often, it is for the job's sake, for money's sake, for the product's sake.

Hence, millions upon millions fill roles such as butcher, baker, or candlestick maker—or, more likely, machinist, bus driver, or librarian.

The roles become stylized, mechanized, and dehumanizing. When they are standardized or professionalized, they are guaranteed to become mediocre. And a job description is much too often a prescription for alienation. So where does a person's sense of pride or "instinct for workmanship" reach fruition? Is it any wonder that almost any analysis, from the most empirical social scientist's to Studs Terkel's more impressionistic one, reveals many people who feel that they are underutilized? Is it any wonder that both unions and companies, recognizing this fundamental severance of pride from job and work from role, focus on specific bread-and-butter issues, beyond-the-job activities, and industrial rhetoric? Is it any wonder that the workplace is a constellation of contradictions? Or is it surprising that the do-it-yourself industry, ironically, has become a billion-dollar one? If workers did not vent their energies and hopes by building boats in their cellars or kites in their garages, how could they maintain their sanity? Or we might ask what is perhaps a more basic question: If one doesn't like one's job, how can he or she tolerate it without developing a kind of occupational and personal schizophrenia? [4]

This is not to overlook the statistics from Sheppard and Herrick or the HEW report that at least half of American workers (40,000,000 plus) *are* satisfied with their jobs. This is not to scoff at the do-it-yourself phenomena; nor is it to denigrate the fantastic momentum of women's handicrafts, which are so significant a part of our cultural heritage. Neither is it to overlook the remaining vestiges of occupational continuity, wherein son and daughter extend their father's or mother's work, or where several generations farm the same area. But even if "only" a few million people feel dehumanized (and the figure will vary with the analyst), we still have a complex problem begging for solutions. It would seem that wherever the touch of industry is felt, whether in our capitalist society or in a modern socialist society such as the USSR or in a remote corner of the Third World that has just emerged from colonialism, the symptoms are the same. At least, conversations with Eastern Europeans and visits to and literature from Africa suggest to me that one of the contemporary human blights, the world over, occurs when people become interchangeable parts, and hence dehumanized. As Robert Schrank suggests after studying the Gaines Pet Food plant in Topeka, Kansas, we may have to admit that some jobs are bound to be wretched.

WHERE THERE'S LIFE . . .

In an essentially optimistic, never-say-fail society, such as the United States tends to be, it is hardly surprising that much energy is devoted to solving workplace problems, both individually and collectively. This assumes many forms. Job mobility for the individual is still a fact of life despite increased specialization, despite the fact that white-collar workers constitute the majority of the work force, and despite structural unemployment and a variety of other economic, social, and political forces that almost discourage work altogether! Every statistic, from unemployment to job-turnover figures, indicates that people frequently change jobs. Data on mobility also indicate constant movement. Recently, considerable attention has been given to the phenomenon of persons in presumably solid and interesting jobs changing careers in the middle of their lives: insurance salesman to medical-school professor, housewife to college administrator, economics professor to opera singer, Trappist monk to book salesman, computer designer to picture-frame maker. Such changes, of course, might move a person from one not necessarily boring job to another of high potential.[5]

But the focus of this book is not on the changing-careers dimension of workplace evolution, interesting and exciting and humanistic though that is; rather, the concern here is to look at the variety of analyses of the problem as well as the variety of organizational, definitional, and motivational applications of ideas about humanizing work. These essays reflect the rich texture of controversy, not only about work itself but also about perceptions of work—by managers, workers, scholars, and journalists. Most of the recommendations are in the context of "job enrichment," "job enlargement," and "participatory management," and do not advocate social revolution or structural social change, although implicit in most analyses and commentary is a high degree of social vision.

Among the critical issues at stake: What impact have the human relationists had after devoting energy to these problems for nearly half a century? What further promise may one find among those specializing in organizational development and organizational behavior? To what extent is it possible to reorganize work to develop human satisfactions of larger proportion and higher quality? And on what scale? Why do men "in charge" so often treat their employees like objects? And how does one go about changing that? How far can democratic decision making go toward changing everything from a television assembly line to the systematized production of insurance policies? Assuming that men and women must work to stay alive (though Howard Radest questions that assumption in the last essay in this book), how can their least-productive resistances be converted into positive behavior? Or should one assume that people do have to work to survive? Is it possible, for instance, to assume that, just as speech, worship, and "due process" are fundamental civil rights, playing and eating might be fundamental human rights? (Again, see Radest.) In a society increasingly devoted to service, will dehumanizing behaviors be "turned around" in different ways, or must we accept the stereotypes suggested by the characterization of social workers in the film *A Thousand Clowns?* How will the new service occupations avoid the elitism, bureaucracy, and demeaning characteristics of the old?

Since women are moving into the work force in increasing numbers, how long can federal, state, and local governments assume a casual posture toward instituting child-care services? Equally fundamental, perhaps, is the question of whether the feminist movement will have an impact on industrial and other work practices, enhancing them with qualities that are traditionally thought of as feminine. With increasing numbers of employees willing to discuss the specifics of their work conditions openly, will such disclosures effect better working conditions? How much effort can we expect from environmental and consumer groups, augmented by laws, to reduce noise levels in factories, improve the notoriously dangerous conditions associated with mining and chemical manufacture (a "new toxic agent is introduced into the workplace every twenty minutes"[6]), reduce accidents around machinery, and in general improve security and health factors in every work space?

How much can we learn from such existing democratic enterprises as some of the plywood companies in the state of Washington or the American Cast Iron Pipe Company in Alabama about employee ownership and its application to the larger world of work? Can the economic-alternatives program of the American Friends Service Committee precipitate enough momentum, if combined with long-standing cooperatives and other profit-sharing efforts, to effect a genuine movement for humanizing work in this country?[7] And what about such prototypes for improving workplace conditions, in the context of major corporate expenditure, as those of General Foods in Topeka, Kansas, Travelers Insurance in Hartford, Connecticut, or Proctor & Gamble in Lima, Ohio?[8] Are these merely isolated instances? Are they worthy of wide replication? Perhaps a more subtle question is: If women and men were paid for doing housework, what social and psychological consequences might result? Would the family be more or less likely to disappear? And what might such an event do to actuarial data pertaining to death?

PERSONAL MOTIVATION

My own early life history was filled with dehumanized work such as lying under automobiles (to earn school money) with water or hot oil dripping into my face as I tried to repair a crankshaft or a muffler; shingling houses and putting up storm windows, with gloves on, in Maine's winter blizzards; "eating" a certain amount of cast-iron dust and dirt while working for six years in a textile machine shop; washing dishes for a tyrannical restaurant owner to earn college meals; working for an authoritarian college president who destroyed more people before my very eyes than I like to think about. Hence the task of assembling this group of essays reflecting a vast range of viewpoints about work was more than a formal or academic exercise; it was a labor for further understanding. And throughout the months of work on this workplace book, I became ever more conscious of the academic setting in which I currently work, where we offer an experimental doctoral program calling for inexhaustible energies and an expenditure of effort beyond any normal expectation. I have wondered how much my own work, where I perceive my life as my work and my work as my life, is brutalizing. And crossing my mind repeatedly: I dictate letters with both compulsion and compassion, keeping one secretary busy most of her working hours. She types them with excellence and loyalty, but I worry. Am I forcing her to become an automaton, an interchangeable part with my dictaphone and her transcriber and typewriter? Does she gain any joy from the process? As I write this, I have not asked her those questions, but I shall. Whose consciousness is likely to be raised more, hers or mine?

STRUCTURE

Humanizing the Workplace is divided into three major sections: the first deals with history, philosophy, and issues related to work; the second, with specific illustrations, both exemplary and incredible; and the third provides a look to the future. Each section is prefaced with comments suggesting the central focus and questions with which the authors are concerned. While the authors do provide us with considerable data, it is my hope that the questions they raise will make a difference in readers' lives, providing ample dimension for rumination, discussion, speculation, and *action*.

NOTES

1. Studs Terkel, *Working* (New York: Pantheon, 1974), p. xi.
2. From cassette available from the Center for the Study of Democratic Institutions, Santa Barbara, Calif., on which Robert M. Hutchins expounds on the philosophy of the hypothetical Dr. Alexander Zuckerkandl.

3. Alan Gartner and Frank Riessman, *The Service Society and the Consumer Vanguard* (New York: Harper & Row, 1974).

4. I have contended for many years that survival in this country depends upon what I call "creative schizophrenia," or the capacity to hold two or more mutually exclusive value systems simultaneously.

5. See Warren Boroson, "New Careers for Old," *Money*, 4, No. 3 (April 1974), pp. 22-26; "Changing Careers at Midstream," *The Humanist*, 34, No. 3 (May-June 1974), pp. 14-23.

6. R. Sherrill, "What's Behind the Failure To Protect the Health of America's Workers," *Today's Health*, Aug. 1972, p. 18.

7. See *Democratizing the Workplace*, a package of materials distributed by the American Friends Service Committee, Cambridge, Mass.

8. See David Jenkins, *Job Power* (Garden City, N.Y.: Doubleday, 1973).

History,
Philosophy,
and Issues

Preface

Roy P. Fairfield

It seems appropriate to open Part I with two essays that throw light on both the research about and the active, practical efforts to effect changes in the workplace during the past half-century; for indeed, 'tis true, as many philosophers have observed, if we disregard history we are doomed to repeat it. Ivar Berg and George Strauss, both eminent social scientists, provide a perspective on new departures toward more-humane working conditions, which are being promoted by organizational psychology and organizational development, two disciplines that only today are coming into their own. Here we see, in brief scope, the contributions of such men as Elton Mayo, Chris Argyris, Douglas McGregor, and Abraham Maslow, to name only a few of the people who have devoted a significant portion of their adult lives to the issues just barely touched upon in the Introduction.

Strauss' essay may seem long for a book of this kind, which can only provide a bird's-eye view of such critical issues in our lives; yet he has done distinguished scholarly work in this field, and his empirically based analysis provides an excellent background for many of the questions other authors raise in later essays. His own speculations and attitudes toward research poignantly delineate the rationale for more research and the importance of all of us seeing the *connections* between understanding work and work itself, between social-science analysis and action based upon it. Nor can one deny the importance of asking: Can or should workers be trained to do unchallenging work joyfully in a kind of *Brave New World* mode? Strauss and others leave us with a crucial query: Isn't social life at the shop, what Robert Schrank calls "schmoozing," a workplace imperative in a society such as ours? Without it, how would we gain perspective on the richness or poverty of *nonwork* life in an environment increasingly homogenized and commercialized?

Irving Bluestone and Franklin Wallick approach workplace problems as labor leaders, officials of the United Auto Workers. While it might be argued that we should have gone further afield to find other articulate persons identified with progressive labor, men such as Harry Bridges or Eric Hoffer, it seemed best to magnify that segment of the industrial world associated with the assembly line. Such a focus may distort, since only a relatively small percentage of people work in such places; yet it does provide a parameter against which to place both concepts of action related to other workplaces. Along with Mitchell Fein, who issues a kind of minority report and questions the behaviorists' and humanists' "right" to redesign work in their own image, Bluestone and Wallick precipitate some fascinating questions: If industrial democracy, in its various unionized forms, has worked, then why are we even asking questions about worker participation in decision making? How democratic can million-member unions be anyway? And why are we relatively free in almost every walk of life, except at work? (As Robert Schrank and J. Davitt McAteer observe, going to the john is regimented, and making telephone calls during working hours is almost impossible for the blue-collar worker.)

To continue: How much worker participation may we project for the American worker in the next decade? Why is humanizing the workplace so much more difficult to negotiate than concrete bread-and-butter issues? Why do academics seem so interested in humanizing work while neglecting, for instance, such dire matters of health as lead poisoning and black lung? What amenities do workers want? Do they want them because they need them? Or because they make invidious comparisons between their own and their managers' privileges and opportunities? Fein suggests that a paradox may exist: Why shouldn't workers have the *right* to be dissatisfied with their work? Of course, nobody aware of labor's battles in other parts of the world can finish reading Bluestone, Wallick, and Fein without inquiring: If American workers don't get what they want through union efforts or management and consultant inventiveness, will they depart from their traditional anti-ideological stance to adopt an ideology for dramatizing and implementing their political power?

Marcus Raskin and Michael Maccoby place the worker in the stream of technology, a stream in which we will all either float or sink. Whereas Raskin's view suggests answers to the question of ideology just raised—he links politics and morality—Maccoby is primarily concerned with worker psychology. Both raise some central questions, which, when answered, may help us all cope. If, for instance, labor leaders held the same philosophy of technology that Raskin does, would they view industrial change as he does? How do their moral assumptions compare? Or, as Maccoby suggests, can we demystify work? If Raskin and Maccoby had been employing a strictly Marxist critique, would they have come out at the same place? I keep asking myself whether or not it is possible for workers to develop a competency based on self-education. Also, my interest in paradox and irony leads me to ask: Why do humans continually and insistently invent machines that are antihuman?

Alan Gartner and Frank Riessman contribute background material at a crucial time in our national life, arguing cogently that out of the sixties came new constituencies and new values leading to a "service society," a "society characterized by an increasing proportion of people producing and consuming services." We have a new kind of worker developing. Gartner and Riessman's thinking and observations take us to the edge of a new vista; but, as I have personally heard them ask repeatedly, can new paraprofessional or other service-related workers overcome the dehumanizing pressures that blue-collar workers have long experienced at the hands of those profiting from the sweat of their brows?

Question, questions, and more questions! Such questions will perhaps become part of the epilogue for the most-concerned readers.

Worker Discontent, Humanistic Management, and Repetitious History

Ivar Berg

We have a way, in America, of rediscovering problems and of simply "updating" the diagnoses of earlier healers, who sought to prescribe homeopathic doses of medications that seemed, at the time, to be specific to the disorders. So it has been, recently, with the problem of work in America. A detached but informed observer sometimes wonders, accordingly, whether the cures are not as problematical as the diseases and whether we would not be well served by a pure-food-and-drug act that looks as *carefully* at prescriptions as diagnosticians look *carelessly* at the pathologies they seek to remedy. A review of the pharmacology relevant to "worker discontent" leaves little doubt that there are elements of malpractice involved, elements not easily isolated or understood without attending to a bit of sociomedical history.

The rash of contemporary studies of employee satisfaction is a manifestation of two earlier and major outbreaks of similar sorts (and with that we may drop the metaphor). These earlier clusters of studies are worth discussing at some length because the newer studies—those dating from the late fifties—have managed to capitalize on the strengths, while obscuring the significant flaws, in the earlier investigations, and have perpetrated the methods, while retaining the assumptions, that marred the pioneering investigations that began with the Hawthorne-plant studies in 1929. Briefly stated, the earlier studies have been "enlarged" by "plant sociologists," who have folded the work of other investigators (whose attentions focused on whole societies) into their own work on social life in the factory and the office. The word "enlarged" is used advisedly here; the work of Geoffrey Gorer, Ruth Benedict, Margaret Mead, Abram Kardiner, Erich Fromm, and that of the authors of The Authoritarian Personality on the "national character" of the Japanese, the Germans, the Soviets, and other nationalities was incorporated into the work-enrichment material of the "factory sociologists."

(It was, incidentally, a redemptive merger for the national-character students, whose "clinical" techniques and very small-sample studies of whole nationality groups came to be regarded with the same suspicions as the too-easy characterizations of Jews by anti-Semites. Thus, the much-criticized work of the psychoanalytically oriented anthropologists could be salvaged, as we will see later, by applying their methods to organizations rather than to whole societies.)

The successes and failures of these continuing efforts have a direct and considerable bearing upon any sophisticated effort to assess the present-day undertakings of a large number of social scientists who may be grouped, quite reasonably, into the "organizational development" school. The related facts—that this school is totally ahistorical, totally without institutional sensitivities, and unconscious of its own intellectual past—heighten the need for a backward look. Oversimplifications will otherwise be repeated, progress in working out solutions to difficult problems in an industrial democracy will be stunted, and culpabilities overlooked.

FACTORY SOCIOLOGY: THE HUMAN-RELATIONS TRADITION

Factory sociology is most conveniently dated from the work of Elton Mayo, a lay analyst, Fritz Roethlisberger, and George Lombard, all of the Harvard Business School; L. Henderson, a physical scientist;[1] and a number of Mayo's and Roethlisberger's students, including a number of today's senior social scientists. Like the "sociotechnical systems" and the "work enrichment" enthusiasts of the 1960s and 1970s, these men of the 1930s had their downfield blockers in industry. Just as today we have Lyman Ketchum, a go-getter with a decent intelligence, an eye for an industrial solution, and a strategic position at General Foods, joining forces with Albert Chernes, an English applied social scientist, Mayo, Roethlisberger, and Lombard had Chester Barnard, James Worthy, and W. J. Dickson, of AT&T, Sears, Roebuck, and Western Electric, respectively.

Mayo and Roethlisberger were quite taken with several sets of ideas, an appreciation of which is crucial to an understanding of the work and the aspirations of those who have continued the work of the pioneers, many of whom today fly the "organization development" colors. First, they were much influenced by Freud's explanations of unconscious processes and especially by his notions about defense mechanisms. Second, they were impressed by Durkheim's notions about *anomie* and the social circumstances that produce the sense of loneliness and isolation comprehended by Durkheim's term, notions that were developed within the context of the French sociologist's studies of comparative suicide rates. Third, they were taken with the central proposition of anthropologists: that all social activities of people, no matter how apparently trivial, serve to "maintain the ongoing functioning of a social system."[2]

Mayo, a lay analyst in Australia, had met countless functionalist anthropologists on their way to and from studies of the social life and rituals of aborigines in the hinterlands, and he was struck by their ideas. Finally, Mayo and his colleagues were in debt to two Harvard Business School articles of faith: first, that men could be trained to become managers through academic programs that go well beyond accounting, finance, and marketing to include psychology;[3] second, that the urge of workers to organize themselves into unions could be countered by "making the pie larger," that is, by increasing the productivity of the factors of production—especially the human factor.

The influences on Mayo, presented here in bare and inadequate outline, were neatly articulated: workers' lack of cooperation with managers, or outright opposition to them, was a special case of an unresolved authority problem with parents; life in industrial society was anomic and the workplace was a potentially therapeutic setting in which compensatory social relations would emerge to replace those fractured by life in urban-industrial centers; workers' behavior, finally, would be understandable to employers if cliques, output restriction, and other "defensive" acts were viewed, like behavior patterns in a preliterate culture, in anthropological perspective.

Of the businessmen, Chester Barnard was by far the most influential. He seized upon the notions of the Harvard Business School professors, weaving their ideas together in one of the most influential books that has ever been written about business, *The Functions of the Executive,* published by Harvard University Press in 1938. This book, which studiously avoids any discussion of unions (even in 1938!), became a bible, a "Marx-for-the-managers"—to borrow an appellation later applied by C. Wright Mills to James Burnham's *The Managerial Revolution.* Drawing heavily on his mastery of telephone-company apparatus, Barnard described the necessity for managers to deal with worker discontent by applying available social-science knowledge regarding workers' needs for "social affiliations" and "democratic supervision."

Both of these could be provided workers so that they would be happier, more productive, and less interested in conflict. "Conflict," with its insidious overtones, was in this tradition very clearly a euphemism for unions.

Unions were ignored in other studies as well. The published report on the Hawthorne experiments appeared in 1938, but the experiments were completed much earlier. The restriction of output by workers, in 1929, was attributed to "nonrational" workers who, according to Roethlisberger and Dickson, "mistakenly" feared that management would revise piece rates if workers produced at higher levels.[4] The effects of depression fears, like unionism, were ignored by these objective scholars. As we will see, this tendency to package anti-unionism and managerial apologetics reappears with the renewed interest in "organizational development."

Like Barnard, the professors considered studies of workers, in which they discovered "social needs" by the bagful, though the researchers had initially set out to study the effects of the physical environment (heat, ventilation, illumination, and so forth) on industrial fatigue. Mayo, in a series of influential books, as influential on "management theory" as those by Barnard, preached the need for arranging capital equipment and for organizing supervisory functions in such a fashion that workers' "social needs" could be filled. An "informal system," said its discoverer, would develop among employees anyway, and the wise manager would recognize that incentive systems, authority patterns, and plant rules are buffered by such "systems," systems designed by workmen to temper the effects of managerial rewards and punishments. Work-group members would adhere to the production standards and other norms of the work group lest they incur the wrath of the system's other members.

This "informal system" could be a gigantic aid to sophisticated managers, wrote both Mayo and Barnard, in that the loyalty of individuals to the work group was a far greater factor in shaping the behavior of employees than were management sanctions. An employee, for example, would let co-workers down only under penalty of social isolation; thus his attendance record and his production record were a function of his social needs and of the degree to which work-group norms were well developed. Such assertions were borne out, at least in the short run, in studies, like those by Lombard, of air-frames manufacturing, where the Harvard professor constructed what is now called a "sociotechnical systems" solution: machines were placed sufficiently close together for workers to talk. The result of this, during World War II, was a social system whose sanctions against absenteeism were far more effective than managerial sanctions.

ORGANIZATIONAL PSYCHOLOGY

Mention of the war is highly relevant here, because it was a time during which factory sociologists became the beneficiaries of two separate and unrelated factors: a change in union attitudes and developments in cultural anthropology. The opposition of unions and "left intellectuals" to the "human-relations movement" melted when all parties agreed that productivity needed to be increased if the United States were to be successful in the great war against fascism. Harold Ruttenberg was one of the first trade-union converts, and his writings incorporated all the relevant citations of studies showing that it was possible to make work life better while making workers more productive. Indeed, the latter was held to be dependent on the former.

Secondly, a group of anthropologists, whose work on Pacific Island cultures helped shape Navy and Marine Corps policies designed to win over or neutralize native populations on the "stepping stones" to Tokyo, came into their own. Their ethnographic methods had already incorporated Freudian thinking, the family being so obviously an important unit in the cultural-transmission process, and they set about to enlarge their intellectual sphere by applying their "psychocultural" approach to the vexing problems of totalitarianism, anti-Semitism, and militarism in Europe and Asia.

Even leading political scientists were taken with the promise that employment of the "culture concept" would facilitate our leaders' postwar capacities to deal with the Soviet Union, and to reform Japan and Germany along more-democratic lines. A whole shelf of books, including those by the figures mentioned earlier, helped explain that the swaddling of Soviet infants contributed to adult stoicism—and vodka consumption—by Soviet adults; that early toilet training in Japan contributed to the orderly, that is, militaristic, Japanese character; and that the patriarchal nature of the German family contributed to the authoritarian German personality to which Hitler successfully appealed.

The data supporting these and related simplifications of complex social systems were scant, if imaginative. Much was made, for example, of an early German film, *The Cabinet of Dr. Caligari*, in which all the themes later embodied in the person and role of Adolf Hitler occurred. Their methods were those of the ethnographer who was accustomed to characterizing a whole preliterate culture on the basis of a period of participant observation with a few families of a particular tribe of South Pacific islanders.

It did not take long, after the war ended, for this effort to fall into disrepute. Teams of social scientists at Russian research centers, particularly at Harvard, Michigan, and Columbia, found little help in these undertakings in their own interdisciplinary efforts to understand the USSR; they soon wrote off the "culture and personality" approach, which many disparagingly referred to as "Scott Tissue sociology."

ORGANIZATION DEVELOPMENT

Back at the ranch, however, the message of the national-character studies seemed to be just what the factory sociologists needed. However, unions were here to stay, and it was inappropriate to regard workers as neurotic aborigines. But by adopting the "psychocultural" model, and even some of its architects, it would be possible to reorganize the concepts of three decades of work, including the wartime work at the Tavistock Institute in the United Kingdom.

Of great moment here was the preservation of the psychological component of the earlier model, dropping, of course, the pejorative implications of the earlier model's view of individual workers. The solution provided two relatively simple steps. First, do psychological studies of organizations rather than of individuals, in plants or study subgroups rather than in whole nations. And the studies came: the Menominee Indians (on and off the reservation), the University of Chicago's divinity and mathematics departments, the Massachusetts Mental Health Center, the Peter Bent Brigham Hospital, a large bank (by Chris Argyris), and a host of others. In each study the organization (hospital, community, department) was characterized in terms of the "psychological demands" it made upon individuals, and an effort was made to determine whether or not the personalities "fit" the structure; incongruencies between structures and personalities would only evoke defense mechanisms, conflict, alienation, and all the rest. The second step was to do psychological studies of managers.

Critics were disarmed by this new synthesis. Whereas the old model devised by the factory sociologists made much of the rationality of managers and the "nonrational" behavior of workers who failed to respond to incentives, absented themselves (and thereby irrationally lost income), and restricted output, the new model made room for the irrationality of managers. According to the organization-development writers, workers were driven to their alienated and unproductive ways by managers who, nonrationally, "structured" their organizations in ways that denied workers their needs for "self-actualization." Human relations had entered a new era, in which its priests and practitioners could follow a doctrine that was apparently evenhanded in its implied castigations.

It will take little imagination to recognize that Scott Myers and Louis

Davis, two of the most notable and successful American spokesmen for the currently evolving model, are well within the two frameworks outlined here, frameworks that were staked out first in the 1930s and then again in the late 1950s.[5]

The basic change that has taken place in the period since the Harvard Business School personnel led the movement involves the redefinition of the psychological problem of work as being one that involves *managers* as well as *employees.* The investigators and publicists have thus gotten part of the way off the hook on which they were deftly placed by the classic critique of the human-relations school by Clark Kerr and his Berkeley colleagues, a critique that deserves careful consideration.[6] By implicating management—first, in the early charges that managers were too prone to adopt an economic model of worker behavior that neglected man's inclination not to live by bread alone and, second, in the later charge that managers' *own* personalities led to authoritarian structures that contributed to worker malaise—the newer investigators appeared to have broadened the front across which we might look for solutions to the industrial problems of workers.

Indeed, there were many who argued, by implication, that the consistent failure of American management to apply the inescapable lessons of the human-relations school's findings was a result of the nonrational nature of managers, a nature that was "uncovered" when the human relationists began psychological assessments of managers and their organizations. These organizations were said to be hierarchical, bureaucratic, rule-ridden, "punishment-centered," autocratic, hyper-rational, but psychologically insensitive and even repressive structures, and were said to be designed by managers who unjustifiably mistrusted employees, feared candor, and were led by their own authoritarian qualities to seal themselves off in the executive suite.

In current discussions of the need for work enrichment and for organizational designs that emphasize the malleability of technical systems, the innocence or nonrationality (or stupidity) of management is not directly attacked. Rather, researchers "share" with putatively reasonable, open-minded, and potent business audiences the promising data on the new Gaines Pet Food plant in Topeka, on experiments at Volvo, Saab, Porsche, Olivetti, and at a couple of Norwegian locations, as well as data on earlier experiments in collieries in the English Midlands and at the Lincoln Electric Company in the United States. The point of these discussions is to demonstrate that social and technical systems must be *articulated,* in order to produce a single sociotechnical system that simultaneously serves human and production goals.

Managers are "stimulated" to think of their options. However, preconference discussions are conducted by the salesmen-investigators among themselves on how presentations may be made to avoid promising too much to would-be clients.[7]

The audiences, incidentally, include many socially conscious younger executives and assorted factotums on the HEW factotum pole. They also include popular journalists without any scientific background who have stumbled upon workplace issues through assignments from their editorial chiefs, and a random assortment of well-intentioned people, who are aided in their expressions of sympathy for troubled employees by jobs that are luxuriously unimpeded by obligations to be productive, critical, or useful. Finally, these audiences include a large number of business executives from the personnel field, all of whom are notoriously impotent in their organizations. These audiences take in these proceedings and carefully jot down the tag words presented on flip charts and electrified transparencies: managerial grids, Theory X and Theory Y, "dollarizing your personal investment," and many more.[8]

MISGIVINGS

A few facts will suggest why skepticism toward the developments outlined is appropriate on the part of those concerned with life in America's workplaces. First, the successful cases that the several traditions can present as evidence of the utility of their curative prescriptions and nostrums are very few in number. The number of American managers who have been willing to act, *in thoroughgoing ways,* on the basis of either the older human-relations or newer organizational-development preachments are very few indeed.[9]

Second, while the number of employers who have incorporated *some* of the ideas, now so highly touted, is very large, there is no evidence whatever that some of the more basic problems are even touched by efforts that yield short-run improvements in morale, absenteeism, or turnover. Consider the magnitude of the chore of "enlarging work" for the two-million-plus college graduates for whom there will be inadequate attrition in the number of persons holding "college-level" jobs to produce enough job openings in the 1970s. Add to this the "college-level" jobs that have been upgraded in terms of entry requirements but not in actual fact.[10]

Third, the evidence advanced, by what is now an international sales force of applied social scientists, that morale is lower, that absenteeism is worse, that turnover is higher in America, is highly suspect. Consider, for example, that a review of the entire published literature on turnover (in an effort to compare the job histories of differentially educated employees up and down the occupational ladder) reveals only a handful of studies of the correlates of turnover and only a slightly larger number of empirical studies of turnover per se.

National data on turnover, collected by the Bureau of Labor Statistics, may not be used to demonstrate that we have, in recent years, entered upon a period that is notable for its negligent job attitudes. Turnover in manufacturing in the period 1951-1969, for example, went down, then up, and is now coming down; the "quit rate" for these employees was 2.9 per 100 employees in 1951, 1.2 in 1961, 2.7 in 1969, and it was 1.8 per 100 workers in 1971, the last year for which "annualized" data are available.

Of turnover and absenteeism among nonmanufacturing employees little may be said. Readers may be more *aware* of the attendance patterns and amount of loyalty of employees in their own organizations today than we were a decade ago, but I will stake my modest professional reputation on the assertion that the patterns have not changed appreciably. Since no helpful public or private data are maintained on these employees, since our own white-collar subalterns' behavior is never closely monitored, and since the few who read these lines are democratic to a fault—they are dedicated "Theory Y" types, who view their charges benevolently and even therapeutically (if only in self-defense)—it is not likely that the author's reputation, such as it is, will be in much jeopardy.

One could go on with misgivings about the anti-union bias that is manifest in the new wisdom about work, but the point needs no belaboring here. The fact is that we are not likely to see the new concern with worker satisfaction move much beyond the "fad" state in which we find them in the United States in 1974. In Western Europe there is full employment and considerable labor unrest. Thus, ten thousand French middle-level, white-collar bank employees struck from January to April in 1974. Under such conditions, supplemented by concerns about "leftist" labor groups, managers will have a slightly more enduring interest in solutions.

One sees no prospects of such developments in the United States. Concern about inflation among employed Americans will generate some visible discontent in the next several years, but its quality and significance will more likely be tempered by employment levels than by employer humanitarianism. Nothing in the earlier developments, outlined above, contradicts that depressing conclusion.

NOTES

1. It was Henderson, more than any other since Wilfredo Pareto, who explicated the relevance of the Newtonian physical-science notion of "system" for

social science. This fact is most important, for with the Newtonian analogy, the social sciences also received the notion of an equilibrium. Attraction to the latter concept led a generation of social scientists to view conflict as an unnatural disturbance of what would otherwise be harmonious, integrated social systems. Exit Marx, unions, and criticisms of management, among other "variables" emphasized by "radical" critics. Henderson was, as indicated, a physical scientist.

2. Thus, the playful pseudopunches that workers gave each other at the Hawthorne works, called "binging," were seen as sanctions calculated to bring a "ratebuster" back in line, thus preserving group integrity and the production quotas that served the social system of the celebrated Relay Test Assembly Room. The workers' production quotas, meantime, were interpreted as the outcome of their distrust of management, distrust born of "nonrational," that is, unconscious, "confusion" about those in authority.

3. This idea, or an earlier version by Frederick W. Taylor, had been challenged by an earlier generation of American businessmen who felt that any such heresy should be resisted on the grounds that ownership, not technical competence, was the source of managerial legitimacy. Thus, Taylor was hauled before a congressional committee when his notions of scientific management received some currency.

4. These experiments have recently been reviewed by H. M. Parsons, who reports after a careful reassessment of both reported and unreported data that the behavior of the Hawthorne workers could more easily be interpreted by reference to earnings than to the sociopsychological factors adduced by the Harvard Graduate School of Business investigators. See "What Happened at Hawthorne?" *Science*, 183 (March 8, 1974), pp. 922-932.

5. The most trenchant of these studies: Edgard Schien's studies of the so-called collaborationist behavior of American POWs captured during the Korean War. A military psychologist who studied the prisoners from the time they were released at Panmunjon, Schien attributed the individualistic and self-preserving behavior of POWs to the clever efforts of their Chinese captors who relentlessly broke up the prisoner groups that might have helped individual GIs to "mobilize their effect" against their captors instead of against each other. Once again, the behavior was not essentially nonrational, that is, disloyal; it was adaptive behavior, given the structure of the prisoners' situation.

6. Clark Kerr and Lloyd H. Fisher, "Plant Sociology: The Elite and the Aborigines," in *Common Frontiers of the Social Sciences*, ed. Mirra Komarovsky (Glencoe, Ill.: Free Press, 1957), pp. 281-309.

7. Readers may read the advance mimeographed assignments given to participants for the various sessions of a conference on work held at Arden House in the fall of 1972, available from Professor Louis Davis, Quality of Working Life Program, UCLA.

8. One such audience recently paid large fees to hear organization developers deal with "The Changing Work Ethic" (Chicago, Dec. 1972). Another audience followed Scott Myers, several weeks later, to Dallas, Texas, to hear a description of work enlargement and other strategies that would help managers avoid unionization of their workers.

9. For a review of the managerial problems some of these and several other experiments in "work redesign" have created, see Richard E. Walton, "Innovative Restructuring of Work," in *The Worker and the Job*, ed. Jerome W. Rossow (Englewood Cliffs, N.J.: Prentice-Hall, 1974), pp. 145-176. Dr. Walton's description raises serious questions in the reader's mind, if not in his, of the seriousness of managerial concern with worker discontent, in contrast, for example, with their own career interests, organizational stability, and similar entrepreneurial questions.

10. See Carnegie Commission on Higher Education, *College Graduates and Jobs* (New York: McGraw-Hill, 1973), chapter 1; and Ivar Berg, *Education and Jobs: The Great Training Robbery* (New York: Praeger, 1970).

Is There a Blue-Collar Revolt Against Work?

George Strauss

In recent years there has been an upsurge of interest in the blue-collar worker.[1] Some have emphasized the "ethnic" revolt against political and social conditions. Evidence of this revolt includes the support for George Wallace in the 1968 and 1972 presidential elections, the "hard-hat" demonstrations of 1970, and the widespread opposition to the bussing of children to achieve racial balance in public schools. Others have stressed the alleged revolt against work, "a new 'anti-work ethic' . . . a new, deep-seated rejection by the young of the traditional American faith in hard work."[2] Although these two phenomena are probably related, my focus will be on the second: revolt against work.

Social critics and representatives of the Establishment alike have warned that worker discontent is increasing rapidly and that workplace reforms are urgently required. "More and more workers—and every day this is more apparent—are being disenchanted with the boring, repetitive tasks set by the merciless assembly line or by bureaucracy. They feel they have been herded into economic and social cul-de-sacs."[3] "The explosive potential of this discontent has the capacity to destroy the fragile facade of American democracy. . . . Positive action [is required] if anything is to be salvaged of the original American dream which dies a little every day in the dismal workplaces darkening the landscape from sea to shining sea."[4]

Source: Reprinted from *Work and the Quality of Life*, edited by James O'Toole by permission of the M.I.T. Press, Cambridge, Massachusetts. Copyright © 1974 by Massachusetts Institute of Technology.

Concern with workplace problems has spread even into the Executive branch. Nixon, on numerous occasions, deplored the apparent decline of the work ethic. In a 1971 speech he said: "Scrubbing floors and emptying bedpans have just as much dignity as there is in any work done in this country—including my own. . . . We must always remember that the most important part of the quality of life is the quality of work. And the new need for job satisfaction is the key to the quality of work."

Not everyone agrees on the extent of the problem. Nor is it clear—even on the assembly line—that workers are as much concerned about the allegedly dehumanizing *intrinsic* aspects of work as they are about traditional concerns like pay, fringe benefits, and job security.

A headline in the *AFL-CIO News* read: " 'Blue-Collar Blues' Overrated: Sociologists Misread Attitudes of Young Workers on Jobs." The accompanying article cites Machinists Union Vice-President William W. Winpinsinger as refuting "the invalid conclusion that today's generation of young workers is rejecting the world of work . . . the real significance of studies showing that one worker in five finds fault with aspects of his job is that 80 percent are satisfied."[5] Much the same view is expressed in the other main AFL-CIO publication.

> Substituting the sociologist's questionnaire for the stopwatch is likely to be no gain for the workers. . . . Much is being made these days in radical-chic academic and intellectual circles of the recent strike at Lordstown, Ohio, Chevrolet Vega plant, where a predominantly young workforce struck over the speed-up safety and other work conditions. The role of the United Auto Workers in formulating negotiable issues out of vague discontents and specific grievances was totally ignored by intellectuals and mass media alike. From the newspaper and magazine accounts one would think that these young workers were on strike not only against General Motors but chiefly against the older workers and their union. Legend now has it that the strike was part of the youth rebellion! In fact it was another strike in the long struggle of auto workers to improve their lot. A similar strike over like issues in Norwood, Ohio, received zero attention. . . . The Norwood workers, you see are older. [6]

Which position is correct? Are we facing a radically new phenomenon, a widespread revolt, particularly by the young, against work or merely a continuation of the age-old struggle of workers to improve their economic positions? Are higher pay, greater job security, and a stronger grievance procedure the answers to worker dissatisfaction—or are more radical measures required?

I will provide a brief overview of the present state of our knowledge of blue-collar attitudes toward work. In so doing I will stress areas of controversy and uncertainty since, despite a good deal of research, our understanding is still very limited. I will discuss in particular issues such as these: How central is work to life? To what extent does boring, unchallenging work lead to worker dissatisfaction? How do people adjust to boring work? Is dissatisfaction with work likely to increase in the future? Is there a revolt against all work, or only against boring, unchallenging work?

A RECENT INCREASE IN DISSATISFACTION?

The evidence we have, though incomplete and contradictory, does not support the hypothesis of a recent substantial increase in blue-collar dissatisfaction with work. Most of the discussion has been based on specific incidents that have made headlines, and there has been too little effort to look at the issues in perspective. The Lordstown strike, for example, made good copy, but strikes over production standards are common in the automobile industry, particularly when new processes are being introduced. Much of the other anecdotal evidence of increased dissatisfaction also comes from automobile plants, which are not representative workplaces since there are few other types of work in which the worker's autonomy is so severely restricted.

What of the statistical evidence? Quit rates in manufacturing went up from 1.1 per 100 workers in the recession year of 1958 to 2.7 in 1969 (but dropped to 1.8 in 1971, went up again in 1972 and quite sharply in 1973, and generally seemed to have moved inversely to unemployment). However, econometric analysis of the 1958-72 period suggests that practically all of the variation can be explained by changes in factors such as unemployment, relative hours and earnings rates, and the age, sex, and racial composition of the work force.[7] (Younger workers, for example—still looking for a career—quit their jobs more frequently than older workers. Thus, quit rates tend to rise when the proportion of younger workers gets larger.) Once factors such as these are taken into account, the remaining trends in quit rates decrease or become insignificant.

Raw absentee rates have shown a slight upward movement. Accident-frequency rates (which measure the number of accidents) have increased quite markedly, but the more significant accident-severity rates (which measure the amount of time lost due to accidents) has remained fairly constant. The rate of productivity growth declined during the late 1960s, but climbed sharply in 1971 and 1972. As in the case of quit rates, however, all these trends can be explained in terms of changes in factors such as hours, pay, the general demographic makeup of the labor force, and so forth.[8] Increased dissatisfaction may have affected worker behavior, but our gross statistical data does not reveal this.

How about opinion polls? Two massive surveys, one conducted in 1969 and the other in 1973, by the University of Michigan Survey Research Center, suggested that there were no significant changes in worker satisfaction during the period that they cover. In fact, insofar as comparisons can be made, attitudes of today's workers toward their jobs are not much changed from worker's attitudes in the 1950s.

Since 1949 the Gallup Poll has been asking, "On the whole, would you say you are satisfied or dissatisfied with the work you do?" The findings of this poll seem to conflict with those of the Michigan group in that, according to Gallup, the proportion of workers reporting themselves satisfied dropped from 87 percent in 1969 to 77 percent in 1973. But the Gallup findings have been subjected to serious challenge. According to one summary:

> Fifteen [probability sample] surveys are available, dating back to 1958. Eight of these were Gallup Polls; seven were conducted by either the National Opionion Research Center or the Survey Research Center of the Universities of Michigan or California. All these surveys shared a single-question measure of overall job satisfaction that made their data roughly comparable. The seven non-Gallup surveys indicated that job satisfaction increased between 1962 and 1964 but has remained unchanged up to the present. A change in job satisfaction over the last few years that appears in the Gallup data is inconsistent with these data. Gallup's "work satisfaction" question was, however, asked of *all* people interviewed (housewives, students, retired people, the unemployed, and so on), not only those who worked for pay. When the Gallup data are reanalyzed, the closer the reanalysis comes to refining the Gallup sample to include only those who work for pay, the smaller the "decline" in job satisfaction over the last several years. [9]

Does this mean that there has been no change in job satisfaction? Not necessarily. The most that can be said is that whatever changes may have occurred have not been great enough to be reliably indicated by our present gross and perhaps inadequate research techniques; all sorts of things may be happening that escape our statistical net.

Though the evidence does not support an assumption of increased dissatisfaction or of the imminent outbreak of revolt, neither does it prove that workers are truly satisfied. Quite the contrary. Though most workers accept—or become resigned to—their lot, the adjustment process is not always easy. It is far more useful, I think, to examine this adjustment process—the question of *how* workers come to terms with their jobs—than to become excessively concerned with short-run indices of morale. But before looking at dissatisfaction with work as such, let me discuss several related forms of dissatisfaction.

OTHER FORMS OF REVOLT

A number of studies have suggested at least some relationship between dissatisfaction with work, politics, society, and even life itself, a syndrome of malaise that has often been called "the blue-collar blues" or alienation.[10] In a society with a short fuse, each cause of discontent tends to exacerbate the others. However, they are far from being identical or even highly correlated (for example, building tradesmen were among the leaders of the hard-hat revolt of 1970, but they hardly rank high in job dissatisfaction).

At least four causes of blue-collar dissatisfaction have been suggested. I will mention the first three, chiefly to indicate their relationship to the fourth—dissatisfaction with work, or the "job squeeze."[11]

The Economic Squeeze

Jerome W. Rossow is credited with this concept. As he put it, the average blue-collar worker "reaches his peak earning power and chances for promotion early in life. Unlike the white-collar worker he earns wages that remain steady even though expenses mount as his children become ready for college or he has to support aging parents." This feeling of being squeezed has presumably been accentuated during the recent periods of combined inflation and unemployment, in which the real income of many blue-collar workers fell or remained constant.

This hypothesis can be disputed on a number of economic grounds[12] but if it is true one thing seems clear: as the blue-collar worker gets older his dissatisfaction should climb. But the evidence from attitude surveys suggests exactly the reverse. In addition, the economic squeeze hardly explains the rise in absenteeism.

The Social Squeeze

The second hypothesis is that blue-collar workers (particularly ethnics) feel threatened by the movement of blacks into their community. Second- and third-generation ethnics who had escaped mid-city slums where their parents and grandparents lived and had settled in working-class suburbs feel their new-found status badly jeopardized.

Further, ethnics who have obtained white-collar supervisory jobs by going to school or gradually working up the seniority ladder find themselves passed over for blacks, whom they feel have failed to earn their rights in the conventional fashion. Compounding this resentment, young middle-class intellectuals seem to despise the very concepts of success that the blue-collar ethnic has suffered for so long in order to achieve. The educational route to success through earning credentials is thus threatened from both above and below. Patience and hard work no longer seem to pay off;[13] manual work appears to be degraded by both schools and society generally.[14] The value of skill differentials in terms of money or prestige has been reduced to the point that even the skilled craftsman, once a man of high social status, is now a nobody.

Dissatisfaction of this sort undoubtedly occurs and very likely has an impact on the workplace. The social squeeze may make the job squeeze less tolerable. According to Ely Chinoy, many blue-collar workers look upon their jobs as temporary, to be endured until something better comes along.[15] Others look at their work instrumentally, as a means toward an end (such as a home of one's own). In either case, if the temporary job becomes permanent or the end turns sour, the willingness to endure may drop precipitously.

A Revolt of the Young?

To what extent is blue-collar dissatisfaction largely a youth phenomenon, an extension of the revolt that took place on campuses? Certainly there is evidence that younger workers are less satisfied with work than are older ones. Some elements of the "youth culture" have spread to the factory; long hair, hip clothes, and the use of drugs are becoming more popular among younger workers. Possibly there is a reaction against the acceptance of authority and the status quo. But one may question the extent to which young blue-collar workers also reject conventional standards of material success. If anything, they are more hostile to student power and blacks' demands than are their blue-collar elders.[16]

Even though it may be difficult to explain blue-collar dissatisfaction in the same terms as dissatisfaction among middle-class youth, there is still a strong possibility that young workers are less willing to tolerate the forms of boring work that their fathers were willing to accept.

THE PERSONALITY-VERSUS-ORGANIZATION HYPOTHESIS

Having disposed of our possibly parenthetical points, let us return to the main question: To what extent is blue-collar dissatisfaction a revolt against work? Over the years, out of the contributions of individuals such as Chris Argyris,[17] Norman R. F. Maier,[18] and Douglas Mc-

Gregor[19] has come a fairly consistent hypothesis that suggests an almost inevitable conflict between organizational and individual needs, especially in mass-production industries. This view, which might be called the personality-versus-organization hypothesis, in oversimplified terms runs as follows:

1. Workers seek social belonging, independence, and personal growth. In other words, they seek to ascend the needs-hierarchy ladder[20] from physical needs, through safety, social, and egoistic needs to self-actualizing needs. "Hierarchy" in this case means that a higher, less basic need does not provide motivation until lower, more basic needs are satisfied, and that, once a basic need is satisfied, it no longer motivates. A critical point is that such satisfactions are desired *on the job.*

2. Organizations, on the other hand, fail to recognize these needs and instead follow Theory X[21] assumptions that workers dislike work and wish to avoid responsibility. In so doing, they force workers to behave in an immature and dependent fashion.

3. As a consequence workers become alienated from their jobs. Either they fight back through union activity, sabotage, or output restriction, or they withdraw and produce no more than a minimum amount of work. Whichever they do, management is forced to supervise them more closely, which in turn makes workers still more frustrated and more likely to fight back or withdraw.

4. The only way to eliminate this vicious circle is for management to adopt Theory Y assumptions about human nature: that people can enjoy work and can exercise self-control and that they are imaginative and creative. Thus, management should develop policies that promote intrinsic job satisfaction and individual development. In particular, management should promote job enrichment, general supervision, and strong cohesive work groups. Higher pay, better job security, and a more effective grievance procedure are not enough.

It is not my purpose to test the validity of this hypothesis here. It does suggest, however, some important questions relating to the role of work in life, and it provides a convenient introduction to the discussion that follows.

EVIDENCE OF DISSATISFACTION

There is considerable evidence that, at least for some workers, dissatisfaction is directly related to short job cycles, surface-attention work, low autonomy and control of the pace of work, and the lack of challenge.[22] Such factors are also related to absenteeism,[23] to turnover,[24] and to strikes.[25] At least two studies suggest that poor mental health is correlated with low-skilled jobs.[26] A different kind of evidence is provided by studies comparing mass-production-assembly-line workers with craftsmen, such as printers, and workers in automated-process technology, such as oil refineries.[27] These studies agree that by all indices job satisfaction is significantly higher for craftsmen than for assembly-line workers. The degree of satisfaction of workers in automated industries is less clear, but certainly it is above that of assembly-line workers.

On the other hand, the need for challenging work needs to be put into perspective. As Table 1, from the 1969 Survey Research Center study[28] suggests, factors relating to supervision, management policies, and the work environment—factors such as having a "nurturant supervisor," receiving adequate help, having few "labor-standards problems" (such as safety hazards, poor hours, poor transportation, and so forth)—all seem at least as closely related to job satisfaction as having a challenging job with "enriching" demands. In other words, improving managerial practices may increase job satisfaction as much as changing the nature of the job can.

Though challenging work is not the sole determinant of job satisfaction, it clearly plays a part for some workers. Granted this, the critical question becomes: How important *is* challenging work for the healthy human being?

THE UNIVERSALITY OF SELF-ACTUALIZATION

Supporters of the personality-versus-organization hypothesis often argue in terms of the Maslow scheme, that is, as individuals mature they seek increasing opportunities for self-actualization: they seek the freedom to be creative, to develop their skills to the maximum, and to exercise personal autonomy. The Maslow scheme is overly simple and can be criticized on a number of grounds. For example, it is stated in a nonoperational manner, which makes it very difficult to prove or disprove, especially since most forms of human behavior satisfy more than one need. Further, there may be substantial differences among people in terms of the relative weight they give to the "basic" needs as against the "higher" ones such as esteem and self-actualization. (Compare Archie Bunker's glorification of basic needs to the poet's or scientist's shunning of such needs and devotion to self-actualization in his garret or lab.) Maslow himself never claimed that all people would wish to climb his ladder, certainly not in the same way. In fact, as his later writings make clear, his "mature," "normal" individual is a rather special breed.

The Maslow scheme, however, is not essential to the broader hypothesis. All that the broader hypothesis requires is that a substantial portion of human beings—for our purposes, blue-collar workers—have a strong need for self-actualization. There can be little doubt that all people have such needs to some extent; the main questions concern how important they are relative to other needs and how people react when they are denied.

The work of David McClelland[29] and his disciples suggests that people do vary substantially in the relative importance they attach to various needs and furthermore that they do not inevitably emphasize self-actualization after lesser needs are reasonably well satisfied.

TABLE 1: Characteristics of Workers or Their Jobs
Most Highly Correlated with Overall Job Satisfaction

Correlation with overall job satisfaction (Jobsat '70)	Correlation with overall job satisfaction (Jobsat '70)
Having a "nurturant" supervisor (one who takes a personal interest in those he supervises and goes out of his way to praise good work) (N = 1237)	.37
Receiving adequate help, assistance, authority, time, information, machinery, tools and equipment to do the job (N = 1494)	.32
Having problems in few labor-standards areas (N = 1511)	.32
Feeling that one's employer handles promotions fairly (N = 1066)	.31
Having a supervisor who does not supervise too closely (N = 1246)	.30
Having a technically competent supervisor (N = 1225)	.29
Having autonomy in deciding matters that affect one's work (N = 1508)	.28
Having a job with "enriching" demands (e.g., a job that demands that one learn new things, have a high level of skill, be creative, and do a variety of different things) (N = 1509)	.26
Receiving more paid vacation time (N = 1270)	.20
Feeling secure against job loss in the possible event that one's job may be automated (N = 357)	.20
Feeling that it would be easy to secure a new job assignment with one's employer (N = 1266)	.20
Working under pleasant physical conditions (N = 1032)	.20

McClelland posits three needs besides physical needs: need achievement, need affiliation, and need power. Persons high in need achievement react well to challenge; those who are low in this dimension are concerned primarily with playing it safe and avoiding failure. Presumably individuals with low need achievement, particularly those with high need affiliation, prefer direction to autonomy. One further point: McClelland's research suggests that these needs are rather easily malleable; a relatively short training course can substantially increase need achievement (and also managerial success). If so, perhaps training can also induce high need affiliation, and workers (shades of Huxley's *Brave New World* and the corporate state) can be trained to prefer unchallenging work.

Aside from this probably extreme interpretation of the implications of McClelland's work, it does seem reasonably clear that because of personality differences people do vary substantially in their needs for challenge and autonomy;[30] the personality differences, in turn, may well be due to variations in culture and child-rearing practices—and possibly to genetic factors. A question to be considered later in this article is whether child-rearing practices may be changing sufficiently to cause substantial differences in attitudes toward work, but for now let us consider a narrower issue: To what extent do cultural differences, especially rural-urban differences, affect worker's attitudes toward challenging jobs?

CULTURAL DIFFERENCES AND THE DESIRE FOR CHALLENGING WORK

A major corollary of the personality-versus-organization hypothesis is that there is a positive relationship between job challenge and job satisfaction and that job enlargement is an almost certain way to raise morale. The findings of Arthur Turner and Paul Lawrence in *Industrial Jobs and the Worker* seriously challenged this assumption. In a study involving eleven firms, these researchers sought to measure the relationship between job satisfaction and the complexity of work. They found as they had expected that small-town workers reacted positively to complex tasks, but to their great surprise urban workers reacted less positively. This unanticipated finding was further supported by a series of articles by Charles Hulin and Milton Blood[31] reporting on a study of 1,900 workers in twenty-one plants in a wide variety of communities. Where urban and slum characteristics were high, the correlations between blue-collar satisfaction and job skills were low or negative, while in more rural areas the reverse was true. The nature and location of the community seemed to make no difference in the case of white-collar workers. Another study[32] is at least partially consistent with these findings: rural workers reacted to job discretion with greater pride in their performance; for urban workers greater discretion was related only to work involvement and to the fact that time seemed "to drag" less often.

This research may be subject to methodological criticism, but assuming that it is valid, there are a number of alternate, though partly contradictory, explanations for these unexpected findings. One possibility is that rural and small-town workers have internalized the old-fashioned Protestant, middle-class ethic, which glorifies work for its own sake and insists on individual achievement. The city worker belongs to a different culture (or is at least alienated from the traditional culture). Why should the urban blue-collar culture be different?

1. Small towns are small, thereby making it difficult for blue-collar and white-collar values to develop in different directions. The city permits greater diversity.

2. Turner and Lawrence point out that their sample of rural workers was largely Protestant and their urban workers largely Catholic (specifically, French Catholic), thus suggesting that the two religions have different values toward work.

3. Alternatively, the differences between the attitudes of urban and rural workers toward their work may not be a matter of religion but of experience. Urban workers, many of whom are blacks or ethnics, may reject the Protestant ethic because their experience has not taught them that hard work pays off.[33] Indeed, rural parents may stress need achievement to their children, while the urban child learns need affiliation or need power.

4. The differences may relate to the Maslow hierarchy. Richard Hackman and Edward Lawler[34] report that urban workers are relatively more concerned with satisfying physical and social, as opposed to egoistic needs than are their country cousins. The explanation for this is unclear, although it is possibly related to the higher cost of living and the greater difficulty of developing meaningful social relations in the city.

A second possible explanation of the urban-rural attitude differences is fairly simple: no one wants unlimited challenge in his life. The research scientist, for example, may relish the novelty and uncertainty of laboratory work, but he insists that his secretary always be on call, that his lab technician give predictable responses, and that his car start with complete regularity. For urban workers, already surrounded with uncertainty, the optimum degree of challenge desired on the job may be considerably less than that of his rural counterpart.

Third, urban workers may be less well endowed than rural workers with manual skills or even intelligence. As a consequence, even relatively simple tasks may seem taxing. (We know that feeble-minded persons often have a relative advantage on simple jobs.)

A fourth explanation is in terms of "equity theory." Challenging jobs usually require more work, and certainly more responsibility,[35] but they command higher status and pay. In rural areas taking on more challenging work may lead to *relatively* greater social and economic payoff than it does in the city, where the highest-paid blue-collar worker may still be quite low on the overall social and economic totem pole; the city worker may decide that the reward for taking on more responsibility may not be worth the effort.

The fifth explanation may be merely a variant of the fourth: work and the job may be much more central to workers' lives in rural areas than it is in big cities, where there are a wide variety of other activities upon which life interest may be focused.[36] This suggests a much broader question to which we now turn: How central is the job in determining satisfaction with life?

THE JOB: PRIMARY SOURCE OF LIFE SATISFACTION?

Must workers satisfy their higher-order needs on the job, or can they satisfy these needs after work, with their family, through hobbies and recreation, or in social and community activities? Arguably, the central focus of many people's lives is not the job, which is seen as merely a way of "getting a living," but the home or the community.

How important is work in human life? Classical Greece devalued work; it was at best *instrumental,* a means to an end. "Gentlemen" in many societies do not work. In the People's Republic of China, on the other hand, strenuous efforts are being made to make all work *expressive,* a valued end in itself. In our society work is more clearly the central life interest of artists and professionals than of laborers. The college professor's career is often both work and recreation; he thinks about his job even when presumably engaged in leisure. His self-image is tied up in work. His friends are likely to be college professors—and they talk shop. To a lesser extent skilled craftsmen behave in the same way. But Harold Wilensky suggests that "Where the technical and social organization of work offer much freedom—that is, discretion in methods, pace or schedule, and opportunity for frequent interaction with fellow workers . . . then work attachments will be strong, work integrated with the rest of life, and ties to the community and society solid. Conversely, if the task offers little workplace freedom . . . then work attachments will be weak, work sharply split from leisure and ties to community and society uncertain."[37]

How do workers respond to jobs that provide little opportunity for being expressive? A few seem to have adjusted easily enough to viewing their jobs as purely instrumental. In my own interviews with factory workers, I often talked to women who repeated variants of "I like this job because it gets me away from the kids and all the pressures at home." Similarly, I know artists who have deliberately taken high-paying but boring jobs in order to earn enough to support their real interests. John Goldthorpe concludes that English auto workers take assembly-line jobs because they view them as an instrument for the attainment of economic ends.[38]

Nevertheless these may be exceptional cases. As Wilensky and others have implied, in our society the nature of one's work, particularly in the case of males, does much to provide meaning in life. What of those for whom the job provides little meaning? Can they trade on-the-job for off-the-job satisfactions? Can the worker who desires but does not find higher-order satisfactions on the job make up for their absence in his off-the-job activities? And if so, at what cost to himself? This is a difficult question to research, to which at least three approaches have been suggested.

Mental-Health Studies

By and large, satisfaction with life seems to be related to satisfaction on the job; that is, those who are unhappy with their jobs are also likely to be unhappy with life in general. This might mean only that some people are perpetual malcontents. Or it may mean that people with unsatisfactory lives *report* dissatisfaction with their jobs, even when their jobs may be identical to ones held by satisfied workers. For example, unmarried workers (who possibly may have less happy lives than married workers) report less work satisfaction than do married workers.[39]

But there is some evidence that workers on objectively less challenging jobs report less satisfying lives. Further, there are the previously cited mental-health studies that suggest that unskilled factory workers suffer from poorer mental health than do those in more skilled work.

Assuming that the mental-health studies are valid, the question remains whether poorer mental health and less satisfaction with life are caused by low job challenge or by other factors. The unskilled or semi-skilled blue-collar worker suffers not just from boring work but from low social status, low pay (at least compared to those with higher-skilled jobs), and relatively irregular work. The latter two factors lead to his or her having a worse standard of living, living in less desirable parts of town, and being less able to afford adequate medical and psychiatric care. Thus, it is far from clear whether poorer mental health is caused primarily by the intrinsic nature of unskilled work or by the fact that such work pays poorly and has low status both on and off the job. Insofar as mental disturbances and dissatisfaction with life are caused by economic and social pressures at home, higher wages may be a better solution than improved human relations or job enrichment.[40]

Recreation Studies

Another approach involves looking at recreation and the use of leisure time. Do those with unchallenging jobs make up for this with challenging recreation and the creative use of leisure time? Of course, answering the question involves value judgments. What the professor-researcher might think creative and self-actualizing, for example, chess, bird watching, mountain climbing, or listening to Bach, the blue-collar worker might find completely boring.

One imaginative study, by Martin Meissner, concluded that workers tend to engage in leisure-time activities that reflect the nature of their jobs.[41] Thus, workers whose jobs permit active discretion tend to spend more time in leisure-time pursuits that also involve discretion, such as participating in organizations, playing sports, homebuilding, and hobbies; those whose jobs permit social activity but not discretion have as their main forms of recreation visiting, outings, "beer and talk," and so forth. And the final category of workers, those whose jobs permit neither discretion nor social activity engage in fishing, religious activities, going for a drive, watching TV and listening to the radio, and similar passive activities. We should, however, be careful not to generalize too much from a single study. Certainly there are those who are able to make up for boring work through creative activity off the job, either at home or in the community. Nevertheless the Meissner study suggests that this sort of adjustment is far from universal; there are large numbers of workers who do not counteract the effects of dull work by active recreation.

Perhaps this should not be surprising. Participant accounts of life in mass-production factories[42] stress the fact that the work pace leaves one so exhausted that there is only enough energy left to drink a few beers or watch television. But there is another, less kind explanation: it is not dull work that causes dull recreation, but dull people who pick dull recreation and through natural selection drift into dull work. In any case, for most workers the quality of life in general seems closely related to the quality of life on the job; the limited evidence that exists does not support the trade-off hypothesis.

The Morse and Weiss Studies

Further evidence of the importance of work is provided by a 1955 study by Morse and Weiss, which asked a sample of male, white workers, "If by chance you inherited enough money to live comfortably without working, do you think you would work anyway?" The vast majority (80 percent) of all respondents answered in the affirmative (see Table 2), even though the percentages were slightly higher for the middle class (86 percent) than for the working class (76 percent). Why would they work? As expected, the main reason middle-class workers would continue working was for "interest or accomplishment," but for the blue-collar worker the main reason was, surprisingly, "to keep occupied."[43] In other words, blue-collar workers would rather work even though working involved just filling up time.[44] This may be a depressing commentary on the meaninglessness of life off the job, but at the least it suggests the centrality of work to the average American white male. It also suggests that workers do adjust to boring work, though perhaps at a cost.

APATHY AS A FORM OF ADJUSTMENT

There are two findings reported in Table 2 that we have not discussed: most blue-collar workers say that they would prefer another job; yet the vast majority report that they are "satisfied" or even "very satisfied"

TABLE 2: SELECTED ATTITUDES TOWARD WORK (percentages)

	Middle Class	Working Class
Would continue working, even if inherited enough not to	86	76
Reasons for so doing		
Interest or accomplishment	44	10
To keep occupied	37	71
Would continue working at same job	61	34
Attitude toward job		
Very satisfied	42	27
Satisfied	37	57
Dissatisfied	21	16

Source: Nancy Morse and Robert Weiss, "The Function and Meaning of Work," *American Sociological Review*, 20, No. 2 (April 1966), pp. 191-198.

with their present work. The second finding is consistent with that of the Gallup Poll mentioned earlier and with almost all other research in this area.[45] In most studies only 10 to 20 percent of those who reply are dissatisfied with their jobs. Even among auto-assembly-line workers, 66 percent report that their jobs are "interesting."[46]

To put the question rather stupidly, does this mean that such a high percentage of blue-collar workers are *really* satisfied with their jobs? I think not. The percentage of those "very satisfied" may be more meaningful, since it is a far less stable figure and varies greatly from job to job. If a substantial proportion of blue-collar workers (1) report being satisfied with their jobs, but wishing to change it, and (2) also report that they would continue working even if they didn't have to, just to fill time, then this can only mean that these workers accept the necessity of work but expect little satisfaction from their specific jobs. Or, to put it in Frederick Herzberg's terms, they are neither dissatisfied nor satisfied; they are apathetic.

The simple personality-versus-organization hypothesis suggests that organizational restraints cause workers to become frustrated and to react to their frustration either by fighting back (through union activity, sabotage, or output restriction) or by producing no more than a minimum amount of work. By 1964, however, Chris Argyris had considerably softened his harshly pessimistic earlier view; he came to realize that many workers seem to adjust to a challengeless work environment.[47] Though such individuals may be psychologically "immature," their expectations of what the job will offer them are low,[48] and they suffer few overt signs of aggression. They do routine jobs in an adequate fashion, though their performance is not innovative and they resist change. These workers may not be overtly dissatisfied but that does not mean that they are motivated.

Implicit support for the Argyris view has come from the reseach of Frederick Herzberg and his colleagues.[49] On the basis of imaginative research, Herzberg concluded that job satisfaction and dissatisfaction are not opposite points on a continuum but in fact are two separate dimensions. "Extrinsic" factors, such as company policy, incompetent supervision, or unsatisfactory working conditions may lead to dissatisfaction. Such dissatisfaction may be reduced by hygienic measures such as fringe benefits, "human-relations training" for foremen, and better company policies, but such measures will not satisfy workers; it will only make them apathetic. For true satisfaction to be obtained, "intrinsic" factors must be provided, such as achievement, accomplishment, responsibility, and challenging work. Note that satisfaction is obtained primarily from the *content* of the work itself, dissatisfaction from its *context*. Only satisfaction relates to productivity; the presence of dissatisfaction may lead to low morale or absenteeism, but its elimination will not raise motivation or productivity. Herzberg concluded that it is a mistake to emphasize traditional "hygienic," "extrinsic" measures, which serve only to make the work environment more tolerable. Instead, management should seek to enrich (not just enlarge) jobs so as to make them seem interesting and important.

Herzberg's work has led to substantial controversy and considerable research. On the whole, those who have used his methodology have obtained his results; those who have used different methodologies have obtained different results. But whatever the research's limitations, most investigators believe that there can be a middle ground between the overly pessimistic view that workers actively fight routine jobs and the overly optimistic one that these jobs make workers truly happy. This middle ground is illustrated by a statement from a blue-collar worker with a routine job, whom I interviewed. The worker told me, in a rather offhand way, "I got a pretty good job." "What makes it such a good job?" I asked. He answered, "Don't get me wrong. I didn't say it is a *good* job. It's an okay job—about as good a job as a guy like me might expect. The foreman leaves me alone and it pays well. But I would never call it a *good* job. It doesn't amount to much, but it's not bad."

This middle ground might be called apathy. The worker's expectations are low, and he accepts his situation. In a sense he has made a bargain with his employer and does not feel badly cheated.[50] Attitudes such as this are not likely to lead to revolt. As Robert Blauner puts it, "The majority of blue collar workers are committed to their roles as producers, and are loyal (though within limits) to their employers."[51]

SUBSTITUTES FOR INTRINSIC JOB SATISFACTION

Too little is known about the process by which workers adjust to boring work, but it is clear that adjustment is easier for some people than for others and in some technologies than in others. At least three factors facilitate the adjustment process.

Social Life

For many workers social life on the job can provide substitutes for satisfactions lacking in the job itself. Even in a humdrum context, people are able to extract surprisingly rich meanings from seemingly trivial events. For example, horseplay, lunchtime card games, gossip around the water cooler, and football pools provide satisfactions, particularly for those with strong feelings of need affiliation. As the job becomes less rewarding, the social group may become more so.[52]

But this is not always the case. Cohesive work groups do not arise automatically whenever the work is boring; jobs differ substantially in the opportunities they provide for social interaction. The automobile assembly line—which permits the typical worker to communicate only with the men directly ahead and behind him in the flow of work—provides less opportunity for social interaction than most other types of work. Similar problems have been created in continuous-strip steel mills, where the work stations have been placed so far apart that workers are unable to communicate with each other.

Success in "bargaining" with management, either formally through the union or informally through such measures as wildcat strikes, can help create group cohesion, just as failure in bargaining can fracture unity. But success of this sort is also partially a function of technology. Leonard Sayles has distinguished between Strategic, Conservative, Erratic, and Apathetic work groups. Only the first two types are successful in terms of bargaining. Members of Erratic groups may work together more closely than members of Strategic groups, but for a variety of reasons differences within these groups prevent them from developing effective teamwork.

Technology is not the only factor limiting the development of social life. High turnover, heterogeneity among employees in terms of age, ethnic, and educational background, and job duties all inhibit the development of cohesive work groups.

Social cohesion is also affected by the opportunity for association off the job. As Robert Blauner has stated: "The evidence of the work literature supports the notion that levels of work satisfaction are higher in those industries and in those kinds of jobs in which workers make up an 'occupational community.' One such industry is mining. Not only is the actual work carried out by solitary work groups, but in addition miners live in a community made up of fellow workers. This kind of 'inbreeding' produces a devotion to the occupation which is not characteristic of many other working class jobs."[53] [See also M. H. Ross' article in this book, pp. 171-179.] Workers who live in isolated small communities, who work odd shifts, or whose jobs frequently take them from home are more likely to develop occupational communities of this sort.

The union also helps provide solidarity, at least for a small group of activists. However, participation in the union is unlikely to be high among groups that are not already socially cohesive. Indeed, substantial evidence suggests that workers who are dissatisfied with their jobs also tend to be dissatisfied with their union.[54]

To summarize, a rich social life on the job can substitute to some extent for boring work. Unfortunately, however, those occupational work groups that have the greatest need for the kind of social support that a cohesive group might provide are frequently the very ones that find it most difficult to develop such cohesion in the first place. There is considerable evidence that cohesion and job satisfaction are postively correlated. The development of cohesive groups may increase interest in the job; on the other hand, the same factors that make jobs less intrinsically satisfying may also inhibit cohesion.

Dreams of Advancement

Ely Chinoy's *Automobile Workers and the American Dream* explains in vivid terms one aspect of how blue-collar workers adjusted in the early 1950s to the frustrations of the assembly line. (Use of the past tense is intentional since this form of adjustment may no longer be feasible.) Despite the seemingly dead-end nature of their jobs, a high percentage of Chinoy's respondents looked upon their jobs as only temporary and dreamed of (or fantasized about) the day when they would be able to quit the factory and set up their own small business or engage in some sort of independent occupation. When the passage of time discredits these dreams, they project their frustrated ambitions onto their children, for whom they make plans for college and escaping the assembly line. In either case, "their daydreams serve as a safety valve for day-to-day frustrations."[55]

Economic Security

The strong unions and the relative prosperity of the 1950s and 1960s brought workers, particularly those with high seniority, considerable job security, protection against tyrannical foremen and arbitrary rules, and an ever growing stream of fringe benefits. These developments led Daniel Bell to conclude: "Workers, whose grievances were once the driving energy for social change, are more satisfied with the society than the intellectuals. The workers have not achieved utopia but their expectations were less than those of the intellectuals and their gains correspondingly larger."[56]

A GAME WITH THE ENVIRONMENT?

Recent research suggests that the process of adjusting to work may be even more complex than had previously been thought. In discussing work attitudes of French white-collar workers, Michel Crozier[57] suggested that "feelings are not the product of circumstances . . . feelings are escape routes . . . [ploys in a] game with the environment." There is no reason to believe that attitude questions are answered with complete honesty or that conscious—or even unconscious—attitudes accurately reflect a worker's objective situation. When a worker reports that he is "satisfied" with his job, it may mean only that his self-respect forces him to answer in this way; work may be so central to life that to report that one's job is unsatisfactory is almost to admit failure in life itself. This is not an attempt to deceive the interviewer; one's need for mental balance (to reduce cognitive dissonance) may require one to believe that he is really satisfied.

If attitudes toward the job represent a game with the environment, then different strategies are possible. Though Crozier's study dealt with white-collar workers in a French company, he suggests strategies that American workers may also be employing. In Crozier's study, lower-ranking employees reported greater satisfaction in working for an insurance company but less interest in their work than did those in higher-ranking jobs. For those of lower ranks—many of whom came from working-class backgrounds—merely working for an insurance company added to their status, even though their particular jobs were menial. Employees at higher levels had the security to cast aspersions on their employers and to suggest they could do better elsewhere. Those at lower levels felt that they could "better safeguard [their] independence by submitting to orders than by seeking to participate in the elaboration of decisions." They preserved their independence not by solidarity but by being apathetic and demanding close supervision; they felt that the permissive supervisor who engaged in general supervision showed "lack of candor" and preferred "the forceful manager who makes clear and categorical decisions. . . . Subservience [is] a marvelous tool by which to control and manipulate management."

Thus for those low-ranking French white-collar workers the strategy was to lie low, to avoid involving themselves in the job, and so to protect their egos. There is certainly a similarity between these workers and their American counterparts who report that they are "satisfied" with their jobs but work only to "keep busy."

Chris Argyris suggests that many lower-skilled workers express the need to "be left alone," "to be passive," and to "experience routine and sameness," and he suggests that these attitudes are caused by the organization's stifling of individual maturity.[58] Kornhauser reports interview responses such as: "There's such a thing as beating your brains against the wall. Some things you just can't change; might as well accept them and adjust yourself to them." Kornhauser calls such "passivity, fatalism, and resignation" evidence of poor mental health. Even assuming that the job caused the attitude (rather than the attitude causing the employee to accept the job), the worker who expresses such attitudes may not be mentally ill but realistic, a shrewd player in the game with the environment, and very healthy indeed.[59]

Apathy is one ploy, resistance is another. Blauner notes that automobile workers, though still on the whole "satisfied" with their work, report greater dissatisfaction than workers in any other major occupation. For the automobile worker "dissatisfaction is a reflection of his independence and dignity . . . This independence and dignity is expressed in other ways besides generalized dissatisfaction. The auto worker quits his job more frequently than other workers. He is characteristically a griper, a man who talks back to his foreman, in contrast to the more submissive textile employee." He also processes more grievances and is more likely to revolt against his union or sabotage the production process. For at least some auto workers, "dissatisfaction is dignity."

The point here is that one should not take expressed satisfaction or dissatisfaction too seriously. A worker may switch quickly from one strategy to another, with little objective change in work conditions. Apathy may quickly change to revolt, just as it did for blacks in America when conditions suggested that that strategy would provide a greater payoff in the game against the environment.

SUMMARY

The evidence is confusing at best. What sense can we make of it?

It seems reasonably clear that not everyone feels oppressed by his or her organization. Dissatisfaction with work seems to be a function of technology. The greatest dissatisfaction is reported on jobs with short job cycles and relatively little challenge and in industries, especially the automotive industry but also in wholesale and retail trade, in which such characteristics are common.

But the degree of job challenge does not alone determine one's attitude toward work. Dissatisfaction is also high on jobs that pay poorly, have low status, and that prevent the development of group life. Supervision is also important, as Table 1 suggests. Some theorists would suggest that good supervision—and, particularly, adequate pay and job security—may be more basic than challenging work.

Personality and culture enter the picture in a puzzling fashion. Two alternative hypotheses are possible.

1. Unchallenging bureaucratic jobs inhibit the normal development of the human personality, thus leading to poor mental health, to apathy, and even to the delusion that one prefers highly structured

work. Persons who work under such conditions redirect, it is argued, their limited energies into activities off the job, into social life on the job, or into sheer fantasy—but never with great success and always with considerable emotional cost.

2. Because of genetic or cultural factors, some people have lower aspirations or less ability to handle challenging work or less need for achievement or more desire to center their lives off the job. Their primary demands from their jobs are economic and instrumental. To the extent they can, they pick jobs that pay well or that make few mental or physical demands.

As inconsistent as these two explanations of the evidence seem, both may in fact be partly true. Whole cultures may adjust, as did blacks until recently, to jobs that provide little challenge, and change "personality" through that adjustment. Whether such adjustment is "healthy" may be irrelevant for our purposes here; the main point is that adjustment can be stable, not leading to revolt unless underlying conditions change.

To put it another way, there are a variety of forms of adjustment to "objectively" unchallenging work, that is, work that most observers—especially college professors—report as unchallenging. Some workers are able to develop rich social lives on the job or are active in their union. Others find a large part of the challenges they desire off the job, through recreation or family activities, though the evidence suggests that for many this recreation may be rather passive in nature. A worker may adjust by dreaming of better work, either for himself or for his children. Alternatively, he may "enlarge" his job through sabotage or output restriction[60] or he may lower his aspirations and delude himself with the belief that he is truly happy—and thus become resigned and apathetic. Finally, he may become a chronic griper or even express his feelings through strikes, absenteeism, or quitting his job, that is, through revolt.

Some of these forms of adjustment are more costly to society and to the individual than are others. Revolt is one possibility, but not the only one. Revolt seems unlikely to increase substantially unless underlying conditions change to make it more attractive than other forms of reaction.

TRENDS FOR THE FUTURE

Have underlying conditions changed? Much of the discussion concerning blue-collar dissatisfaction assumes that it has intensified in recent years. Although we have little evidence so far suggesting that dissatisfaction with work has increased, there are a number of hypotheses available to explain such dissatisfaction, if and when it becomes apparent. Why should such a change occur?

One possibility is that the characteristics of work itself have objectively altered. Other than gross census data about occupational distribution, we have little evidence about changes in the nature of work. Possibly there has been some movement away from assembly-line work and toward process automation. If so, as was pointed out previously, this change might actually result in increased satisfaction. More likely, the change in the nature of jobs has been too gradual to lead to any sharp change in the degree of satisfaction.

On the other hand, there have been some changes in the job environment: managers, as well as workers, are better educated; unionism and the human-relations movement have had an impact; and although we have little firm evidence, we have every reason to believe that workers today are better treated by their bosses, that company policies are more humane, that safety hazards have been reduced, and that job security has improved. Herzberg's "hygienes" are more prevalent, thus making the job more tolerable.

The biggest changes, however, have occurred in the work force.

Younger Workers

Because of demographic shifts, we have seen a substantial reduction in the average worker's age in many industries, especially in the automotive industry. This reduction in age may have had an impact on job satisfaction. Since the first studies were made, young people have registered less satisfaction with their work than did their elders; not only is youth more restless, but younger employees usually work at less interesting jobs, receive lower salaries, and have less job security—and yet, if they are married and have children, they may have the greatest needs. During the late sixties, according to the Gallup Poll, morale fell much faster among younger workers than among older ones. Possibly these younger workers were influenced by the generally more permissive environment that accompanied the student revolts. Certainly, among the current generation of younger workers, the personality-versus-organization conflict is particularly acute.

But this trend toward a younger work force may reverse itself. The bonanza crop of postwar youth (born 1946-51) that entered either the workplace or college during the hectic years of 1964-69 is now in its mid-twenties. By the mid-seventies, the post-World-War-II baby was rapidly approaching the so-called untrustworthy age of thirty, burdened down, no doubt, by children and mortgages.

Better Educated Workers

In 1948, the average education of the employed labor force was 10.6 years; in 1972, it was 12.4. Twenty-six percent had had some college. The educational level had climbed much faster than the demands of most jobs. Almost a million people with three years of college are in unskilled and semiskilled occupations. Understandably, there is evidence that where job level is held constant, education is inversely related to satisfaction.

Cognitive dissonance is at work here. The extra investment involved in increased education has given rise to increased expectations that have not been met in practice. For these workers education has not been a route to success.[61] A substantial proportion of workers, especially those who report "some college," feel that their skills are underutilized on the job.[62] Among whites, those thirty years of age or younger with "some college" reported the greatest dissatisfaction overall.

Education may have two other effects. It may increase the worker's opportunities to find meaningful recreation off the job, which suggests that he will more easily make a tradeoff between boring work and interesting leisure. On the other hand, it may also reduce his sense of alienation and increase his sense of control over the environment. To the extent the second proposition is true, he will be less likely to adopt a strategy of apathy in the game against the environment and may be more inclined to engage in active revolt.

Movement up the Maslow Hierarchy

All during the 1940s and 1950s, workers named steady work as the most important thing they wanted from their jobs. A comprehensive 1957 study, which summarized the extensive literature, listed job factors influencing satisfaction in roughly this order: job security, opportunities for advancement, a progressive company and good management, good wages, and intrinsic work—with intrinsic work coming fifth.[63] By sharp contrast, in a 1969 survey interesting work came first and job security was rated seventh; six of the eight top-ranking aspects of work related to job content.[64]

These data may be but statistical artifacts (see the different ranking in Table 1), but if confirmed by other evidence they suggest a substantial shift in the value-ordering of American workers, one that is consistent with the Maslow hierarchy. After all, this is the first generation not to grow up in the shadow of the Great Depression; the specter of job insecurity may have been licked. With low-level needs largely fulfilled,[65] workers may be in a position to demand satisfaction for their egoistic and self-actualization needs. If so, such workers are less likely to be apathetic or even to settle for a job that offers a high income and a rich social life but no intrinsic satisfaction. For such workers, money alone may no longer be sufficient motivation—or, as economists put it, it may have a declining marginal utility.

Two studies seem consistent with this view. The first, by Charles Hulin, suggests that when work content is held constant, job satisfaction is negatively correlated with community income. In other words, as the community grows more prosperous and the worker's job remains unchanged, his satisfaction drops. The second, by Richard Hackman and Edward Lawler, tends to confirm the commonsense expectation that the relationship between job challenge and job satisfaction is highest when workers are motivated to satisfy higher-order needs.[66]

Fewer Escape Routes

Chinoy suggested that one escape route of the automobile worker was to dream of setting up his own business. (Other studies suggest that in some industries ambitious workers once felt they had a real chance to move into management.) One may wonder whether these escape routes still are psychologically meaningful—even for workers with some college education.

A REVOLT AGAINST ALL WORK?

We come to a final difficult question: If there is to be a labor revolt at all, will it be against all work or only boring work?

A case can be made for the possibility of a revolt against all work. The Hulin and Blood studies suggest that a significant portion of our population rejects the Protestant work ethic and feels no increase in satisfaction when given challenging work. In addition, certain segments of our youth culture have "dropped out" of the "rat race" (consider the college-educated hippie postman or candlemaker). To some extent there seems to be a drop in competitive motivation and belief in the work ethic among college students.

But by and large, this case is weak. As suggested earlier, workers from the city slums whom Hulin and Blood studied may have given up and settled for steady but boring jobs. Their children, better educated and having grown up in greater economic security, feel more in control of their destinies and reject their father's low-risk solutions. If those at the bottom of the social pyramid—blacks, Indians, and Chicanos—can revolt, why not those slightly higher up? [67]

Anyway, the youth culture may not represent a revolt against all work, but only against meaningless work.[68] Witness the rise of handicraft industries.

Earlier I argued that too many sociologists apply professors' standard values in judging the plight of blue-collar workers. But as the worker becomes better educated and more affluent, he may become more like the professor. Possibly. But as long as access to education in our society remains relatively open, the vast majority of those who *really* want white-collar, professional, or managerial jobs will obtain the education required to get them. (Mine may be an elitist view.) When almost everyone has a high-school education, the social and psychological meaning of that degree may drop, as will the expectation that it should guarantee meaningful work.

CONCLUSION

Recent political developments do suggest some sort of socioeconomic revolt among blue-collar workers, or perhaps among lower-middle-class groups generally. (But, given the Nixon landslide, it would appear to be a strange revolt—a revolt against change rather than for it.) However, the evidence is less clear about a sudden increase in dissatisfaction with work. The two phenomena may be related, but they are not identical.

A boring job is a boring job, but some adjust to it more easily than others. Businessmen, economists, and politicians have now begun to talk about job enrichment as the remedy for a host of maladies, even as a means of making price controls work. It is not clear that all workers want job enrichment or that job enrichment alone, without increased wages, increased promotion opportunities, and a higher social status for blue-collar work would resolve such blue-collar dissatisfaction as does exist. On the other hand, job enrichment may require redesigning production processes and may reduce technological efficiency. Further, it may necessitate readjustment (inevitably upwards) of pay scales, retraining of management, and possibly reduction in the rigidity of our seniority rules. The net advantage of job enrichment, either to our economy or to our society, may be low.[69]

NOTES

1. As yet the interest seems greater among journalists and politicians than among social scientists. Indeed the whole development has come as a surprise to social scientists, whose interest in blue-collar attitudes and behavior peaked

during the 1940s and early 1950s. During the late 1950s and 1960s, our interests tended to climb the status ladder from blue-collar workers to supervisors and then to managers and professionals, while as variables our concerns were more and more centered on motivation, productivity, and organizational climate.

2. *Economist*, April 30, 1972.

3. Harold L. Sheppard and Neal Q. Herrick, *Where Have All the Robots Gone? Worker Dissatisfaction in the Seventies* (New York: Free Press, 1972).

4. Harvey Swados, "Foreword" in Sheppard and Herrick, *op. cit.*

5. *AFL-CIO News*, Jan. 27, 1973, p. 5.

6. Thomas R. Brooks, "Job Satisfaction: An Elusive Goal," *AFL-CIO American Federationist*, 79, No. 10 (Oct. 1972), pp. 1-8.

7. Lloyd Ulman, Robert Flanagan, and George Strauss, *Worker Discontent: Where Is the Problem?* (Berkeley: Institute of Industrial Relations, Univ. of Calif., 1974).

8. *Ibid.*

9. Thomas P. Quinn, Thomas F. Mangione, Martha S. Mandilovitch, "Evaluating Working Conditions in America," *Monthly Labor Review*, 96, No. 11 (Nov. 1973), p. 39.

10. Sar Levitan, *Blue-Collar Workers: A Symposium on Middle America* (New York: McGraw-Hill, 1971); Stanley E. Seashore and J. Thad Barnowe, "Demographic and Job Factors Associated with the 'Blue-Collar Blues'" (Mimeo., 1972); Sheppard and Herrick, *op. cit.*

11. The social historian may note that public concern with the other forms of dissatisfaction antedated concern with work dissatisfaction by several years.

12. Levitan, *op. cit.*

13. Edward Ransford, "Blue-Collar Anger: Reactions to Student and Black Protest," *American Sociological Review*, 37, No. 3 (June 1972), pp. 333-346.

14. But note the resurgence of interest in crafts and other manual activities among middle-class youth.

15. Ely Chinoy, *Automobile Workers and the American Dream* (Garden City, N.Y.: Doubleday, 1955). The extent to which blue-collar workers have lost faith in the American Dream remains to be tested. Offhand it would seem that they believe in it more than do hippies.

16. Ransford, *op. cit.*

17. Chris Argyris, *Personality and Organization* (New York: Harper & Row, 1957).

18. Norman R. F. Maier, *Psychology in Industry* (Boston: Houghton Mifflin, 1955).

19. Douglas McGregor, *The Human Side of Enterprise* (New York: McGraw-Hill, 1960).

20. Abraham Maslow, *Motivation and Personality* (New York: Harper & Row, 1954).

21. McGregor, *op. cit.*

22. Robert Blauner, *Alienation and Freedom* (Chicago: Univ. of Chicago Press, 1964); Charles R. Walker and Robert Guest, *The Man on the Assembly Line* (Cambridge: Harvard Univ. Press, 1952); Seashore and Barnowe, *op. cit.*

23. Walker and Guest, *op. cit.*; Arthur Turner and Paul Lawrence, *Industrial*

Jobs and the Worker (Boston: Harvard Grad. School of Business Administration, 1965; but see Maurice Kilbridge, "Do Workers Prefer Larger Jobs?" *Personnel*, 37, No. 5 (Sept. 1960), p. 45.

24. Charles S. Telly, Wendell French, and William G. Scott, "The Relationship of Inequity to Turnover Among Hourly Workers," *Administrative Science Quarterly*, 16, No. 2 (June 1971), pp. 164-172.

25. Leonard R. Sayles, "Wildcat Strikes," *Harvard Business Review*, 32, No. 6 (Oct. 1964), pp. 84-92.

26. Arthur Kornhauser, "Mental Health of Factory Workers," *Human Organization*, 21 (Spring 1962), pp. 43-46; Gerald Guerin, Joseph Vernoff, and Sheila Field, *Americans View Their Mental Health* (New York: Basic Books, 1960).

27. Blauner, *op. cit.*; Jon M. Shepard, "Functional Specialization and Work Attitudes," *Industrial Relations*, 8, No. 2 (May 1969), pp. 185-194.

28. Survey Research Center, University of Michigan, *Survey of Working Conditions* (Washington, D.C.: U.S. Department of Labor, 1971).

29. David McClelland, *The Achieving Society* (Princeton, N.J.: Van Nostrand, 1961).

30. One study, for example, suggests that workers who have a high need for independence and weak authoritarian attitudes are likely to respond to consultation with their supervisors by being more satisfied with their work; those with low needs for independence and strong authoritarian values are less likely to respond in this manner. See Victor Vroom, *Some Personality Determinants of the Effects of Participation* (Englewood Cliffs, N.J.: Prentice-Hall, 1960).

31. See Charles Hulin and Milton Blood, "Job Enlargement, Individual Differences, and Worker Responses," *Psychological Bulletin*, 69 (1968), pp. 41-55.

32. Gerald I. Susman, "Job Enlargement: Effects of Culture on Worker Response," *Industrial Relations*, 12, No. 1 (Feb. 1973), pp. 1-15.

33. As far as ethnics are concerned, this explanation would seem to fly in the face of the "social squeeze" hypothesis, which argues that ethnic blue-collar discontent arises because blacks threaten their achievements. It should be noted that the Hulin and Blood sample excluded blacks.

34. J. Richard Hackman and Edward E. Lawler III, "Employee Reactions to Job Characteristics," *Journal of Applied Psychology*, 55 (June 1971), pp. 259-286.

35. According to the 1969 study, jobs that are high on "enriching job demand" are also high on "job-related tensions."

36. It should be noted that Jon M. Shepard's research seems to contradict all these explanations. His findings suggest that job satisfaction is positively correlated with job challenge, even for alienated workers. See "Functional Specialization, Alienation, and Job Satisfaction," *Industrial and Labor Relations Review*, 23 (Jan. 1970), pp. 207-219.

37. Harold Wilensky, "The Uneven Distribution of Leisure," *Social Problems*, 9, No. 1 (Summer 1961), p. 522.

38. John H. Goldthorpe, "Attitudes and Behavior of Car Assemblers: A Deviant Case and Theoretical Critique," *British Journal of Sociology*, 69 (Jan. 1966), pp. 41-55.

39. Survey Research Center, *op. cit.*

40. Research into the question makes it abundantly clear that unskilled workers are not the only ones to suffer from poor mental health. Depending on what study one looks at or what mental-health index is used, one can conclude that executives, clerical personnel, salespeople, and lower-level supervisors all suffer from one form or another of below-average mental health. The 1969 study concludes that those in higher-status occupations suffer more from job-related tensions; those in lower-status occupations, from somatic complaints. (Survey Research Center, *op. cit.*)

41. Martin Meissner, "The Long Arm of the Job: A Study of Work and Leisure," *Industrial Relations*, 10 (Oct. 1971).

42. For example, Studs Terkel, "A Steelworker Speaks," *Dissent*, 19, No. 1 (Winter 1972), pp. 9-20.

43. This answer is consistent with Gerald Susman's findings (*op. cit.*) about urban blue-collar workers.

44. In the 1969 University of Michigan survey (Survey Research Center, p. 61) 67.4 percent of the respondents answered in the affirmative the question, "If you were to get enough money to live as comfortably as you would like for the rest of your life, would you continue to work?" And yet, doubt can be cast on both of these studies, in the case of automobile workers, an exceptionally large proportion of whom elected to take early retirement when this option became available in 1970.

45. Results of the 1969 manpower study: 46.4 percent, "very satisfied"; 39.0 percent, "somewhat satisfied"; 11.3 percent, "not too dissatisfied"; 3.2 percent, "not at all satisfied." The only report that I know of in which less than a majority expressed satisfaction was the 1965 Gallup Poll, in which only 48 percent of the black respondents expressed satisfaction (compared to 87 percent for whites). Arguably, this exceptional finding represents an attitude toward life or toward politics rather than toward the job.

46. Blauner, p. 204.

47. Chris Argyris, *Integrating the Organization and the Individual* (New York: Wiley, 1964).

48. Or, to put it another way, since their expectations are low, it requires relatively little objective satisfaction for them to report themselves "satisfied."

49. Frederick Herzberg, *Work and the Nature of Man* (New York: World, 1966).

50. This does not mean that workers never feel cheated. Quite the contrary. Tyrannical actions of individual foremen, efforts to speed up the production line, and so forth, can often lead to feelings that the basic bargain has been broken. My point is merely that available evidence suggests that a broad spectrum of workers are at least resigned to their lot.

51. Blauner, p. 181.

52. See particularly, Donald F. Roy, "'Banana Time': Job Satisfaction and Informal Interaction," *Human Organization*, 18, No. 4 (Winter 1959-60), pp. 158-166.

53. Blauner, p. 351.

54. Leonard R. Sayles and George Strauss, *The Local Union*, rev. ed. (New

York: Harcourt, 1967).

55. Blauner, p. 120.

56. Daniel Bell, *The End of Ideology* (New York: Collier Books, 1960).

57. Michel Crozier, *The World of the Office Worker* (Chicago: Univ. of Chicago Press, 1971).

58. Chris Argyris, "The Individual and the Organization: An Empirical Test," *Administrative Science Quarterly*, 4, No. 2 (1959).

59. Frederick Herzberg (*op. cit.*) looks upon mental health and mental illness as two separate dimensions (making the same distinction he makes between job satisfaction and dissatisfaction). Presumably Kornhauser's workers are neither healthy nor ill. A broader question concerns the way one characterizes the deviant worker who makes work central to his self-image in a situation where most of his peers seek satisfaction elsewhere. In a crazy world, what is sanity? (See *Work in America*: Report of a Special Task Force to the Secretary of Health, Education, and Welfare (Cambridge, Mass.: MIT Press, 1973), pp. 84-85.

60. William F. Whyte, *et al., Money and Motivation* (New York: Harper & Row, 1955).

61. Better-educated workers may demand higher wages just to counteract their boredom. Indeed, they may compare their wages with those of their age group who have "made it" in white-collar work.

62. Survey Research Center, *op. cit.*

63. Herzberg, *op. cit.*

64. Neal Herrick, "Who's Unhappy with Work and Why?" *Manpower*, 4, No. 1 (Jan. 1972), p. 5.

65. Arguably, blue-collar workers now receive middle-class wages and now want middle-class-type jobs. Such a view would seem to be inconsistent with Rossow's economic squeeze.

66. Hackman and Lawler, *op. cit.*

67. Interestingly, the generation gap in terms of job dissatisfaction is far greater among blacks than whites.

68. Meaningful work may mean more than challenging work. It must serve some broader social or aesthetic end.

69. Most of the discussion regarding worker dissatisfaction and job enrichment seems to be centered on manufacturing, yet there is good reason to believe that an ever increasing percentage of the nonchallenging jobs in our society will be in the service industries.

If there is to be a revolt, what will the role of the union be? The union movement is structured today to obtain greater income and job security for its members, not to demand more challenging work—to satisfy economic and security needs, not needs for self-actualization. Indeed, the prevailing mode (on the part of both unions and their members) has been to resist any change in jobs unless liberally compensated. Union leaders merely echo the feelings of rank-and-file workers in viewing management as an enemy; but as long as these attitudes prevail, the kinds of participative management envisioned by proponents of job enrichment may be difficult to obtain. Even where workers genuinely want job enrichment they may be very suspicious of the motives of the management that seeks to introduce it.

Worker Participation in Decision Making

Irving Bluestone

The history of mankind has been marked by struggle between those who govern and those who are governed. In each major conflict, regardless of time, place, and circumstances, the voice of rebellion against authority has manifested itself in the cry for freedom, liberty, human rights, and human dignity. The underlying motivation is the desire for the right to participate in the decisions that affect one's welfare.

Monarchs once claimed to rule by the "divine right of kings." And who would be so brave as to challenge the right of rulers claiming divine guidance? Yet challengers there were, and challengers there will be. The yearning of people to have something to say about how they will be governed is unceasing, even as history records setbacks along the road.

The same drive that has moved people and nations toward political freedom exists as well in the workplace—between employer and employee. The owner of capital in the early years of the Industrial Revolution assumed the same mantle in his firm as had monarchs in an earlier day. We are, of course, familiar with the oppression and oppressiveness in the factories of the early Industrial Revolution. Control over the employees was almost absolute—short of the worker's right to quit and take a chance of being blackballed from other employment.

Source: This article appeared in The Humanist, September-October 1973.

49

Zachary U. Geiger, proprietor of the Mt. Cory Carriage and Wagon Works, listed rules and regulations for his employees in April 1872. Today they appear ludicrous, yet they were the norm in their day.

1. Employes will daily sweep the floors, dust the furniture, shelves, and showcases.

2. Each day fill lamps, clean chimneys and trim wicks; wash the windows once a week.

3. Each clerk will bring in a bucket of water and skuttle of coal for the day's business.

4. Make your own pens carefully. You may whittle nibs to your individual taste.

5. This office will open at 7 a.m. and close at 8 p.m. daily except on the Sabbath, on which day it will remain closed.

6. Men employes will be given an evening off each week for courting purposes, or two evenings if they go regularly to church.

7. Every employe should lay aside from each pay a goodly sum of his earnings for his benefits during his declining years so that he will not become a burden upon the charity of his betters.

8. Any employe who smokes Spanish cigars, uses liquors in any forms, gets shaved at a barber shop, or frequents public halls will give good reason to suspect his worth, intentions, integrity, and honesty.

9. The employe who has performed his labors faithfully and without fault for a period of five years in my service and who has been thrifty and attentive to his religious duties and is looked upon by his fellowmen as a substantial and law-abiding citizen will be given an increase of 5 cents per day in his pay providing that just returns in profits from the business permit it.

Contrast this relationship with the following. In 1967, the UAW was negotiating with each of the three big automobile companies—General Motors, Ford, and Chrysler. These negotiations took place separately, since the auto industry and the UAW do not engage in industry-wide national contract bargaining. When the contracts were about to come to their terminal date (each of them had the same date of termination), the union proposed to each automobile company that the contracts be extended on a day-to-day basis while negotiations continued toward a conclusion. The companies refused this proposal. As a result, the contracts expired, and the workers were free to strike at any time. One of the union's tactics was to curtail overtime work in order to forestall the buildup of car inventories.

In one of the plants, the local management called a meeting with the committee after the workers had walked out rather than work overtime. The management said to the committee: "You fellows won't let us set our own schedules; so, okay, you set the schedules."

The chairman of the union committee pondered this a moment and then asked, "You mean you want to give up management's prerogative to schedule overtime? You want the workers to make that decision?" The company spokesman replied, "Look, we are asking you to do it." The union chairman, without blinking an eye, retorted, "The hell with you. You set the schedules, and we won't work them!"

AUTHORITARIAN RULE IN THE WORKPLACE

In a society that prides itself on its democratic system of freedom for the individual and rejection of dictatorial rule, the workplace still stands as an island of authoritarianism. The organizational mold of business, especially big business, and the material objective of maximizing profits serve to obstruct, or at least deter, the fulfillment of democracy in the workplace. In fact, the workplace is probably the most authoritarian environment in which the adult finds himself in a free society. Its rigidity leads people to live a kind of double life: at home, they enjoy a reasonable measure of autonomy and self-fulfillment; at work, they are subject to regimentation, supervision, and control by others.

A society anchored in democratic principles should ensure each individual the dignity, respect, and liberty worthy of free people; it should afford opportunity for self-expression and participation in the shaping of one's own life. At work, however, personal freedom is severely curtailed, each worker having to adapt himself to tasks, work speeds, and behavior decided upon by others or by machines.

The American way of life rests on the concept that in public life the "governors" are subject to the will of the "governed." In the private life of business, however, leadership does not stem from the confidence of the "governed" (the workers); rather, it is directed toward protection of the interests of the firm, most often against the "governed," whose activities and patterns of life at work are organized, directed, and dominated by the "governors."

In a democracy, the rules of society are fashioned with the consent of those who must live by them, and the individual is guaranteed a fair trial and is "innocent until proved guilty." In the workplace, management decides the rules to be lived by, then exercises its authority to impose sanctions in cases of individual transgression.

The argument used to support authoritarianism in the workplace is that the organization of production and the goal of maximizing profit make it mandatory. Ownership means control. Ownership means rule by decree. Thus, the pattern of relations between the "governors" and the "governed" in business is contradictory to democracy.

Moreover, the power of ownership is reinforced in society by custom, tradition, and law. The rights of property often supersede the rights of people, and these property rights are buttressed by protective legislation.

This is the heart of the problem that labor-management relations must grapple with. Workers who organize into unions bring an increasing measure of democracy into the workplace. In the broadest possible sense, this is an essential task of unionism and collective bargaining. Moreover, once organized, the workers, as citizens, move to alter the law and to make the rights of people superior to the rights of property and profit. This, too, is an essential task of unionism.

Present-day industrialized society holds to certain economic precepts. Among them are: (1) technological progress is inevitable and desirable; (2) a better living standard for all depends on increased productivity and an expanding gross national product; (3) the purpose of business is to make and maximize profit.

Thus, the underlying thrust of our economic system, anchored in these precepts, has motivated management to develop a production system that is maximally advanced technologically, with maximum production at the lowest possible unit cost, and with maximum profitability.

The pursuit of maximum profit received remarkable stimulus with the advent of industrial organization and its system of production. Very soon, individuals and their needs became extensions of that tool. Skills were broken down to the least common denominator so that humans became as interchangeable as machine parts. Specialization through fractioning the job into the simplest, most repetitive acts of performance reduced skill requirements to the minimum. This production process evolved into scientific management.

The granddaddy of the principles of scientific management, Frederick Taylor, once observed that the average workingman is "so stupid and so phlegmatic that he more resembles the ox in his mental makeup than any other type." Obviously, this is more than mere exaggeration. It is a cynical expression concerning human beings who happen to be workers.

Over the years, scientific management evolved refinements that have robotized workers, removing to the greatest degree possible requirements of education, knowledge, skill, creativity, brain power, and muscle power. The assembly line, with its repetitive, monotonous sameness, developed into the ultimate symbol of scientific management. Taylor's principles have served industry well as a guide toward ever increasing productivity, lower unit costs, and higher profits. They also dovetailed neatly into the concept of "profits before people."

WINDS OF CHANGE IN THE PRODUCTION SYSTEM

Times and circumstances are now beginning to modify the eighty-year-old practices of refined technology—in part because workers' attitudes toward the meaning of work are changing, but also because society as a whole is paying closer attention to the total environment and the quality of life.

About the time that Henry Ford announced the "five-dollar day," he remarked, "The assembly line is a haven for those who haven't got the brains to do anything else." His "enlightened" wage scale was accompanied by rules reminiscent of Geiger's rules of 1872. Mr. Ford's hiring practices were strict and stifling. No women were to work in his factories; they belonged at home in the kitchen and with their children. Men who failed to support their dependents would find no work at Ford, nor would divorced men or others who were "living unworthily"—those who smoked or drank hard liquor. Once hired, the workers were subjected to a spy system. "Social workers" on the Ford payroll visited workers' homes and reported on living habits: Did the man raise his own garden as instructed? Did his family house male boarders (which was taboo)? Did the worker complain to his family about his job and factory conditions? And so forth.

Today, the employer no longer has control of the worker outside the workplace, and unionization has wrested from the employer a measure of the control he exercises at the workplace. The next step is to provide the worker with a more meaningful measure of control over his job through participation in decisions affecting the job.

Contrast Henry Ford's stifling authoritarianism with the words of Richard Gerstenberg, chairman of the board of directors of General Motors Corporation, in 1972: "Productivity is not a matter of making employees work longer or harder . . . We must improve working conditions and take out the boredom from routine jobs . . . We must increase an employee's satisfaction with his job, heightening pride of workmanship, and, as far as is feasible, involve the employee personally in decisions that relate directly to his job . . ."[1]

Within its limited meaning, this statement marked an unfashionable awareness of Robert Heilbroner's thesis that ". . . the ultimate challenge to the institutions, motivations, political structures, lifeways, and ideologies of capitalist nations is whether they can accommodate themselves to the requirements of a society in which an attitude of 'social fatalism' is being replaced by one of social purpose."[2]

Mr. Gerstenberg's statement hopefully represents a conscious departure from the historic trickle-down theory that profits come first, that profits exemplify good in themselves and can only redound to the benefit of all society. Yet, more income and more material wealth, in and of themselves, do not guarantee a life of satisfaction or worth, and certainly cannot compensate for lives converted into deadened extensions of the tools of production.

New directions emerge as new problems arise. Cracks are occurring in the traditional discipline of the workplace. Absenteeism has been increasing. The Monday and Friday absentee is more commonplace. Tardiness also shows a generally upward trend. Labor turnover increases. Job boredom and repetitiveness are accompanied by "job alienation." Departure from the "work ethic" in turn results in a deterioration of production and quality. Workers feel a loss of individuality, dignity, and self-respect. Job dissatisfaction grows, and workers question the current ways of doing things as they seek to change the inflexible restrictions the production process puts upon them.

In 1969, the Survey Research Center of the University of Michigan reported the results of a study of 1,533 workers at various occupational levels. It concluded that workers ranked interesting work and enough equipment, information, and authority to get the job done ahead of good pay and job security.

An extensive study by Harold Sheppard and Neal Herrick, *Where Have All the Robots Gone?*, concluded that job dissatisfaction is indeed widespread—and not only among blue-collar workers; that workers entering the labor force are increasingly anti-authoritarian, better educated, less income oriented than past generations of workers, and more resistant to meaningless, repetitive, and boring job assignments. They expect to enhance the quality of their working lives.

Each year, the Gallup organization has been taking a poll aimed at determining "job satisfaction." Between 1969 and 1971, those indicating satisfaction with their work dropped by seven points, from eighty-eight to eighty-one. Still further, the Bureau of Labor Statistics indicates that absentee rates have increased an average of 35 percent since 1961.

One significant aspect of American life that has been undergoing rapid change relates to freedom to enjoy the autonomy of self-employment. In 1950, 16 percent of the labor force was self-employed. This figure dropped to about 12 percent in 1960, and to 8 percent in 1970. Thus, the percentage of the self-employed dropped by half in two decades. Increasingly, people have been losing even this bastion of control over their working lives.

A study undertaken by HEW, published in 1973 as *Work in America*, leaves no doubt that worker dissatisfaction with jobs, both blue-collar and white-collar, is widespread, is on the rise, and presents an urgent problem for management, union, and government. The report notes:

"And significant numbers of American workers are dissatisfied with the quality of their working lives. Dull, repetitive, seemingly meaningless tasks, offering little challenge or autonomy, are causing discontent among workers at all occupational levels."[3]

The report makes a point that the failure to solve this problem will mean increased social costs. It points to the relationship between job dissatisfaction on the one hand and mental health, alcohol and drug abuse, heart disease, early death, and other factors on the other; it concludes that unless the situation is corrected society can expect these costs to impose an increasing tax burden on the total community.

It is important to understand that reasonable satisfaction with meaningless, repetitive work may simply mean that man, highly adaptable creature that he is, has made his peace with an unhappy situation. There is strong evidence that workers write off deadening jobs as "inevitable" and seek their satisfaction in other pursuits. The HEW study makes a point of the relationship between the meaninglessness of the job and the adverse effect on the physical and mental well-being of the worker.

It is also important to note that workers who have been given the opportunity to enlarge their horizons at work, to participate in the decisions affecting their jobs, and to lend their innovative input toward getting the job done have a focal point against which to compare their previous work experience. These workers usually do not want to return to the simple monotonous tasks of little or no responsibility. They have tried a better way and they like it.

The increase in job dissatisfaction is not only rooted in the production system of scientific management; it feeds as well on the growing cynicism and frustration that citizens express toward public life. An increasing number feel alienated toward their government and public leaders as they become more remote from decision making in a complex world and as they sense their inability to affect economic and political decisions. With the exception of a Ralph Nader, the average citizen feels impotent to influence the direction and thrust of society.

How widespread are complaints about the hypocrisy of elected leaders and the disillusionment over promises made but never kept? And how often are voices raised against corruption, dissembling, and the lack of moral leadership "on high"? Until Watergate, even political spying, bugging, and bribery on a large scale raised less of a ripple than a deep freezer or a vicuna coat. It is too early to assess the long-term impact of Watergate on these feelings of impotency and disillusionment.

It is axiomatic that people respond more affirmatively to their role in society as they share in the opportunity to participate significantly in decisions affecting their welfare. History teaches, moreover, that at some point people who are denied this opportunity will reach out to grasp it.

This is equally true in the workplace. The stirrings of job dissatisfaction, in my judgment, relate in large measure to denial of participation in the decision-making process, denial of the opportunity to be creative and innovative and to control the machine, instead of being controlled by it.

The ferment of union activity in the 1930s and 1940s consolidated the organizing strength of industrial workers. It was the first stage toward accomplishment of a larger goal: industrial democracy. It provided the base on which workers were then able to improve their standard of living, win better working conditions, and achieve a greater measure of dignity and security as important members of society. Every gain constituted an incursion into the traditional authority wielded by management. The vast array of benefits won in collective bargaining over the years relates essentially to protecting the worker and his family against the hazards of economic insecurity. Workers, young and old, continue to aspire toward a better life, to be won at the bargaining table and through legislation. Their unions will, of course, persist in innovative collective-bargaining efforts as well as in improving upon already established benefit programs. They mobilize politically, cognizant of the intimate relationship between the bread box and the ballot box.

There is little need to spell out the enormously important progress workers have made through their unions. In *quantitative* terms, organized workers have won, and continue to win, a larger share of economic well-being. Unorganized workers have, of course, reaped the advantages of the gains made by unionized workers. Working conditions have also been vastly improved under the pressure of collective bargaining. Yet in *qualitative* terms, workers have not made as marked progress and are still struggling to play a more meaningful role in the decisions that affect their welfare in the business enterprise. Emphasis on qualitative improvement of life on the job is, I believe, the next step on the road toward industrial democracy.

WHITHER WORKER PARTICIPATION?

Two distinct, somewhat overlapping directions are indicated. One relates to "managing the enterprise"; the other relates to "managing the job." The latter is part and parcel of the former, but it is of more immediate concern to the worker.

Experiments with worker participation in "managing the enterprise" are under way in Yugoslavia (worker control of management), Germany (*Mitbestimmung*—codetermination established by law), Sweden (voluntary acceptance of worker representation on a company's board of directors), and Israel (union owned and operated cooperative enterprises). But in the United States, labor contracts, with their hundreds of provisions establishing and protecting workers' rights, leave substantially to management the "sole responsibility" to determine the products to be manufactured, the location of plants, production schedules, the methods, processes, and means of manufacture, as well as administrative decisions governing finances, marketing, purchasing, pricing, and the like. Unions traditionally have moved in the direction of improving wages, benefits, and working conditions. Generally, they have left "managing the enterprise" to management, only *reacting* to managerial acts objectionable to the workers. They have not embraced a political philosophy to motivate their overall policies and programs. This is not to say that American unions have no socioeconomic-political concepts. Quite the contrary; but they are not married to an "ism" governing and directing their behavior.

Rather, American unions move to meet practical problems with practical solutions. It is highly improbable that they will approach the problem of worker participation in decision making via fierce ideological struggle founded in socioeconomic theory. They are not prone to beat their wings in ideological or doctrinaire frustration. Where workers feel victimized, they combine their forces to correct the situation, case by case, problem by problem. Gradual persistent change, not revolutionary upheaval, has marked the progress of the American worker. When explosions occur, as in the 1930s, they are responses to specific problems and are searches for specific solutions. We can anticipate that worker participation in managing the enterprise or job will manifest itself in a similar way.

Decisions regarding purchasing, advertising, selling, and financing, for instance, are far more remote from the immediate problems facing the worker than are decisions concerning his or her job. In the vast range of managerial decisions, the immediacy of impact on the worker varies enormously. Thus, the average worker in a gigantic enterprise usually displays less interest in the selection of the chairman of the board than in the amount of overtime he receives.

What direction, then, will the drive toward worker participation in decision making take? To begin with, it seems safe to say that any further encroachment on so-called management prerogatives will spell "revolution" to management, while to the worker it will simply represent a nonideological effort to resolve a bothersome problem.

Certain areas of possible confrontation come to mind. By way of example, management makes a decision to shut down a plant or move all or part of it to another location, often hundreds of miles away. The union bargains for severance pay, early retirement, the right of the worker to transfer with the job and to receive moving allowance, and so forth. But the worker, often with long years of service, is the victim of such a decision. He is permanently thrown out of work, or even if he is given the right to transfer with the job, he must pull up stakes, cut his roots in the community, leave friends, perhaps break family ties, and begin a new life in a strange place, with no assurance of permanence. Management wields the decision-making authority; the workers and the community dangle at the end of that decision.

Similarly, management generally controls the final decision to subcontract work or to shuffle work among its facilities in a multiplant corporation. The worker faces the ultimate insecurity. Management also holds the authority to discipline. All places of work (as in society at large) require rules and regulations for people to live by; but discipline can be a fearful weapon in the hands of a ruthless employer, even when subject to a collectively bargained grievance procedure.

Production scheduling can be a serious source of friction. In an auto-assembly plant, for instance, changes in line speed to meet changes in production schedules or changes in model mix require rebalancing of jobs and operations. This in turn gives rise to disputes over production standards and manpower. Frequent changes in line speed or model mix disturb agreed-upon settlements about production standards and manpower agreements, often resulting in crisis bargaining and, on occasion, strike action.

The never ending yet necessary introduction of technological innovation and the concomitant alteration of jobs, cutbacks in manpower, and effect on skill requirements are a constant source of new problems, emphasizing the concern workers naturally have for their job security. Furthermore, the call for excessive overtime is a constant source of unhappiness and discontent.

These are but a handful of the kinds of confrontation issues that directly affect workers and that are increasingly subject to "worker participation" bargaining.

Other types of issues, also relating directly to life in the workplace, will command attention, for democratizing the workplace carries considerations beyond the worker's immediate job. The double standard for managers and workers is being questioned. Symbols of elitism, traditionally taken for granted in industrial society, are challenged: salaries and their normally recognized advantages (versus hourly payment and the punching of time clocks), paneled dining rooms (versus spartan cafeterias), privileged parking facilities nearest the plant entrance, and so forth.

Democratizing the workplace may entail organizing the work schedule to enable the worker to manage his personal chores: visiting the dentist or doctor, getting his car repaired, visiting his children's school during teaching and conference hours, for example.

Worker participation in decision making will be demanded more often with regard to those aspects of working life most immediately and noticeably affected. "Managing the job" is more immediate and urgent. Worker concern for "managing the enterprise" is more variable and is best measured by the immediacy of impact on the worker's welfare.

Increasing attention is currently being devoted to this problem of "managing the job." Rising rates of absenteeism, worker disinterest in the quality and quantity of production, job alienation, and the insistence on unit-cost reduction are motivating some employers to re-evaluate current practices and customs governing management-worker relationships. Concurrently, workers rebel against the authoritarian atmosphere of the workplace and the subordination of their personal dignity, desires, and aspirations to the drive for more production at lower cost; they find little challenge, satisfaction, or interest in their work. While the worker's rate of pay may dominate his relationship to the job, he can be responsive to the opportunity for playing an innovative, creative, and imaginative role in the production process.

One of the essential tasks of the union movement is to "humanize the workplace." A pleasant, decent management is desirable but does not alter the basic managerial design. "Human engineering" concepts may make for more comfortable employer-employee relationships, but here, too, managerial administration of the workplace remains fundamentally unchanged. "Humanizing the workplace" not only must include the normally recognized amenities of life in the workplace but it also must move to a higher plateau and relate to job satisfaction—a closing of the widening gap between the mechanization of production by scientific management and the worker's participation in the production and decision-making process. "Humanizing the workplace" in this sense represents one additional step toward the fulfillment of industrial democracy.

But humanizing the workplace must not become simply another gimmick designed essentially to "fool" the worker by having as its primary goal or hidden agenda an increase in worker productivity. Manipulation of the worker will be recognized for what it is—another form of exploitation; it will breed suspicion and distrust.

In this regard, Delmar Landan, an expert in personnel development for General Motors, has said: " . . . where we have to aim is participation—it is the only way to work in this increasingly complex society. The man at the top can't have all the answers. The man doing the job will have some of them."[4]

Worker participation in decision making about his job is one means of achieving democratization of the workplace. It should result in a change from the miniaturization and oversimplification of the job to the evolution of a system embracing broader distribution of authority, increasing rather than diminishing responsibility and accountability. It should combine the imaginative creation of more-interesting jobs with the opportunity to exercise a meaningful measure of autonomy and utilization of more-varied skills. It requires tapping the creative and innovative ingenuity of the worker to the maximum.

Hundreds of experiments have been and are being undertaken in American industry, following the European lead. They are directed toward opening up opportunities for meaningful worker participation. The HEW report describes some of them. In the auto industry, the industry with which I am most closely associated, a myriad of demonstration projects are under way. They cover innumerable facets of the problem and some are a sharp departure from the assembly-line concept.

It is too early to describe precisely what form or forms humanizing the workplace will take. Certain criteria, however, deserve serious consideration.

1. The worker should genuinely feel that he or she is not simply an adjunct to the tool, but that his or her bent toward being creative, innovative, and inventive plays a significant role in the production (or service) process.

2. The worker should be assured that his or her participation in decision making will not erode job security or that of fellow workers.

3. Job functions should be adapted to the worker; the current system is designed to make the worker fit the job, on the theory that this is a more efficient production system and that, in any event, economic gain is the worker's only reason for working. This theory may be proved wrong on both counts.

4. The worker should be assured the widest possible latitude of self-management, responsibility, and opportunity to use her or his brain. Gimmickery and manipulation of the worker must be ruled out.

5. Changes in job content and the added responsibility and involvement in decision making should be accompanied by upgrading pay rates.

6. The worker should be able to foresee opportunities for growth in his or her work and for promotion.

7. The worker's role in the business should enable her or him to relate to the product or services rendered, as well as to their meanings in society; in a broader sense, it should also enable her or him to relate constructively to her or his role in society.

The union, as the workers' representative, will naturally share with management in implementing these and other criteria. But crisis negotiating—settling a wage dispute before a midnight strike deadline—is not the time to seek precise means of humanizing the workplace. This task requires careful experiment and analysis. While issues of economic security (wages, fringe benefits) and continuing encroachment on what management terms its sole prerogatives will remain adversary in nature, there is every reason why humanizing the workplace should be undertaken as a joint, cooperative, constructive, nonadversary effort by management and the union. The initial key to achieving this goal may well be open, frank, and enlightened discussion between the parties, recognizing that democratizing the workplace and humanizing the job need not be matters of confrontation but of mutual concern for the worker, the enterprise, and the welfare of society.

NOTES

1. Richard C. Gerstenberg, speech to the Annual Meeting of the American Publishers Association, New York, April 26, 1972.
2. Robert Heilbroner, "The Future of Capitalism," World Magazine, Sept. 12, 1972, p. 30.
3. Work in America, Report of a Special Task Force to the Secretary of Health, Education, and Welfare (Cambridge, Mass.: MIT Press, 1973), p. xv.
4. Delmar Landan in Judson Gooding, The Job Revolution (New York: Walker Publishing Co., 1972), p. 111.

Work with Dignity

Franklin Wallick

Humanization of work means many things to many people. To some it means giving workers a variety of jobs to do to break a dull routine. To others, humanization means job enlargement, increased responsibility, no more time clocks, an opportunity to air and settle grievances, a living wage, a battery of fringe benefits, and a workplace environment free of noise, dust, bad ventilation, and other health hazards.

Boredom on the job has become a media catchphrase, and numerous worldwide experiments are being made to find ways to make workers happier on the job. We are told that a generation of younger workers is in revolt against the traditional work ethic, a claim dramatized by the Lordstown, Ohio, strike of 1972, when young long-haired workers spat out their resentment against the drudgery of the faceless assembly line. [See Bennett Kreman's "Search for a Better Way of Work," pages 141-150.]

A strike involving less articulate, less flamboyant, middle-aged workers erupted at Norwood. Ohio, over the same issues that flared at Lordstown. Although the strike lasted one hundred and seventy days, it was not considered hot news, and few newspaper and television reporters paid much attention.

There are other symptoms indicating that all is not well in American industry or commerce. Absenteeism rates are high. Labor turnover con-

Source: This article appeared in The Humanist, September-October 1973.

founds bosses. Drug addiction is common. There are even rumblings of trouble in Japan, where workers cheerfully sing the company song at the beginning of each workday.

Some excellent experiments in work enlargement and enrichment are being made in Norway, Sweden, Yugoslavia, and in the United States. But how much of this is somebody's hobbyhorse and how much is for real? Many union officials are profoundly skeptical of the whole humanization trend. To some, it seems to be a way to get more out of the workers without paying them more. Some experiments are conducted in nonunionized settings, often in an effort to prevent unionization. Naturally this alienates union people even more from the so-called humanizers.

Are we talking about a significantly youthful revolt? Is it a generation problem? Considerable research suggests that today's younger workers are less authoritarian, more acute in their perceptions, and less willing to take the conventional wear and tear of work than those in the past. My own union's president, Leonard Woodcock, thinks that the symptoms we see are more a result of a worldwide malaise than a unique characteristic of young workers. Certainly the Norwood strike bears this out.

One indication that a serious problem exists has been pointed out by Douglas Fraser, a UAW vice-president and the union's chief negotiator with the Chrysler Corporation. Fraser reports that in a recent year Chrysler was forced to hire forty-four thousand workers in order to maintain a work force of one hundred thousand. This large turnover cut across age groups, reflecting a deep malady that begs for a cure. For this reason, auto management is as eager to find answers as are the workers and the union.

Malcolm Denise, a Ford Motor Company vice-president, has been very candid in discussing the discontent problem with some of his fellow Ford executives. In 1969, Denise observed: "Our new work force has had a costly and unsettling impact on our operations. More money, time, and effort than ever before must now be expended in recruiting and acclimating hourly employees; quality-control programs have been put to severe tests; large numbers of employees remain unmoved by all attempts to motivate them; and order in the plants is maintained with rising difficulty."[1]

At a recent seminar, an official of a large corporation said: "The enemy is Frederick Taylor." I found that statement fascinating, because for many years Frederick Taylor was the epitome of efficient management—time study and the whole efficiency craze—which finally drove our union and many others into the training of time-study stewards so that we would be able to fight back. Mr. Taylor's method was to break one job into tiny pieces, and then assign workers and machines so that a single worker would do a single piece. The management official who deemed Taylor the enemy told how his company had been plagued with faulty production, worker chaos, and heavy turnover because they would assign more than twenty people, for example, to work on one local telephone directory for several small towns in Indiana. Under this official's direction, the entire setup was changed. A single person was assigned to do the whole directory, and it became "his" or "her" directory. Mistakes were minimized, job satisfaction soared, and turnover declined. This was a white-collar operation, substantiating my original thesis that we are talking not only about the "blue-collar blues" on the traditional assembly line but also about work in any place with any kind of collar, blue or white.

Some of the experimental projects used as showcases in the United States are clearly designed to keep unions out. They are not overtly anti-union, but management seems to think that a neat little dash of work humanization will forestall any bid for unionization. Although we can learn from these experiments, healthy labor-management relations cannot develop in enterprises without unions or where unions are subverted.

Too many in management still think that unionization of their business represents some failure on their part. I would argue quite the contrary: only through a trade-union relationship can a company establish the kind of nonmanipulative and democratic link to its workers that is both civilized and equitable. The most enlightened management will provide less than a full voice for workers until it has the benefit of a union relationship.

That brings me to the general trade-union attitude toward what we call "humanization of work." If you were to take a poll today, you would find most union officials turning thumbs down on humanization of work as a prime bargaining issue. A number of articles in the labor press poke fun at the boredom syndrome, which has fascinated contemporary thinkers. I don't happen to agree with them, but that is the way they look at it.

Merely redesigning jobs, without raising incomes or improving the quality of the work environment, would be resisted vigorously by the unions. "Nobody is approaching me," said Doug Fraser, "and asking to humanize my job. But they are trying to clean up and make safer the places where people work. And, in the auto industry, they are asking for a pension they can live on after thirty years of service."[2]

Today, more than 60 percent of American working families have incomes that are less than the Department of Labor's standard for an intermediate family budget. Therefore, income is, and will remain, a prime goal for most unions.

Working people have a canny knack for knowing what is possible; and, if there is skepticism today by workers and their leaders, it may simply be that no worker wants to take a leap that may not improve the current situation. However, many of the humanization experiments, in little fragmentary ways, are yielding valuable insights into better ways of organizing work.

Possibly because no one has found a magic formula for taking boredom out of work, the big issues in our industry are "thirty years and out," elimination of compulsory overtime, and health and safety on the job. These are the issues raised again and again at special conventions by both skilled and unskilled workers in recent years. This does not mean that we should turn our backs on the boredom issue. Far from it. We are merely saying, if I read worker sentiment correctly, that we must keep our eyes on new job-design experimentation. We must insist that the union become a full partner in anything that management proposes, and we will not settle for less than the best. What irritates us in the UAW is the unilateral method of imposing new techniques upon workers. This can be a sinister manipulation in the absence of union consultation and planning.

"Historically," says Irving Bluestone, "the slogan has been to let management manage, and the workers will react to what they don't like. Yet, at some point, workers will want to and should participate in broader areas of decision making (product, product design, etc.) and not merely some of the tinkering which the job-enlargement people are talking about these days."[3] Any union or management that moves in the direction Mr. Bluestone suggests is not reshuffling jobs to make people happier in superficial ways. It is, instead, fundamentally changing its direction toward democracy in the workplace. Some management people who delve into these arcane matters of humanization think this way, too, but it often comes out differently in print and in practice.

Humanization of work is not a fit subject for crisis bargaining. Management has as much at stake in getting some answers as do the workers and the union. If Chrysler has to hire forty-four thousand workers in a single year to maintain a work force of one hundred thousand, then something is drastically wrong at Chrysler; and both the company and the workers have an equal stake in discovering what it is. We do not want to raise false hopes. We do not believe we can usher in an industrial utopia overnight. Nevertheless, we are going to keep the pressure on for something better, and we are keeping close watch on everything industry is doing. They often do more than meets the eye!

My own special concern is occupational health. I worked as a UAW lobbyist in Washington to help enact the Occupational Safety and

Health Act of 1970. In the ten years I have lived in Washington and worked for the UAW, no other single legislative accomplishment has more potential for good among working people and there is nothing of which I am prouder. The implementation of this act leaves much to be desired. But this law, even with an unsympathetic administration, has done a great deal to lower noise levels, clean up air, and monitor hazardous substances in the workplace. Still, the federal government estimates that four hundred American workers die every day from health hazards on the job. Assuming a two-thousand-hour work year, this is fifty deaths an hour. Such an insidious threat to life and limb represents a great challenge to the industrialized world.

A number of landmark workmen's-compensation cases have been settled recently: more than one million dollars for lung damage to thirty-two workers in Wisconsin and a large payment for lung damage to a coke-oven worker in Pennsylvania. We have black-lung compensation in federal law, and a new move is under way to pay workers' compensation for any lung disease acquired on the job. One expert estimates that more than two billion dollars in compensation could be paid under present state laws for occupational loss of hearing, if workers knew their rights and sought to use them.

The disease and carnage of the workplace present a great challenge to labor, management, government, and the world of science. The UAW has led a number of health and safety strikes. In a lead-batter plant in Delaware, one of our unions called a strike in order to improve standards for protecting workers from the ravages of lead poisoning. There are close to a million workers exposed to dangerous levels of lead in the United States, and the strike in Delaware is a harbinger of more to come.

I am dwelling on my pet subject, occupational health, because I am bothered by the great attention that academic circles and the public press give to humanization of work, while it is difficult to arouse scholarly and media concern over the safety and health hazards that are a daily problem for millions of the people I represent. It is easier to worry about boredom and forget noise, to write about monotony and ignore dusts, to fret about dull jobs and not mention fumes on the job. I submit that all of these ought to be the concern of academics and the media, as well as labor and management. Certainly the credibility of those who worry about humanizing work would be stronger if they pushed for occupational safety and health with the same vigor they now devote to the cause of job enrichment.

Working people are demanding more pay, but they are also demanding better working conditions; our technological capability for attaining a pollution-free working environment is at hand.

In the early seventies, an Upjohn Institute survey showed some interesting findings when a cluster of questions were put to company presidents, union stewards, and both blue- and white-collar workers. Blue-collar workers (who were questioned in personal interviews, while the others were questioned by mail) all said that "good health and safety practices" ranked as their first priority; "opportunity for the individual worker to achieve and grow on the job" and "contingency protections like workmen's compensation" came next; "adequate income" ranked last.

It can be argued that these were well-paid workers and therefore that they did not see money as an important goal and, further, that it is only one man's survey. I think, quite to the contrary, that noneconomic problems loom big in workers' lives, and it behooves labor bureaucrats like myself to listen and do something.

The world does not stand still, and the world of working people is not an endless quest for more money. The environmental movement has made all of us, in office buildings, in our homes, and in factories, sniff the air with greater vigilance. It is not uncommon today for union stewards to carry noise meters to work in order to measure the level of noise pollution on their jobs. Millions of workers are simply no longer fatalistic about the danger and grubbiness of work. There *is* a danger, I fear, that the humanization craze can become merely a cosmetic to hide low pay and health hazards on the job.

What we need is a wholesale attack on all working-class problems: the poor quality of neighborhoods and schools (workers are often trapped in ugly urban situations from which upper-middle-class families can escape by moving to the suburbs); extra-heavy tax burdens (a working husband and wife pay more than their fair share of social-security taxes, and the federal tax structure is not fair to workers); inadequate transportation (getting to and from work is often a major problem for working people); few outdoor recreational opportunities (workers have more leisure time); poor air and water (workers' homes are often downwind from the city's worst polluters).

The American worker has been catered to, put down, caricatured, and even worshipped. Both political parties pay lip service to the hard-working American. Humanization of work, using insights gained from the dozens of experiments being conducted in the United States as well as overseas, can be part of a new strategy to honor hard work, to give it dignity, and to enrich the lives of working Americans with more than a new round of superficial panaceas.

NOTES

1. Malcolm Denise, remarks at the Ford Management Conference, White Sulphur Springs, W.Va., Nov. 10, 1969.

2. Douglas Fraser at a conference of UAW skilled-trades members, Feb. 1973. Fraser wrote me subsequently: "I was making the point that workers' perception of humanizing the workplace was making the workplace safer and cleaner, more relief time, more holidays, more vacation, shorter work week, and early retirement. I was making the point that the workers had not yet thought through and perhaps not even begun to think through how a job can be restructured to give the worker a greater feeling of satisfaction and accomplishment. Thus, my point was that not a single worker had come up and asked me what I was going to do about enriching his job, nor had any worker approached me with specific recommendations as to how his job could be enriched."

3. Irving Bluestone, speech entitled "Worker Participation in Decision Making" given at the Institute for Policy Studies, Washington, D.C., March 2, 1973. It is available upon request from the UAW General Motors Department, 8000 E. Jefferson St., Detroit, Mich. 48214.

The Myth of Job Enrichment

Mitchell Fein

Practically all writing that deals with worker boredom and frustration starts with the idea that the nature of work in industry and offices degrades the human spirit, is antithetical to workers' needs and damages their mental health, and that the redesign of work is socially desirable and beneficial to workers. Curiously, however, this view is not supported by workers or their unions. If workers faced the dire consequences of deprivation projected by the behaviorists, they should be conscious of the need to redesign and enrich their jobs. (The term "behaviorist" is used in this article to include psychologists, social scientists, and others who favor the redesign of work and job enrichment as a way to enhance the quality of working life. Many behaviorists, in fact, may not hold these views. Still, there is a sharp difference of opinion between what workers say they want and what behaviorists say workers want.)

WHO SPEAKS FOR WORKERS?

Workers' feelings about their work and what goes on at the workplace are expressed quite freely by workers themselves and their spokesmen in the unions. Since no union has yet raised the issue of work boredom and the redesign of jobs, is it not reasonable to assume that the

Source: This article appeared in *The Humanist*, September-October 1973.

question is not important to workers? Workers are not bashful in their demands, and worker representatives are quite vocal in championing workers' needs. One might argue that workers do not comprehend the harm that is done to them by their work and that they must be shown that many of their problems and troubles really stem from the nature of their jobs. But that assumes that workers are naive or stupid, which is not the case.

The judgments of those advocating job changes derive from people whom Abraham Maslow would characterize as "superior people (called self-actualizers) who are also superior perceivers, not only of facts but of values, . . . their ultimate values [are then used] as possibly the ultimate values for the whole species."[1] These advocates of change maintain that healthy progress for people is toward self-fulfillment through work, and they see most jobs as dull, repetitive, seemingly meaningless tasks, offering little challenge or autonomy. They view the nature of work as the main deterrent to more fulfilling lives for the workers and the redesign of jobs as the keystone of their plans for accomplishing the desired changes.

Paul Kurtz has stated: "Humanists today attack all those social forces which seek to destroy man: they deplore the dehumanization and alienation of man within the industrial and technological society. . . . and the failure of modern man to achieve the full measure of his potential excellence. The problem for the humanist is to create the conditions that would emancipate man from oppressive and corruptive social organization, and from the denigration and perversion of his human talents. . ."[2] Humanists' goals and behaviorists' objectives appear similar. Both accept Maslow's self-actualization concepts as the preferred route to fulfillment. But by what divine right does one group assume that its values are superior to others and should be accepted as normal? Both the selection of goals and attitudes toward work are uniquely personal. The judges of human values have no moral right to press their normative concepts on others as preferable.

SATISFACTION AND ACHIEVEMENT

The fundamental question is whether or not the nature of work prevents people from achieving the full measure of their potential. When behaviorists view people at work, they see two main groups: those who are satisfied and those who are not. They examine the satisfied and like what they see. These are eager, energetic people, who are generally enthusiastic about their jobs and life in general. The behaviorists hold them up as ideal and prepare to convert the dissatisfied.

In contrasting the satisfied workers with the dissatisfied ones, behaviorists see the nature of the work performed as the main difference. So they propose to change the work of the dissatisfied to more closely resemble that performed by the satisfied. But there is a large "if" in this approach: What if the nature of the work is not the reason for the satisfaction?

It could very well be that the satisfied have more drive, which creates greater material wants and higher goals, which in turn motivates them to make more-effective efforts in the workplace and to bid for more highly skilled jobs, and so on. Restructuring the work and creating new opportunities may make some people enthusiastic, but to what extent is the nature of the work the determinant of a person's drive?

There are no data that definitively show that restructuring and enriching jobs will increase the will to work or give workers greater satisfaction. Similarly, I have not seen any research data that show that a person with drive is deterred from reaching his potential by the nature of the work.

I believe that ethical considerations alone should keep behaviorists from setting up their values as the ideals for society. In addition, I will attempt to demonstrate that the behaviorists' views on redesigning jobs are misguided; they do not understand the work process in plants, and they misjudge workers' attitudes toward their jobs.

WORKERS' ATTITUDES TOWARD THEIR WORK

A 1972 Gallup Poll found that 80 to 90 percent of American workers are satisfied with their jobs. A 1973 poll by Thomas C. Sorenson found that from 82 to 91 percent of blue- and white-collar workers like their work. He asked, "If there were one thing you could change about your job, what would it be?" He found that "Astonishingly, very few mentioned making their jobs 'less boring' or 'more interesting.' " [3]

Behaviorists and humanists find it difficult to understand how workers can possibly say they like their work when it appears so barren to intellectuals. This view was recently expressed by the behavioral scientist David Sirota, after making a study in a garment plant. He was surprised to find that most sewing-machine operators found their work interesting. Since the work appeared highly repetitive to him, he had expected that they would say that they were bored and that their talents were not fully utilized. These workers' views are supported in a study by Emanuel Weintraub of 2,535 female sewing-machine operators in seventeen plants from Massachusetts to Texas. He found that "most of the operators like the nature of their work." [4] What the behaviorists find so difficult to comprehend is really quite simply explained: Workers have similar attitudes toward their work because *they are not a cross-section of the population, but rather a select group.*

There is greater choice in the selection of jobs by workers than is supposed. The selection process in factories and offices goes on without conscious direction by either workers or management. The data for white- and blue-collar jobs show that there is tremendous turnover in the initial employment period but that the turnover drops sharply with time on the job. What occurs is that a worker comes onto a new job, tries it out for several days or weeks, and decides whether or not the work suits his needs and desires. Impressions about a job are a composite of many factors: pay, proximity to home, nature of work, working conditions, attitude of supervision, congeniality of fellow workers, past employment history of the company, job security, physical demands, possibilities for advancement, and many others. Working conditions may be bad, but if the pay and job security are high, the job may be tolerable. To a married woman, the pay may be low, but if the job is close to home and working conditions are good, it may be desirable. There are numerous combinations of factors that influence a worker's disposition to stay on the job or not.

There is a dual screening process that sifts out many of those who will be dissatisfied with the work. The process operates as follows: The worker in the first instance decides whether or not to stay on the job; management then has the opportunity to determine whether or not to keep him beyond the trial period. The combination of the worker's choice to remain and management's decision regarding the worker's acceptability screens out many workers who might find the job unsatisfying.

R— Some workers find highly repetitive work in factories intolerable, so they become truck drivers, where they can be out on the road with no supervisor on their back all day. Others prefer to work in gas stations, warehouses, retail stores, and other such places. Increasingly workers are taking white-collar jobs that in many ways are similar to repetitive factory jobs but which have cleaner physical surroundings and better working conditions. In times of high unemployment, workers stay in safe jobs for continuity of income; but, as the job market improves, the rate of turnover increases and selection of jobs resumes.

There would undoubtedly be much greater dissatisfaction among workers if they were not free to make changes and selections in the work they do. Some prefer to remain in highly repetitive, low-skilled work even when they have an opportunity to advance to more-highly skilled jobs through job bidding. A minority of workers strive to move into the more skilled jobs, such as machinists, maintenance mechanics, setup men, group leaders, and utility men, where work is discretionary and the workers have considerable autonomy in the tasks they perform.

The continued evaluation of workers by management and the mobility available to workers in the job market refine the selection process. A year or two after entering a plant, most workers are on jobs or job progressions that suit them or which they find tolerable.

However, the work force in the plant is not homogeneous. There are two main groups, the achievers and the nonachievers. Their attitudes toward work and their goals are vastly different. A minority of the work force, which I find to be 15 percent, have a drive for achievement and identify with their work. These workers' attitudes match the ideal projected by behaviorists. They dislike repetitive work and escape from it by moving into more-skilled jobs, which have the autonomy and interest they look for in their work. Only a minority of jobs in industry and offices are in the skilled category, and fortunately only a minority of workers aspire to these jobs. About 85 percent of workers do not identify with their work, do not prefer more complicated and restructured jobs, and simply work in order to eat. Yet they, too, like their work and find it interesting.[5]

For different reasons, both groups of workers find their work interesting and satisfying. The work of the 85 percent who are nonachievers is interesting to them though boring to the other 15 percent. And the 15 percent who are achievers find their work interesting, though it is not sufficiently appealing for the majority to covet it. The selection process does amazingly well in matching workers and jobs.

What blinds behaviorists to this process is their belief that the achievement drive is an intrinsic part of human nature, that fulfillment at work is essential to sound mental health, and that, given the opportunity, workers would choose to become more involved in their work and take on larger and more-complicated tasks. Once behaviorists take this view, they cannot understand what really happens on the plant floor or why workers do one thing rather than another.

WHY DO BEHAVIORISTS CLAIM TO SPEAK FOR WORKERS?

Behaviorists' insistence that they know more about what workers want than workers themselves is largely based on a number of job-enrichment case histories and studies of workers over the past decade. It is claimed that these studies show that workers really want job enrichment and benefit from it. But when these studies are examined closely, four things are found. (1) What actually occurred was quite different from what was reported by the behaviorists. (2) Most of the studies were conducted with hand-picked employees, usually working in areas or plants isolated from the main operation, and they do not reflect a cross-section of the working population. Practically all are in nonunion plants. (3) Only a handful of job-enrichment cases have been reported in the past ten years, despite the behaviorists' claims of gains for employees and management obtained through job changes. (4) In all instances, the experiments were initiated by management, never by workers or unions.

The *Survey of Working Conditions*, conducted for the United States Department of Labor by the Survey Research Center of the University of Michigan, contained serious errors.[6] The General Foods-Topeka case reported by Richard E. Walton[7] [discussed at some length by Robert Schrank on pp. 119-140] omits important information that shows that the sixty-three workers for this plant were handpicked from seven hundred applicants. Texas Instruments, which conducted the longest and broadest experiments, only attracted 10 percent of its employees to the program.[8] The Texas Instruments cleaning-employees case, as well as others, was grossly misreported in HEW's *Work in America*.

There are no job-enrichment successes that bear out the predictions of the behaviorists, because the vast majority of workers reject the concept. A small proportion of workers who desire job changes are prevented from participating by the social climate in the plant. They find involvement by moving into skilled jobs. Perhaps behaviorists do not recognize the moral issues raised by their proposals to redesign work—for example: intrusion upon a person's right to personal decisions; exploitation of workers' job satisfaction for company gains; distortion of the truth.

The boundless wisdom of this country's founders in separating religion from government and public practices has been revealed in countless ways. But along comes a new faith that proclaims that people should derive satisfaction from their work. When up to 90 percent of workers are reported to be satisfied with their work, the behaviorists say that workers do not really know what satisfaction is and that they will lead them to a superior kind. This sounds oddly like the proselytizing of a missionary. If behaviorists called for making enriched work available for those who want it, I would support them because I believe a minority of workers do want it. But I oppose foisting these practices on workers who do not call for it. In any case, I believe the minority has all the enrichment they want.

Exploiting workers' job satisfaction for management's gain can backfire dangerously. Workers expect management to develop new approaches and production processes to increase productivity; they are prepared for continuous pressure for more output. But when these

changes are designed primarily to create a more receptive worker attitude toward greater productivity, they may see that they have been
"had." If management's gains are real, while workers' benefits are only
in their minds, who has really benefited? The behaviorists now say that
workers should also share in productivity gains. But these statements
have come late and are couched in such vague terms as to be
meaningless.

When a supposedly good thing must be put into fancy wrappings to
enhance it, something is amiss. Why must the job-enrichment cases be
distorted to make the final results appealing? Why must behaviorists
use phrases such as "work humanization" to describe their proposals,
as though work were now inhuman? Workers understand the meaning
of money, job security, health benefits, and retirement without fancy
explanations. If the enrichment and redesign of work is such a good
thing, why is it rejected by those who would benefit from it? The so-
called new industrial democracy is not really democracy but a new
autocracy of "we know better than you what's good for you."

NOTES

1. Abraham Maslow, *The Farther Reaches of Human Nature* (New York:
Viking, 1971), p. 10.

2. Paul Kurtz, "What Is Humanism?" in *Moral Problems in Contemporary
Society: Essays in Humanistic Ethics*, ed. P. Kurtz (Buffalo: Prometheus Books,
1973), p. 11.

3. Thomas C. Sorenson, "Do Americans Like Their Jobs?" *Parade*, June 3,
1973.

4. Emanuel Weintraub, "Has Job Enrichment Been Oversold?" an address to
the 25th annual convention of the American Institute of Industrial Engineers,
May 1973, *Technical Papers*, p. 349.

5. A more complete discussion and supporting data for the 15/85 worker
composition is contained in M. Fein's "Motivation for Work," in *Handbook of
Work Organization and Society*, ed. Robert Dubin (Skokie, Ill.: Rand-McNally,
1973).

6. *Survey of Working Conditions* (Washington, D.C.: U.S. Dept. of Labor,
1971). These errors were disclosed in my analysis in "The Real Needs and Goals
of Blue Collar Workers," *The Conference Board Record*, Feb. 1973.

7. Richard E. Walton, "How To Counter Alienation in the Plant," *Harvard
Business Review*, Nov.-Dec. 1972, pp. 70-81.

8. Fein, "Motivation for Work."

Thinking About Technology—
Subjectively, Objectively

Marcus Raskin

THE SUBJECTIVE

It is impossible to begin a discussion of technology without a realization of one's own impotence in the face of what social organization has created with technology. Specifically, the ordered activity that produces things and tasks—whether atomic bombs, tanks, laser beams to sew back the retina of the eye, or the ordering of men to develop rules and regulations through bureaucratic structures—leaves one quite aghast at knowing where to turn or what to say.

Each day appears to be another horror. And yet I sit here consuming technology—typing on an electric typewriter and listening to Horowitz repeat Schumann's "Fantasy," thereby allowing me to hear it in my head. I am transported through technological means, reaching toward the soul of my existence. And, as I write this and think about the potentiality, I see us chained by a technology that is used as the instrument of the strong, the aggressive, the dionysian, perhaps by the murderer, to transform the culture and life of others.

I think about the excrescence of our civilization visited on others through massive removal of people from the villages of Indochina, the bombing study at Cornell, the development of communications and logistics so that wars like Vietnam can go on forever without too much

Source: This article appeared in *The Humanist*, September-October 1973.

fear of opposition from anyone. They are the remote wars fought technologically, the ground upon which a culture grows. My mind wanders to the Jason Study, whereby one's own acquaintances, even friends, who knew the madness and moral bankruptcy of the bombing in Indochina, attempted to put forward their own plan of action, the electronic barrier. In 1967, the year the antiwar resistance began to reach out, America's great scientists, men of purpose and decency, found that they were less than what they thought they were, because they were called upon to fulfill a role. Seeing politics and power as a function of problem solving and puzzles, they were the natural allies of state power. Their task was to recommend a better way of killing. "Better things for better living through chemistry"—or electronics—or fences.

I think of Jacques Ellul's point that when the worker returns from his eight-hour machine task, "free" to discuss the painful vexations of his work, he is assaulted by the television set. I think of my view that people become part of the Dream Colony, nonexistent. They exist as a continuation of the corporate dreams canned for them. Furthermore, they are silent; they speak less than ever, without the grunts or sparkle of complaint once shared with the family. And in bars they sit silently in dread, hoping that this is the best of all worlds. Otherwise, what is it all for?

I think of the story that the treasurer of the Institute for Policy Studies told me. A black mayor of a town in Mississippi comes to Washington for a meeting. His assistant needs him. The assistant tells the police chief, who puts out a message through the FBI and other police stations. He is found within fifteen minutes through his rented car fifteen hundred miles away and asked by the Washington police to pull over. I learn that the ALERT system, of which this is an example, was implemented by an FBI chief. Technology in the service of the state, of the police, of order.

I think of Milton Kotler visiting Boston University, Martin Luther King's alma mater, where the administration was supposedly trying to find "community" and an "answer" to the urban "tragedy." He walks into a confrontation between the students and the administration. The students do not want the Marines on campus. The president says the Marines have a right to be there. (Shouldn't students be allowed to recruit for their ideas in a Marine camp in exchange for the right of recruitment on their own turf?) The president then tells the students to disperse or he will call in the police. They say they won't disperse. The president, a man of his word, calls in the police, while the FBI takes pictures of the protesting students. Heads are busted. And the dean, asked to mediate by the students, refuses. He says it is the president's "show." As heads are busted, the dean comes forward with a socio-technological correction. He says that the police should have used hoses rather than clubs. Uses of technology, and technology itself, become the instrument of moral evasion.

Earlier in the day, a graduate student of obvious promise comes to see me about the importance of developing nonlinear modes of thought. This means the development of the right side of the brain as against the conceptual side on the left, so that man does not destroy himself. I say to her that we have been taught that it is the irrational we must fear, that in writing *Being and Doing* I realized that the rational is built into the faulty superstructure. Is there, I wonder, a nonlinear part to our thought that shows a direct relationship between a new knowledge and the empathic feeling and which will somehow, like a powerful gaseous substance, blow away the technology of war, record keeping, files, parasitical activity, and everything else that props up a colonized system in which each does the other's life, each becomes more hidden from the other, and each knows the other only through the hierarchic other?

The irrational is reflected in the work of the Rand Corporation, which, during the fifties and sixties, developed means of employing the economy for nuclear war and developed limited and counterforce war strategies and budgets to go hand in hand with that purpose. Indeed, there the universities stood, employing knowledge and quanification, prediction and materials, method and procedures for murder and destruction. And if it was not for the purpose of seeking or preparing for war—that is, if all of that war preparation was a put-on—we are left with another devastating question: What has it meant to develop a whole internal culture and economy around the ideas "as if" and "non-use," where people live off the death instinct because there is no other "work"?

I stop typing for a moment, rub my eyes, and remember that I have glaucoma. I think about my drops and recall the story about how some people on the West Coast have formed a corporation to work out the technology of the delivery of drugs to the body so that trauma does not occur to the body. Each time I take the drops, there is the shocking sensation that would be avoided if there were a "finder" in the drug. And I recall that the West Coast group is a profit-making corporation. Who gets those profits? Why has nothing been produced yet? What does it mean that we continue to work on innovation of product or, better stated, on products where the differences may be important or may be marginal but finally are inessential? Why are we inundated with the novelties of packaging and advertising that teach us what we are through the products that we buy? How strange it is that our genius at packaging is filling up our garbage cans and will now flood our cities? How can we ever maintain all those machines and support these systems of our cities—the subways, hydroelectric plants, radar screens, sewers, and garbage cans?

I remember a discussion in Cuernavaca. My wife and several new-left writers were with Ivan Illich talking by candlelight. He says we must end schooling and insists on the notion of giving everyone a medical kit. Imagine everyone in the world having medical kits. Is this possible? Is this a joke? Could we give everyone medical kits? And, if we did, what then? Would the Club of Rome say that we were allowing too many people to live?

I think of the Nicaraguans, who had one hell of an earthquake. They are to be pitied. Their government is fascist, yet people all over the world, governments as well, send them food. People try to give, acting out of a moral sensibility, but there is no will, political or otherwise, to get the food to the needy. And there is no technology, no adequate distribution system that would reflect this genuine sensibility of humanity.

And then there is the green revolution: increasingly it is seen as a Rockefeller plot to use Rockefeller oil and tankers to get big farmers to drive out small farmers, changing the diets and the crops of the wretched, destroying many different strains of grain for a few strains that can easily be wiped out in a drought or by disease. Who or what is the end we are attempting to serve with our technology? And what about those who make and use machines as their work? What happens to the person who made the grooves in Horowitz' recording? Does he or she get to control anything?

THE OBJECTIVE

Traditional philosophers often state that moral good and evil reside in the *use* of things by those who are free. In our own time, using and making a thing defines the contours of freedom. Consequently, we are even more puzzled and chagrined at the daily life of our society, since we are sure that what we do and make defines our freedom. Today, complex social organization lays out roles and functions in which the particular task and the division of labor that people find themselves accepting in order to survive prevents them from knowing the sum of what they do or the whole process in which they participate. The citizenly activity that could give meaning to freedom in a contemporary context of deliberation and execution does not exist, and hence the content of politics (deciding what is made and used) is aborted. Political association becomes a function of seeking power. In other words, politics, which should help the individual relate his material condition to the thing he makes, its purpose, and the way he lives, is robbed of that meaning. Politics retains its machiavellian meaning as the art of manipulation and the struggle for power among the few, outside of any forums that would generate serious dialogue or inquiry. Neither in the university nor the courtroom, the coliseum nor the neighborhood bar, is there a forum for such considerations.

The worker in the factory and the secretary in the office may feel the uselessness of the task and the madness of the thing made or done. However, neither is able to find a political expression or a forum, whether it be a union, assembly, or political party, which would change the material condition of his or her existence. The result of this sorry state is that the individual, encased in his colonized role, is stopped from using his unique human ability—that of making moral judgments. Once this happens, two wretched results emerge, which are important to consider in the context of technology: "neutral" tools, and things that can be used for good *or* evil—usually for evil. Since there is no collective or cooperative motive to act or think otherwise and people are defined as "specialists," each alienated from the other, evil technological processes become the usual practice of society. A chain of destructive creativity occurs, such as the arms race and hierarchic organization. This destructive creativity is the ground of our public life. The underlying concept of the interchangeability of parts and ideas, without anyone either comprehending or caring about purpose and effects, systematically undermines people's judgment and comprehension of the meaning of what they do and make and, hence, of the technology used. What flows from our present difficulties?

We have moved to a new level. Many now believe that making and *consuming* (not using) things defines our freedom. Yet there has been no concern with the moral questions surrounding the issue of production and consumption. It has been assumed that making and consuming are moral rewards, being good in and of themselves. Our "science" of economics has asserted that the making of more nuclear weapons, the development of more bubble-gum factories and the like, all contribute equivalently to the gross national product and "growth."

We need to ask whether or not certain forms of social organization and the creative results upon which such organizations act must be restrained because they have a criminal result. Technology and its forms become questions of value and purpose to be judged accordingly. This notion is not new. Some believe that the Greeks went further. Yves Simon, the Thomist philosopher, pointed out that Greek artisans restrained their own creative ability, apparently fearing that great power would be placed in unworthy hands if they continued their researches and inventions. It is, I suppose, why Aristotle commented that, even though we know we can do or make something, we must still question whether we should go ahead and *do* it.

But, as I have said, we do not have the forum to ask such questions. Presently, very few people understand the technology of today, and even fewer have been allowed to discuss the "ought" questions that surround the making and doing of particular products and services. Thus, expertise is divided among a few, and the rest of the people in the society understand very little of how things work. A society that fears *political* revolution commits itself to daily *technological* revolution, hindering human beings and further abstracting corporate or organizational forms or functions that are to "control" revolutions. The result is a society of the colonized, without forums for debate and deliberation or technical comprehensions of their machines or their own "ends" or purposes.

The enlightened belief that scientific and technological discoveries would break the authoritarianism of man's domination over man has not proved correct in practice. This failure has meant that we are now forced to deal with not one but two problems: the first is that technology has not liberated people, and the second is that we are still trying to find ways of democratizing relationships among people. The present situation, in which technology attempts to develop as many possibilities as it can that are profitable to particular corporate and governing elites, requires that we now develop an alternate technology that we may refer to as the *value and logic of stopping.*

We need to find a "valuelogic" that makes clear to us what we do not want, why we do not want it, and what the consequences will be of such a technology of stopping. Attempts along this line can now be found among people who argue ecological questions, the relatively arid stance of economic growth, and other such matters. In the development of a "valuelogic" of technology, we must comprehend the importance of three principles, at least two of which may contradict each other, which of course means that in practice a balance must be found between them.

1. *Certain activities may be elongated with the understanding that particular projects do not have to be completed by one person* or a small group in a short period of time. Instead, the projects themselves are reflective of the human spirit, which continues from one generation to another. In practice, for example, the development of a city or a theory of knowledge, or the building of new human relationships, are things that are directly related to the flow of human experience, past and future. They are beyond the present. One problem of technology is that it telescopes or collapses time and space so that our own con-

sciousness is isolated. We come to believe that each thing that we do stands as an isolate without any connection to anything else. Our tasks or projects must be finished by us and, if possible, used by us. While there is no escaping the technology of the immediate, in which our consciousness is infused with the belief in the present as the only human reality, we need to find ways of ensuring that technology not be used only as a telescoping experience, in which a few people are able to fly from one part of the world to another in a few hours or in which the work of billions of people from one generation to another is destroyed within an hour at the order of a president or a leader who uses nuclear weapons. The relativity of time and space should not defeat the continuum of man's projects through history and the future. Otherwise, what should be valued will give way to the selfish and the immediate.

2. *The fruits of technology and the effects of it may be shared;* but, in the context of a highly centralized society, technology itself reaches for solutions that require highly centralized, pyramidal activities. Thus, we need to investigate all highly complex, expensive technologies that either require or create huge bureaucratic and hierarchic organizations while utilizing immense resources from the community. Technology and the workplace are, of course, integrally related. The result is consideration of the kinds of machines that are made to do a variety of tasks. For example, the standards of technology in space flight seem far more humane to those who are users of space technology than the technologies that have been developed in factories and for assembly lines. Their development governed by the notion of ever increasing profits, the types of machines used in our plants seem peculiarly antihuman. We may see this in many ways. From the noise of a pneumatic drill to the crude modes by which automation now replaces workers with machines, leaving them without a place in the productive life of the society, the development of machines and technology starts from fundamentally colonizing attitudes. Our machine-age mind is limited in terms of what is considered and produced, by the structure of capitalism and state power.

This problem is also one for socialist countries and, most important, for any working class that strives for liberation. Simone Weil has said: ". . . any change in the relationship between the classes must remain a pure illusion, if it be not accompanied by a transformation in technical processes, expressing itself in entirely new types of machinery." Such machinery, from the worker's point of view, should not do physical harm to the worker, but should be useful for a variety of different tasks, so that workers can use machines as they see fit and as the productive need requires. Workers should be able to understand, if not reconstruct, and fix their machines when necessary. Finally, the machine and its process should be one that can be defended and changed in public forums with workers and "consumers" present. Once such a series of changes came into being, the worker could begin to control his work situation and therefore be able to warrant directly to users the worth and purpose of the product. The worker and the technician will have developed their own code of ethics and system for accounting to the public.

3. *Therefore, it becomes important to think about how we may distribute knowledge and technical power* to different individuals and groups in the society so that it is not concentrated in one place or with one group. As part of the Encyclopedia of Social Reconstruction, attempts are being made at the Institute for Policy Studies to develop intermediate technologies that would be held in the public domain and controlled at the simplest social and communal level. Our hope is to develop a humane technology whose process is readily understood and which fits into the daily lives of people. In other words, the question of limits and size becomes crucial. Hence, there is less likelihood that a particular neighborhood will build a nuclear weapon instead of a solar-energy system for laundry. In this regard, therefore, the moral relationship to the kind of technology we develop has to do with what we see as the purpose of a society and, indeed, for us as individuals, the purpose of humans. By asking such questions about purpose and ends, we may begin to change our means, those activities that supposedly are instruments to our purposes, even though the purpose or end disappears and we are left to become our own instruments.

Who Creates
New Technology and Why?

Michael Maccoby

Why are new technologies created? It is sometimes argued that they are simply the inevitable result of scientific advancement. According to this view, a scientific discovery results in a new and better way of doing things. The new technology may be resisted by traditionalists who do not know how to use it or whose position is threatened by it, but gradually it prevails because it is better. Such a view is misleading. New technology is not created merely because of new scientific discoveries, even though they are essential to technological innovation. On the other hand, many discoveries and new technological possibilities are buried in reports or memos from corporate scientists, never to be developed or produced, even though they might have led to better ways of doing things. And this does not even take into account the work of noncorporate scientists that is never utilized.

Although it is risky to generalize about technology, since the term covers such a wide range of objects and systems, the creation of most new technology in the United States is determined by two main demands that are, to a certain degree, interrelated but are sometimes in conflict. They are the demands of the state—that is, the federal government—and those of the large corporations.

Above all, the state demands new weapons, strategic advantages,

Source: This article is based on the author's contribution at the seminar entitled "Technology and the Future of the World" at the Korcula Summer School in Yugoslavia, August 1973.

and internal-security systems (including listening devices and computerized control of information). Two motives that move the state to demand new technology are "security" and prestige (or glory).[1] These motives introduce a powerful irrational potential into the creation of new technology. In the realm of foreign policy, there is never enough security or military superiority against powerful opponents, particularly when each state is not sure about the capabilities of the others. In the realm of domestic policy, even the most embryonic opposition might conceivably grow into a threat to the security of the state, so that all sorts of spying and data-processing technology can be justified. Preoccupation with both internal and external security is, of course, magnified when policies of the state are aggressive and make enemies.[2]

The desire for prestige and glory can energize a limitless hunger for new technology. This is generated by bureaucratic processes, although the character of the presidency makes a difference.[3] John F. Kennedy and Lyndon B. Johnson, more than Dwight D. Eisenhower or Harry S. Truman, were motivated by the desire to be "first" in the world. The fantasy of earlier times—to reach the moon—became a high priority for these glory-seekers and in turn supported development of new technology. The excessive demands of the state for both security and glory lead to the irrational dictum that anything that *might* increase security or glory *should* be built. The state thus pressures or seduces industry to meet its demand for new technology, and in so doing threatens to aggrandize most technological development.

The second demand—that of the corporations to optimize growth and profits—is subject to more constraints than are state demands. In order to prosper, corporations must sell technology to buyers who can use it. Although there is a certain irrational element in the businessman's desire to buy technology that is glamorous, novel, and exciting (though it may be no more efficient than other products), most sales of new technology are made to other companies and bureaucracies (the state as employer), who buy the product because it promises to maximize predictability and control over the production process. They believe this will increase efficiency and, in the case of the private sector, profits. For these consumers, glamour is secondary, although it may be a consideration in buying the latest "hardware" with the "sexiest" packaging. Thus, corporations specializing in research and development tend to create technology that can be sold.[4]

In some cases, technology created by the state's need for security or prestige has been adapted by corporations to increase predictability and control over the production process, as in the case of computers, airplanes, communications satellites, and so forth. The state and corporations may have similar interests, but this is not always the case. The symbiosis may become a millstone around the corporation's neck when the state demands that more and more resources be committed to specialized products, such as rocket ships and nuclear weapons.

There are at least three reasons why the state's demands damage corporations. First, because of national security, new technology for the state cannot be sold to other potential buyers. Since the corporate goal is to widen markets constantly, corporations' wish to grow inevitably conflicts with the priorities of the state. Corporations would like to sell new technology to semihostile states like the People's Republic of China or the USSR and treat other states as customer corporations rather than as rival nations, but the state emphasizes national security over corporate profits.

Second, corporations find that dependence on the state encourages bad business practices. Building whatever is technically possible is poor business for a company competing in a tight international market. The demands of the state for total reliability in such hardware as missile backup systems and spaceships lead to so great a cost and require such expensive servicing that no one but the state could afford them. When a company dependent on the state tries to diversify, it might usually unlearn these uneconomical habits. Furthermore, financial dealings with the state are different from most other business practices, since companies often bid low and raise prices later as the state asks for changes incorporating the newest technological ideas or tactical considerations.

Third, dependency on the state is risky, since a change in national policy can suddenly upset all corporate planning. For example, Congress might cut the military budget, thus ending corporate projects that cannot be sold to anyone else. Thus, the demands of the state can weaken the corporate economy by cramping planning processes and endangering the competitive position of highly technological companies. Those corporations that have been most dependent on the state have often ended up ill equipped to compete in a competitive world market where most buyers are not interested in glory or destructive power.

In sum, scientists and engineers who create new technology in the United States and other highly industrialized nations such as the USSR are governed in their work principally by demands to strengthen the state and corporations. The result of their creation of new technology over the past century has been increasingly to centralize power and put it in the hands of managers who can make decisions that affect the vast majority of the population.

A MORE HUMANE TECHNOLOGY?

The key to developing a more humane technology in all spheres of life may be the technology of production. In the "technology of production," I include both mechanical-electrical-chemical processes *and* the systems of management in factories and offices that organize this hardware. The development of productive technology in the twentieth century—from assembly lines and time-motion industrial engineering to continuous-process factories, computers, and sociotechnical management—has been a series of innovations in both types of technology, which for the most part go together.

Not only does the technology of production determine conditions under which people work, but it is also a key factor in forming new social conditions. This is because a particular technology favors some kinds of people over others, by requiring certain schooling or the proper attitudes to fit the requirements of the production process.

The interrelation between technological development and the organization of production requires a fuller analysis than is possible here. New technological advances—such as the development of electronic components for cheap minicomputers or photoengraving processes that replace hand-circuit assembly—change the whole nature of work and the type of workers required.[5]

The motives for developing new technology, from the assembly line to the computer, have not been to further the human development of the individuals who work with it. While some technological developments may have humane consequences (such as doing away with undesirable jobs or increasing communication), most managers who create new technology rarely think of the human consequences of what they are creating. They are neither inclined by character nor educated to consider how new technology affects emotional health and human development. Most never consider love of life versus mechanized attitudes, psychological activeness versus passive consumerism, or greater social equity versus inequity and resentment. Managers generally believe they are benefiting humanity by creating jobs, making life easier for people, increasing communication, and generally raising the standard of living.

But even in cases where they believe they are helping people by creating a new technology, social goals do not determine the priorities of what is built. The priority is what promises to increase profit or what is demanded by the state. Some of the more progressive managers know that modern technology of production has in fact dehumanized both workers and managers by mechanizing and fractionating work at the bottom and provoking overcompetitiveness at the top. But they do not go further to relate this knowledge to social-psychological effects: lack of responsible citizenship from those who have no say in the workplace, deadening of sensibility due to loss of craftsmanship and the inability to determine the pace of one's work and life according to one's individual rhythm. And ultimately we have a society of hostile classes: At the top are the owners and managers, the winners, who are detached technocrats, all head and little heart, who run the machines and then go home to comfortable, protected enclaves; and at the bottom are the "losers," the human robots in factories and offices who are made so passive and bored by their work that they can be "turned on" only by drugs or sadistic excitement. And on the fringes of the system are the "useless" people, who increasingly act out their resentment in "meaningless" destructiveness.

Is there any way to move in a more progressive direction? How can a technology that will benefit human development be created in America? According to this analysis, one part of the answer lies in changes in the conditions that determine corporate decisions about what to build. (A complete answer must also relate to decisions of the state.)

The customers of the new technology are usually corporations that maintain that they buy that which is more "efficient" and which therefore promises them greater profits. But any new technology will be efficient and profitable if and only if three social conditions are met. One condition is the availability of skilled workers, technicians, and professionals who can use the technology. Hence, such technology requires an educational system to train workers. The second condition is that society accept the new technology rather than declare it illegal because it pollutes, poisons, or limits the freedom of some for the benefit of others. The unwillingness of society to pay the human costs of factories that pollute has begun to modify the development of new technology; this same principle might someday be applied to the psychological costs of dehumanizing technology in factories.

The third essential condition relates to the attitudes of workers who operate the new technology, who must be at least willing to work with the technology, and in some cases they must want to work with it. If the "proper attitude" is missing, the technology, however mechanically advanced, will become inefficient. If rejected by the workers, technology that is efficient one day can become inefficient and unprofitable the next.

For example, the assembly line, like other forms of "scientific management," is efficient only if workers are willing to adapt or resign themselves to such dehumanized work. In the case of the assembly line, in contrast to other forms of work requiring more craftsmanship, workers do not have to be highly motivated, but they must at least be willing to comply.[6] As long as workers accept the authority of management and engineering science, the assembly line can then be considered relatively efficient technology, inasmuch as control over each worker is maximized and he or she beomes an interchangeable part of the machine.[7]

The idea that a particular technology represents the highest scientific level it is possible to attain may serve to reinforce the authority of management and the compliance of the worker. The worker reasons that if prestigious engineers and scientists knew better ways to build technology, they would do so. Who is he to argue with engineers and scientists? Although workers object to extreme speedups and other unbearable conditions and express their dissatisfaction in negative ways (output restriction, slowdowns, absenteeism, and at the extreme, wildcat strikes), they are inclined to accept technology as the inevitable means to maximum production, which gives them the income to buy the goods they want.

What happens when the attitudes of workers change and they reject totally the role assigned to them by the production technology? This is happening today in Sweden and Norway, where workers refuse to take jobs that make them into passive parts of a machine. The pressure to redesign the technology of production could be resisted if companies hired foreign workers. But both the Swedes and the Norwegians fear the resulting social problems, since they have had unfortunate experiences with Southern Europeans and Asians imported to do their dirty work. Instead, the state has supported scientists and engineers in creating both new material and organizational technology that permits greater autonomy and individual development at work.[8]

In the United States today, workers are increasingly dissatisfied with the dehumanizing effects of technology. But in accepting the authority and inevitability of science-technology-management, most workers protest only when the speedup becomes too great or the grievances pile up. Otherwise, they adapt to "reality" and in some cases manage to remain relatively happy, due to their own inner strengths and lives outside work. As a result, workers are caught up in a process where, instead of demanding more humane working conditions, they demand more money to buy the consumer goods or entertainment that compensates for their suffering at work. And to get more money, they must agree to technological changes that further diminish their sense of autonomy and craftsmanship. They see no alternative.

For this reason, a majority of workers still report that they are satisfied with factory work. But this "satisfaction" is belied by data on alcoholism, drug taking, emotional symptoms, and other counter-productive behavior. Furthermore, the same workers who say they are "satisfied" in general are critical about specific conditions, such as lack of autonomy, disrespectful supervisors, speed of work, and so forth.

Recently I visited an assembly plant where my managerial host maintained that the workers had no complaints. Walking along the line, he stopped to introduce a cheerful-looking young black worker. "Why are you here?" the worker asked me. "To learn about how the work affects the workers." "Don't go away," he said as he rushed to do his job. (A car came by each minute and the weld took about forty seconds.) Back again, he said, "The job isn't backbreaking. In the eight years I've been here, they keep making it easier. It's just that it destroys the mind, it's so damn boring."

The manager had chosen a cheerful worker to demonstrate his point. (Most workers looked bored and unhappy.) But his cheerfulness testified not to the working conditions but to his ability to transcend them.

For most people, the cost of adaptation is the crippling of personal development; for many, it is frozen rage that deadens life. If this statement sounds ideological, one need only study cases where technology and work organization have been redesigned to increase autonomy and democracy, with the result that workers have begun to experience the liberation of themselves, with a flowering of ideas and energy.

If dissatisfaction with work can be focused on creating a more humane and democratic technology of production, the result might be an increasing liberation of energy and a stimulation of ideas to humanize society. How can one expect workers or managers to support human social experiments and to oppose the irrationality of the state if their work demoralizes and reinforces mechanized, authoritarian attitudes? How can one expect workers to develop greater concern for products that aid rather than undermine human development if their work does not encourage dignity and responsibility? How can one expect workers to care about others' suffering if nothing is done to change the conditions that make workers sick and angry? To become aware of all that serves full human development, one must first realize that boring work destroys the mind. The bored worker is likely to opt for a culture that compensates for the destructiveness of work by escapism—which is also destructive of one's full development but is at least pleasurable.

Responsibility in a full social and civil sense depends on the ability to be responsible for both oneself and what one produces. Although most work—even work in more democratic workplaces—is far from this ideal, the process of awakening to responsibility begins with the demystification and reconstruction of the workplace.

The possibility of such a sociopolitical process developing in America depends upon focusing the dissatisfaction with dehumanizing work on a positive program. This growing dissatisfaction appears to be the result of converging trends. On the one hand, chances for self-employment continue to disappear, and many workers brought up with the attitudes of independent farmers or craftsmen are being forced into factories, where they resent mechanized tasks, although they may accept the work as relatively well-paying and not too difficult. On the other hand, there is a new self-affirmative attitude on the part of the traditional working-class and white-collar workers. Increased schooling and participation in the social movements of the 1960s have raised their aspirations and made them critical of irrational authority. [9]

These two types of workers—ex-independents and newly self-affirmative—share a dissatisfaction with dehumanizing work, although they might disagree on issues of social welfare or social justice. For example, southern rural workers who are suspicious of social-welfare programs, fear black progress, and support higher military spending are at the same time deeply dissatisfied with uncraftsmanlike work. They favor experiments that give them more say in running the factory. A movement to humanize technology could gain their support and in the process educate them through the experience of struggling for a more just and humane society.

Such a movement would also gain many allies from progressive managers who, in their own lives, value the opportunity for creative work and learning and who recognize the dehumanizing effects of the mechanized organizational system. [10] The impulse to humanize work appeals to the most progressive side of the managerial character. Many managers are indifferent to other social issues that might concern them, such as the impact of their products on the environment and the public, the quality of life in their communities, and military and foreign policy. But they *are* concerned with the quality of work, mainly for themselves but also for others, since work is vitally important to their own sense of well-being and self-realization.

Projects in which productive technology (including organizational systems) has been designed to maximize or optimize worker well-being have been instituted by progressive managers in the belief that they can mix idealism with practical management and by so doing make the workers more satisfied as well as increase profits. While there is some question as to whether technology can be humanized and profits maintained in all industries, according to our analysis, as workers become more self-affirmative and critical of dehumanizing technology, it will be increasingly inefficient to maintain such a technology. Companies will then have to accept new constraints if they are to make any profit at all. A change in workers' attitudes can change what is efficient and thus modify the nature of the demand for technology. As a result, corporations that create technology will have to make a more humane product if they are to remain competitive.

An objection that might be made to the argument presented here is that corporations will retain defensive options against worker demands for a humanized workplace. Instead of creating more humane technology, they can automate, thus eliminating workers, or, failing this, they can move their plants abroad. In regard to automation, it would be to the workers' long-range benefit to automate the worst jobs, but there are limits to what is possible as long as so much industry is based on product innovation. Constantly changing tools would be prohibitively expensive in many industries, such as automobile manufacturing where model changes are the rule. Even if the decreasing cost of mini-computers should significantly increase the possibilities for automation, mechanistic organizations are prevalent in office and service work, as well as in factories. Automation technology is very far from replacing a majority of the work force. Even where such technology has proved most successful (as in continuous processing), workers are needed; in fact, they work best under conditions that maximize autonomy and chances for individual development.[11] As for the second option, many companies have already opened plants abroad, seeking cheaper and less-demanding labor. Of course, this creates new problems of communication, of dealing with foreign governments, and so forth, quite beyond the scope of these observations. A larger production exodus from the United States would effect not only workers but also managers, and would spark a strong political reaction.

The foregoing analysis suggests a process of creating a general demand for technology that intentionally serves human development rather than merely profit, glory, or security. Such a process, beginning in the workplace, requires a political struggle that can be energized only by the demands of the people most closely involved, including progressive engineers and managers as well as production workers. Such a struggle must encompass the corporate organization, the factory, and the labor union. It must also draw support from intellectuals, particularly scientists and educators, who can share their knowledge and in the process expand their own function and relatedness to social progress.

In this endeavor to create a humane technology, it seems to me that the social scientist has a role with at least three functions. First, he can study the concrete relationships between technology, work, and the individual, and then communicate these findings to workers in a clear and penetrating way to enlarge their understanding. Once the social scientist becomes engaged in a dialogue with workers and progressive managers, the latter can help him or her design studies to clarify relationships that workers may sense but be unsure about. These might include a problem such as the differential effects of certain kinds of organization and technology on both experience and physiological measurements and health.[12]

Second, the social scientist can help to create alternative models of technology and organization that challenge the authority of dehumanized technolgy and authoritarian management. An interesting example of the power of a new model—even, in this case, the *idea* of a model—was the strike of the General Motors Assembly Division at Lordstown, Ohio, in 1972. What began as a more or less typical strike against a speedup and harsh disciplinary practices took a different form when workers heard that more humane ways of organizing an assembly line existed in the Volvo plant in Sweden. The more radical demands sparked by this knowledge of an alternative soon died down, partly because the workers learned that the Volvo project was still just an idea and not a reality and partly because the time was not yet ripe to demand systemic changes requiring both new technology and managerial philosophy. The dissemination of information about the Swedish innovations in the technology of production probably led to the 1973 contract between the UAW and Chrysler, in which the union assumed joint responsibility with management for developing and evaluating experiments "in improving the work environment as a means of making work a more satisfying and stimulating experience."[13]

Social scientists have a third function. As new psycho-socio-technical models are constructed, they can subject them to systemic study, analyzing the interrelated principles that determine the system to discover human consequences—particularly whether or not they allow independence and stimulate democratic cooperation.

Without such analysis, workers may be mystified by programs and rhetoric that promise more than they deliver. On the one hand, new programs announced as "humanistic" may be manipulative attempts to buy increased productivity, while at the same time they undermine the struggles of organized labor for security and equitable pay. On the other hand, increased self-management or "workers' control" may be disillusioning if the technology remains dehumanizing. If workers lack the education and means to reorganize the work process, self-management tends to become a form of human relations rather than a stimulus to develop one's skill, knowledge, and sense of self through work. Only when workers learn that it is possible to reconstruct the workplace according to principles that optimize individuation and democracy, as well as security and equity, will they know that it is in their self-interest to demand that all forms of technology be created to stimulate and not cripple their development.

NOTES

1. Left out of this analysis is the state's capacity to better life by creating new technology, for example, in medicine. This is a complex subject, since (1) new humane technology may in fact strengthen some elements of society versus others (see the work of Ivan Illich); and (2) at the present time, the state spends relatively little on developing humane technology.

2. A primary preoccupation with security is, of course, even more characteristic of the Soviet Union than of the U.S., and is more of a determining factor in creating new technology. For an illustration, see A. Solzhenitsyn's *First Circle* (New York: Harper & Row, 1968).

3. See Richard Barnet, *The Roots of War* (New York: Atheneum, 1972).

4. In some corporations, good ideas that might be profitable are never produced because they cannot be sold *within* the company. Internal selling in some cases may be even more difficult than selling the product to an outside customer.

5. This process is not simple to describe since it requires complex psychological as well as structural analysis. For example, in the U.S. corporate system, innovative technology favors people who are themselves willing to try new things and who are motivated by participation in fast-moving, competitive teams. See Michael Maccoby, "'Winning' and 'Losing' at Work," *Spectrum*, July 1973.

6. When the assembly line and other forms of scientific management were first introduced in the United States, many craftsmen fought against these innovations on the grounds that they were dehumanizing and antidemocratic. See, for example, Milton J. Nadworny, *Scientific Management and the Unions* (Cambridge, Mass.: Harvard Univ. Press, 1955).

7. A similar analysis could be made of the efficiency of computerized clerical work, telephone switchboards, and the organization of development projects in electronics or aerospace, which are "efficient" only so long as they find workers willing to accept fragmented jobs that allow little autonomy or learning. For example, a recent consultant's report advised the telephone company that a "successful" employee is "one dependent upon and yielding to authority rather than autonomous; socially unobtrusive rather than exhibitionistic; persistent and enduring in her approach to work; and conservative in her life-style, more conforming than innovative or rebellious." Cited by Harold L. Sheppard in "A Simple Simon's Partial List of Issues About the Current Controversies Surrounding the Quality of Working Life," paper presented at the 25th meeting of the Industrial Relations Research Association, Toronto, Dec. 28, 1972.

8. The Norwegian Industrial Democracy Project directed by Dr. Einar Thorsrud is a prime example of a state-supported program to develop a new technology of production. It should be noted that the imported Third World workers in Western Europe are increasingly objecting to dehumanizing technology.

9. See Michael Maccoby and Katherine A. Terzi, "Character and Work in America," in *Exploring Contradictions: Political Economy in the Corporate*

State, ed. Philip Brenner, Robert Borosage, and Bethany Weidner (New York: David McKay, 1974) for a fuller discussion of these trends.

10. See Alfred T. DeMaria, Dale Tarnowski, and Richard Gurman, *Manager Unions?* An AMA Research Report (New York: American Management Association, 1972), which reveals that a high percentage of managers surveyed are even willing to join a union to increase chances for learning and craftsmanship, as well as to have security, equity, and democratic relations in their work.

11. A well-known example is the General Foods Pet Food plant in Topeka, Kansas, described by Robert Schrank on pp. 119-140.

12. I participated in two types of meetings, one organized by Neal Q. Herrick and sponsored by the U.S. Department of Labor and the other a meeting sponsored by the UAW with technical, office, and professional workers, where workshops were held discussing effects of technology on emotional and physical well-being. At the UAW meeting, after I gave a talk on this subject, groups of workers met in small workshops to discuss the issue in the light of their own experiences. These discussions led to ideas for studies and for experiments in reorganizing work.

13. Similar agreements have been negotiated with the other automobile companies.

The Culture of the Service Society: The Value Explosion of the Sixties

Alan Gartner and Frank Riessman

During the Era of Protest [the Sixties], practically all non-economic status relationships were challenged and extensively modified: the relationships between whites and Blacks, parents and children, teachers and pupils, policemen and citizens, officers and soldiers, bishops and clergy, the artist and his [sic] audience, the government and its citizen, and most important of all, men and women. As the protest movement gained momentum and took new forms, some of its theorists were inevitably drawn into challenging the legitimacy of all authority, however derived.[1]

Since the 1960s there has arisen a broad range of new values and related movements. New words and demands have entered our consciousness and to some extent our lives: alienation, personal liberation, encounter, the quality of life, male chauvinism, counterculture, ecology, malaise, life-style, growth centers, self-actualization, meaningful work, participation, and more. These words have been embodied in many cases in the various movements of the 1960s and the early 1970s—the student movement, the black and minority Third World movements, the women's movement, the ecology movement, the consumer movement, the human potential movement, and so on.

How are these various themes and movements related to changes in our emerging service society—a society characterized by an increasing proportion of people producing and consuming services, as well as reading about and thinking about services, a society in which services are extremely important for economic stability and social and political control?

It is possible, of course, to believe that the new values are only accidentally related to the changes in our social structure. Or, that they represent a counterrevolutionary reaction to the changes, as was earlier suggested by Brzezinski,[2] who saw the counterculture largely as a reaction similar to that of the Luddites, who reflected their own obsolescence by attacking the advances of their society but who really wished to stop history. Or, as does Daniel Bell,[3] who writes of the disjuncture of social structure and culture in modern society—and by "social structure" he means the post-industrial knowledge explosion and by "culture" he is referring to the modern counterculture emphases of the youth.[4] Or it is possible to take the views of Charles Reich[5] and Theodore Roszak,[6] who see the modern values as highly revolutionary, reflecting a moral rebellion against the bankruptcy of corporate liberalism, the establishment, or the "welfare-warfare" state, where real human needs are neglected by large-scale organizations that dehumanize their members. This view is rooted in the belief that there is a new affluence (the "post-scarcity" society), which has made unnecessary the old repressive values that were linked to economic scarcity.

It is clear that both groups—the Brzezinski-Bell counterrevolution theorists and the new revolution theorists, such as Reich, Roszak, and others—are looking at the counterculture in different ways. Reich and his group view it as highly positive and in the historical vanguard, but the Brzezinski group sees it as counterrevolutionary, anachronistic, regressive. They see the disjuncture as temporary, while the Reich group sees it as the forerunner of the future and perhaps as the predeterminer of a changed society.

The Brzezinski group stresses the major social transformations undergone as we move from an industrial to a post-industrial, technotronic society, which they view as highly rationalized and characterized by high productivity, automation, increased leisure time, rapid rates of social change, and a rational administration, largely of a hierarchical, disciplined character. Enormously high levels of education will be required and the power will lie with those who possess educational capital. The knowledge industry will be the central motor of historical change. Basically, there will be a technical-managerial approach to the solution of human problems, rather than one related to power and conflict, or ideology. The counterculture people see the key modern development as being the post-scarcity society, although it is not entirely clear how this post-scarcity base (which is, of course, far from fully actualized) specifically produces all the new modern values.

There is no question that both groups are pointing to aspects of change and potential change in the modern society. We would suggest, however, that a more specific analysis, based upon the emerging neocapitalist service-society formulation, can explain more effectively not only the counterculture values of the youth, but the whole wave of new consciousness that goes far beyond the oppositional youth dimension. Moreover, we will attempt to classify not only the range of new value syndromes but also the specific limits of their institutionalization. That is, while we believe that the new values are very important, have had a significant effect upon the consciousness of many groups in our society, and are spreading to other groups contagiously, nevertheless, the full expression of these values in practices and institutions is limited by the power and influence of the corporate state. Despite this, however, these new developments have considerable power and cannot easily be violated, as we shall see.

VALUES AND MOVEMENTS OF THE SIXTIES

In our view, major themes and values characteristic of the service society surfaced sharply in the 1960s, particularly around the various movements of that period: the civil-rights, black-power, consumer-protection, ecology, youth, free-speech, peace, welfare-rights, and community-control movements, and the demands for rights and entitlements by large numbers of people ranging from patients and prisoners to homosexuals.

It is our contention that the values of the sixties are being contagiously institutionalized in everyday life, in people's life-styles, behaviors, and consciousness. Institutionalization, of course, has a double edge. On the one hand, it typically waters down a value and weakens, in some respects, the value it had in its original, more pristine mobilizing form. For example, the demand for participation and community control in the 1960s had a much sharper edge than it does in the 1970s. On the other hand, the very fact of institutionalization and acceptance is a strengthening feature, a feature that would be much stronger still, if the basic economic structure were to change.

Much of the discussion of the 1960s focuses on the counterculture and the so-called opposition youth. Bell, Brzezinski, Herman Kahn, and others disconnect the counterculture from the values and movements we have mentioned, and tend to fasten their attention on a limited range of counterculture features. We are much more interested in the larger configuration and the various value syndromes emanating from these movements. The syndromes that we shall describe below frequently overlap, the lines of difference are blurred, and in many cases it is possible to combine different value elements to construct a different syndrome.

Our intention is to demonstrate in a broad way that these value patterns are related to significant service-society features—in some cases that they are derived from various vanguard groups, such as women, youth, minorities; that they function in many ways to support the new service (relational) work and the requirements of that work; and finally that, more nonspecifically, they are related to the new importance of the consumer role in society and the nature of consumer time, which is open, unbounded, less structured. In a sense, then, our analysis suggests a convergence of many different elements in the service society. This accounts for the speed and force with which these values developed in the 1960s and the fact that they are spreading further in the 1970s, despite the decline of the movements of the sixties and the general backlash against them.[7]

The so-called counterculture values are spreading, particularly in the workplace, in the women's movement, in population groups that are typically more middle-class and traditional, in mainstream education, in the media—in short, in everyday life and its reflected human relations. Our analysis, then, is very different from those of Bell and Brzezinski, who largely see the new values as a disjuncture, lacking in social-structural dimensions, independent of and unrelated to social forces, and, in some cases, downright anachronistically dysfunctional.

What are the new value themes and how are they related to the emerging service society? As we sketch out the various value configurations, it will be clear that there is considerable overlap among them; the boundaries that we suggest are tentative working definitions. It will also be apparent that different vanguard groups—sometimes blacks and other minorities, sometimes the youth, sometimes the women— are central to particular value syndromes.

RIGHTS, ENTITLEMENTS, AND PERSONAL LIBERATION

Perhaps one of the most important syndromes, and one that affects the others very much, is the extension of rights and entitlements to a variety of groups, beginning with Third World minorities and extending to students,[8] women, old people, homosexuals, children, welfare participants, prisoners, patients, and so on. In the sixties, in particular, there was a great expansion of many rights: the right of students to participate in the decisions of the university, rights for the poor, the right to information about products, the right to a fair hearing for welfare recipients, and of particular interest, various personal-autonomy rights with respect to sex, family, and birth control.[9] It is noteworthy that in some areas these rights are being extended in the seventies to certain rights that women are demanding, the right of the educationally handi- capped to education, the right of the mentally ill to rehabilitation, the right to higher education as expressed in the Higher Education Act of 1973, the right not to be discriminated against via tests, and so on. Many of these rights relate directly to services such as education, health, rehabilitation, and so forth.

ACCOUNTABILITY AND RELEVANCE

The rights of the receivers of service—consumers—relate very much to a new trend with regard to professional practice and credentials. The new demand was clearly for relevance, accountability, and vitality of the service, whether it be education, health, mental health, or whatever. With a real concern that services "deliver," a new service conscious- ness was arising in critiques of professional practice, particularly in the critique of teachers at all levels from elementary school through grad- uate school.

As in the case of rights and entitlements, the spearheading move- ment was that of Third World minorities, particularly the blacks, and the thrust here spread to other groups—other minorities, youth, women, and so forth. This theme received much of its power from parent and community groups along with enlightened professionals and the alter- nate-institution people, who were looking for new kinds of human ser- vices that worked, that were humane, nonbureaucratized, not de- fended by tradition, secrecy, and mystique. One of the major demands was to demystify the professions; new kinds of professionals emerged in law, medicine, journalism, architecture, and so forth.[10]

SELF-ACTUALIZATION, AUTONOMY, AND INDIVIDUALISM

Another major value theme has to do with the development of the in- ner life, with growth, self-expression, and personal liberation. Here the theme overlaps with the first theme concerning rights. This syndrome is expressed in the desire for open classrooms and free schools, the re- emergence of progressive education, and the desire for spontaneity, openness, informality, and freedom.

New forms of psychotherapy have appeared, though frequently they are not called that at all: growth centers, alternative states, encounters, sensitivity groups, consciousness raising. The opening up and discov- ery of the self along with the expansion of consciousness is primary, and so the interest in drugs has spread. Anything that interfered with this development was looked at askance—tradition, control, discipline, structure, form, rationality. This trend has clearly been led by the affluent young and their parents in different forms and directions, but their personal liberation owes much to the blacks.

The wish for emotional expression spills over into many areas, including style and culture and, most clearly, sexual relations.

A wide variety of social changes have occurred, including greater explicitness in, observations of, and research into sexual activities (for example, contrast the more open response to the far more explicit work of Masters and Johnson to that which greeted Kinsey's work); wider attention to sex on the stage, in movies, and in print; greater acceptance of various unconventional living arrangements;[11] legal changes regarding private sex acts among consenting adults; changes in abortion laws; increased availability of contraceptive devices. In examining attitudes, while age is a differentiating factor, the break is between those under and over forty-four years of age, not at some younger level.

Morton Hunt, writing in *Playboy*, states that within the context of the continuing dominance of heterosexual marriage, there is greater "spontaneous and guilt-free enjoyment of a wide range of sexual acts in the context of the emotional significance of sexual expression."[12]

THE QUALITY OF LIFE

Concern for the quality of life has both external and internal dimensions. Externally, the concern is directed toward ecology, the environment, and Nader-oriented issues regarding commodities and services. Internally, it is directed toward the expansion of consciousness, the use of leisure and art, and much of the inner self-expression described above. It was largely led by the affluent young and their parents.

THE EGALITARIAN-ANTIHIERARCHICAL THEME

Major criticism has been directed at traditional, hierarchical authority and discipline found in the family, school, workplace, and church.[13] There has been a sharp drop in respect for and trust in the basic institutions of society. For example, a study by the Center for Political Studies at the University of Michigan, found that trust in basic governmental institutions, between 1958 and 1972, dropped among whites from 50 percent support to barely 5 percent, while among blacks the drop was from 50 percent support to nearly 50 percent estrangement. Among all age groups support dropped over the course of the four waves of interviews conducted between 1958 and 1972; while youth have been more estranged than older persons in each succeeding wave, by 1972, people in the fifty to fifty-nine, sixty to sixty-nine, and seventy and over age brackets ranked even lower than youth in estrangement.[14]

In the early forties Erich Fromm[15] analyzed and criticized irrational authority; today however there appears to be a tendency to attack all authority and all discipline indiscriminately. A neoanarchism has emerged, with a powerful pro-humanism that emphasizes the "natural man" and spontaneity; this has extended to small groups, communes, networks, and communities where the good life could be lived.[16] The central enemies were bureaucracy and bigness, formality and structure. A strong Rousseauean component has been revitalized.

An effort was made to build alternative institutions, frequently on a nonhierarchical basis. This movement quite obviously was led by the affluent young, although some of its antibureaucratic overtones have spilled over into various functioning institutions where professionals and service workers are employed. It is frequently directed at alienation and powerlessness.

THE INTERPERSONAL-PSYCHOLOGY THEME

If physical science is the center of Brzezinski's technotronic world and engineers and scientists are the center of Bell's post-industrial society, then psychology and the behavioral revolution are the centers of the service society. Its prophets are Abraham Maslow, William C. Schutz, and Carl Rogers; the key words are self-actualization, encounter, human potential, and joy. The service society is a relational society, and the new humanistic psychology is concerned with interpersonal relations, self-development, and sensitive awareness of others, especially at the nonverbal level. *Psychology Today* is a key magazine bringing the behavioral-revolution message to vast numbers of people who are concerned about sexual expression and many of the other new values. The expansion of psychological knowledge into everyday life is very impressive. This theme is voiced to a great extent by affluent professional adults.

WORK AND PLAY

Work and leisure or play are frequently blurred in the new work theme. Self-expression is crucial to both, as is a nonhierarchical orientation. This is perhaps best exemplified in the free-school movement. Systematic, disciplined hard work is looked upon askance. Work, rather, is to be self-actualizing, joyful, nonhierarchically organized, an expression of the self, and it should be as free and autonomous as possible.

Other dimensions of the new work syndrome emphasize that it should be meaningful, useful, community serving, participatory, satisfying, and nonbureaucractic. Expression of this theme comes from two different directions: on the one hand, there are the affluent adults and the young with their alternative institutions, and on the other hand, there are the Third World minorities; both groups are increasingly opposed to dead-end, boring, meaningless work. In addition, there are the professionals, who feel that their training, skills, and human potential are not utilized in highly bureaucratic work structures.

THE SERVICE-ADVOCACY THEME

The sixties saw a great deal of concern about human service, particularly by the young, who were concerned about working in the ghetto, helping the poor in direct, nonprofessional ways. This is also reflected in the whole new-professional movement described by Ronald Gross, where large numbers of young professionals select and recast their work in a noncareerist, serving mode.[17]

THE ANTICONFORMITY, ANTIMATERIALISM THEME

This powerful theme developed initially among the young but spread via various alternative therapeutic institutions to adults who increasingly rejected the acquisitive life, the rat race, conformity, competition, manipulation, and even in some cases, material values. A new humanism has appeared, concerned with enjoying life and people, leisure and art, inner experience and nature, and living for oneself rather than conforming for success. This dovetails with the antihierarchical, the self-development, and the quality-of-life themes.

> The old culture, when forced to choose, tends to give preference to property rights over personal rights, technological requirements over human needs, competition over cooperation, violence over sexuality, concentration over distribution, the producer over the consumer, means over ends, secrecy over personal openness, social forms over personal expression, striving over gratification, Oedipal love over communal love, and so on. The counter culture tends to reverse all these priorities.[18]

THE IDENTITY, SELF-DETERMINATION THEME

The black-power movement, which spearheaded the slogan "Black Is Beautiful," is illustrative of this identity theme. Reversing the traditional racism and the more modern environmentalism, which in one way or another has represented blacks as inferior, the new theme went beyond a vague cultural pluralism, and it was argued instead that blacks have a unique identity that was, indeed, very positive and healthy. This identity was based upon deep traditions—African and others—that emerged from a long history of struggle against oppressive majorities and their oppressive cultures. The theme was reflected at both the political and cultural levels: with the accenting of physical and cultural characteristics, the demand for black-study programs, the political rejection of alliances, and a preference to go it alone, at least as a first stage. The emphasis was on group identity and self-determination, and there was a strong rejection of potential contamination by nonblack groups.

The theme spread rapidly to other minorities, such as Chicanos, Puerto Ricans, American Indians, and, more recently, has been expressed in the women's movement, with its desire for female identity, self-determination, and personal liberation. The idea leads to a powerful attack on all discriminatory ideology that, whatever its presumed objective, winds up putting down the group in question, whether it be on the basis of the IQ of blacks, the sexuality of women, or whatever. The particular significance of this theme is that it does not attempt to "explain" inadequacy but essentially denies presumed inadequacy and reinterprets the phenomena.

THE NEXUS

We come now to the key question: What is the relationship of these various value patterns to the emerging service society?

At the simplest level of occupational determinism, one could argue, of course, that a good number of the new value syndromes are directly reflective of and useful to the new service occupations. "An individual now talks to other individuals rather than interacts with a machine and this is the fundamental fact about work in the post-industrial society."[19]

Obviously in such a relational, interpersonal society, humanistic psychology and the whole syndrome related to it is likely to come to the fore. The need for sensitivity to others and great awareness of oneself not only are useful in relation to service work but also have wide applicability in sales, advertising, personal services, and so forth.

Another key syndrome relates to the need for creativity, self-actualization, and development. These characteristics are much in demand, not only in the professions and human services but also in the knowledge sectors.

Creativity should not be controlled and manipulated on a hierarchical basis. The creative person needs lots of freedom, room to grow and express himself, rather than traditional restrictions, boundaries, and controls. Permissiveness in child rearing and the revival of progressive education are in many ways consonant with the development of the new creativity that is so needed in service occupations, as well as in educational fields and in people's expanded leisure lives. The new occupations require more autonomy. Again, one of the rallying cries in the professions is the accusation that the emerging bureaucracies have stifled the creativity that service workers have been trained to bring to their jobs and that they expect of them. Andre Gorz has been among the most prominent theoreticians to point out this powerful source of alienation within the educated labor force in the workplace. [20] He notes that workers in scientific and cultural industries experience the impossibility of putting their creative abilities to work and thus tend to rebel against the bureaucracy, a rebellion that, incidentally, may be more fully expressed by their children, who are presumably being prepared for similar labor by educational institutions. The socialization of children requires a good deal of openness, creativity, and informality, but these qualities run counter to the atmosphere found in the traditional, rigid, test-bound, grade-oriented authoritarian school.

While some of the new values can be partially explained by their suitability to the new work structures and work lives of service workers, a more generalized, nonspecific mode of explanation is necessary to understand fully the many value dimensions. In essence, we are talking not only about service occupations or even services sectors; we are talking about the service society. The service society is characterized by features that go beyond the characteristics of specific service occupations. And so, our interpretation must be much more attentive to the nonspecific, indirect effect of the service society on emerging values. Nevertheless, specific occupations and their socialization functions are not irrelevant.

Much of the thrust of the new values comes from the various groups we have mentioned, not so much in their service-work roles as in their consumer roles. Thus, it is particularly important to understand the special role of a consumer in the service society, because the values put forward by Third World minorities, students, women, and other groups cannot be entirely explained in terms of their noninvolvement in the industrial sectors, but must be particularly understood in the light of their roles as consumers and potential service workers.

SIXTIES INTO SEVENTIES EQUALS ?

It is fashionable to believe that the values and movements that emerged in the 1960s are lost, wiped out, violated, or rejected. There is some superficial basis for this view, in that the cutting edge of the movements and their related values are no longer on center stage. The counterculture, welfare rights, the youth movement, community control, and black power seem thoroughly distant. The blacks are quiet, the youth are back in school, and the counterculture has become spiritual. A new privatism prevails, sometimes masked as personal liberation. Still, the consumer movement and Ralph Nader go on; the environmental movement in some ways is stronger than ever; the women's movement is still on the rise and has won many victories; there are more blacks in elected office than ever before in American history; the mainstream school system is adopting open-classroom types of organization. Consumer participation on corporation and community boards continues high; schools have been highly sensitized, as have other institutions, to community pressure; open enrollment remains, if not as strong as it once was. The encounter movement is spreading; more people are involved in growth and development activities than ever before; and the acceptance in everyday life of the counterculture's values and ethos is truly amazing. For example, we have seen the acceptance and use of marijuana, new sex customs, abortion, liberated speech.

What all this means, it seems to us, is that the basic thrust of the 1960s and the service society (and consumer values) has not been lost by any means. True, some of the values are vulgarized, commercialized, and watered down, but others have been institutionalized, accepted into consciousness and everyday life; they have deeply affected human relations and some have contagiously spread to new areas, including the workplace.

CONCLUSION

The consumer role that is becoming increasingly dominant in modern life is characterized by much more unstructured time in which the individual feels freer to make choices, to do his or her own thing, to live his or her life-style. He or she can be less concerned with organization, hierarchy, tradition. The consumer role permits more interest in growth, self-development, expression, liberation, personal rights, the environment, and nature. In some cases this leads to a tremendous privatism, personalism, and hedonism, while in other cases, consumers' demands for accountability of services and quality of goods attracts them to Nader, the environmental movement, participation in school activities, and so forth.

The consumer is seen in many roles: taxpayer, student, volunteer, housewife, community board member, parent, patient, client, customer, media viewer, welfare recipient, unemployed worker, and pollee. In a sense, of course, everyone—worker, taxpayer, voter—is a consumer, and much more time is spent in the consumer role in our society. But the worker-consumer in the traditional industrial structure is greatly constrained by the rules and pressures of organization. The consumer as student, welfare recipient, woman-at-home—while surely under pressure—is less constrained by the rules and requirements of organized work. These groups, in addition, are also largely politically disenfranchised; they are, in some sense, "unnecessary people," in Jean Miller's terminology,[21] dispensable as far as production is concerned (although very necessary as consumers). They are, in turn, less integrated into production and work processes, less socialized by these processes, and more open to new trends, feelings, and ideas derived from neighbors, peers, the media, consciousness-raising groups, and so on. Consumers are constantly overstimulated to purchase goods with greatly expanded credit, but the inflationary economy typically cheats them at the point of consumption. The "unnecessary people" are, however, very necessary to stabilize the economy, not as worker-producers, but as consumer-buyers of overpriced, overadvertised products.

It is clear, then, that the value configurations we have been describing are overly determined, in part by the consumer culture, in part by the intrinsic human potential and character of service work (a kind of occupational determinism), and in part by the groups in our society who are most involved in service work and in disenfranchised consumer roles—the women, the youth, and the minorities—the consumer vanguards, so to speak.

NOTES

1. Theodore Caplow, "Toward Social Hope," *Columbia University Forum* (Winter 1973), p. 3.

2. Zbigniew Brzezinski, *Between Two Ages: America's Role in the Technetronic Era* (New York: Viking, 1970).

3. Daniel Bell, *The Coming of the Post-Industrial Society* (New York: Basic Books, 1973).

4. Kenneth Keniston, *Youth and Dissent* (New York: Harcourt, Brace, 1971).

5. Charles Reich, *The Greening of America: The Coming of a New Consciousness and the Rebirth of a Future* (New York: Random House, 1970).

6. Theodore Roszak, *Where the Wasteland Ends* (New York: Doubleday Anchor, 1972); *The Making of a Counter-Culture* (New York: Doubleday, 1969); *Sources* (New York: Harper & Row, 1971).

7. It should be noted of course that there were other elements and events in the 1960s that played a special role in the rapid development of some of these

values; for example, the war and the draft, the Third World, the development of the "pill," and the rapid expansion of the power of the media, which gave special attention to new movements, new ideas, new values, new themes, and new words.

8. In the past four years, according to a Harris Poll, those who felt that "student demonstrators who engage in protest activities," and "blacks who demonstrate for civil rights," did more harm than good dropped by 33 percent and 32 percent, respectively. New York Post, Oct. 1, 1973.

9. By 1972, 71 percent of a representative sample of white adults favored birth-control-education programs in public high schools. This was up 10 percent over two years earlier. A majority of both men and women, Catholics and non-Catholics, favored free birth-control services for teen-age girls who requested them. This percentage, overall, in 1972 was 54 percent, up from 38 percent in 1970. "Contraceptive Education for All Teens, and Services on Request Favored by Most Adults," Family Planning Digest, 2, No. 5 (Sept. 1973), Table 1.

10. See Ronald Gross and Paul Osterman, The New Professionals (New York: Simon and Schuster, 1972).

11. Between 1960 and 1970, the census reports an 820 percent increase in unmarried couples living together, compared with a 10 percent increase in married couples living together. No doubt, part of this increase simply indicates more openness in reporting such an arrangement. But those who so report may be only a portion of those who live together.

12. Morton Hunt, "Sexual Behavior in the 1970s," Playboy, 20, No. 10 (Oct. 1973), p. 207.

13. In response to a Harris Poll, those who felt that "people who don't believe in God" did more harm than good had dropped by 32 percent in the past four years. New York Post, Oct. 1, 1972.

14. Newsletter, Institute for Social Research, Univ. of Mich., 1, No. 18 (Spring-Summer 1973), pp. 4-5.

15. Erich Fromm, Escape from Freedom (New York: Holt, Rinehart, 1941).

16. See Murray Bookchin, "On Spontaneity and Organization," Liberation (March 1972), pp. 5-17.

17. Gross and Osterman, The New Professionals.

18. Philip Slater, The Pursuit of Loneliness (Boston: Beacon, 1970), p. 100.

19. Bell, The Coming of the Post-Industrial Society.

20. Andre Gorz, Strategy for Labor (Boston: Beacon, 1967).

21. Jean Baker Miller, "On Women: New Political Directions for Women," Social Policy, 2, No. 2 (July-Aug. 1971).

Some
Specifics

Preface

Roy P. Fairfield

Let us now move from the general to the specific, from analytic and philosophical vistas to concrete instances and images. Eight authors bring their perspectives to many of the issues that the foregoing authors have raised.

Robert Schrank is one of the country's foremost specialists in problems of the workplace. Veteran of many workplaces himself—having sat on both sides of the negotiating table—and participant in more workplace conferences (both American and international) than he may even remember, he has a viewpoint from which to analyze and evaluate. His description and critique of the Gaines Pet Food plant in Topeka, Kansas, thought to be one of the most avant-garde operations in American industry, is vivid and incisive. As we finish reading such an account, those of us who are veterans of traditional factories will probably resolve to stop at Topeka to see this plant in operation. But it is one thing to describe a factory, from whatever angle of vision; it is quite another to see it in both historical and current perspective. We must thank Schrank especially for putting the Gaines operation into the context of an analysis by Richard Walton, a Harvard social scientist working on work problems. And in view of Schrank's pessimism about the nature of industrial design, we must question the assumptions upon which his dim view is based. Must a design be absolutely rigid if we are to produce millions upon millions of nuts and bolts, cars and lamps, toasters and saws? If so, then how do we account for the "ingenuity" or even such an accidental redesign of work spaces and functions as that reported by Bennett Kremen in his conversation with workers at the Vega plant in Lordstown, Ohio? And, had any of us been working with Myra Peabody, who recounts her nightmarish days at the General Dynamics boatyard, could we have redesigned such a workplace and established spheres of trust between workers that would have alleviated anger and alienation? Or would we be tempted, as perhaps some managers would have been, to discount Ms. Peabody's perceptions as slightly "wacky"?

The two articles etching some of the dimensions of coal miners' lives and dilemmas help explain the public image of a difficult and demeaning occupation and the cultural setting where they spend their lives. Some may feel that focusing upon such severe tasks may distort. After all, with an increasing number of persons working in a service society (wearing white and pastel collars to boot), should we worry about an occupation in which the preponderant number of people are invisible? My answer is a resounding yes! As much attention should be given to this minority as to any other minority in the country (after all, every work group is a minority) when one group of humans is affecting another group of humans adversely. McAteer's anecdote about the drinking water, however small it may seem, is unfortunately all too symbolic. Few of us will forget Bloody Harlan County, in eastern Kentucky, from the newspaper and history books, if not from direct contact. One wonders if it would be necessary for workers to challenge management authority if there were more worker participation in decision making? Nor can one but wonder how far we may be from another Bloody Harlan when a mine manager tells a television reporter, "You're not going down into the mine because *I say you are not going!*" Where are human concerns when such arrogance of power is as demonstrable as in the drinking-water incident or in the manager's response to the reporter's interest in the story under ground?

The eight hundred thousand workers whom Jack Russell highlights may constitute only 1 percent of the work force, but as a type they remind us of the many kinds of migrant workers in this country. Although street-corner workers, dehumanized by the daily shape-up, are highly visible, few members of the populace, even congressmen, seem to see them. Yet they are reminders of vast numbers of invisible workers in this country, the men, women, and children who follow the crops north, from tomato picking in Florida to cherry picking in Michigan, people who have harvested the very food on our tables while harvesting little more than a shameful way of living for themselves. And while Cesar Chavez and other migrant heroes have provided the country with a new view of these workers and have helped them earn their rightful wages, schools, and dignity, still, as Jack Russell points out so well, there is an urban blight that needs a Chavez. So much more so for the racist and sexist implications of the phenomenon.

The last two articles in Part II may seem poles apart: garbage collecting and office design. But both reflect human adaptation and imagination. Ed Walsh has done an important service in damaging a stereotype. He suggests that the joy of working, even though it is doing dirty work, may be found in camaraderie and good-humored competition (more of what Schrank calls "schmoozing"), as well as in picking up a paycheck. Meanwhile, Walter Kleeman has given us a glimmer of hope by presenting many ways for office workers to escape the sterility of wall-to-wall standardization of office artifacts. Nobody can avoid making connections between his view of the "social water hole," the miners' drinking-water problem, and the problem of relieving themselves that garbagemen face when they can't find a john along their routes.

With more space it would have been fun to discuss more specifics: how Proctor & Gamble designed a plant at Lima, Ohio, intended to stimulate relationships among people and effect autonomous group behavior that would help them determine the nature of the work environment; how Travelers Insurance Company in Hartford, Connecticut, made a structural change in their key-punch operation to integrate workers into the total process rather than fragment their lives by doing bits and pieces; how Corning Glass rearranged work crews in Medford, Massachusetts, and Fort Lauderdale, Florida, to give employees a sense of being totally involved with the product rather than merely working on one sliver of it; or how groups of workers in England and France seized their plants "illegally" for "work-ins" that eventually made them owner-workers and responsible for feeding the phoenix they resurrected from the ashes. And what was the impact on Swiss workers of their taking a five-minute break for folk dancing? Also, the worker-exchange program that Robert Schrank discusses in Part III raises many questions about the potential for cross-cultural influence and change, when the workers of one country gain new perspectives on their own jobs by taking a long look at other modes of work organization in other cultures. In the long run, what they see and do may even undermine Schrank's less than optimistic viewpoint.

On Ending Worker Alienation: The Gaines Pet Food Plant

Robert Schrank

General Foods Corporation is probably best known to the average person for Post breakfast cereals and Jello. They also make pet food. The Gaines Pet Food plant in Topeka, Kansas, is a tiny segment of one hundred and twenty employees in a multinational corporation whose annual sales exceed two billion dollars.

In the recent discussions about the quality of working life, the Topeka plant has repeatedly been cited as a prototype workplace. Writing in the *Harvard Business Review,* Richard E. Walton, for example, cited the Topeka operation as an example of "How To Counter Alienation in the Plant."[1] This essay is about a recent visit I made to the Topeka plant. It is also a review of some of the issues involved in rising worker dissatisfaction.

The Topeka plant has been in operation since January, 1971. Lyman Ketchum, who became manager of the original Gaines Pet Food operation in Kankakee, Illinois, in 1966, is largely credited with planning and developing the Topeka plant. Ketchum described the Kankakee Operation as it was when he took over. "At the time, rapidly expanding volumes caused overtime operations. Kankakee had a young work force with 53 percent of the males under 28, and 35 percent of the females under 28. It was a capable work force. Rapid turnover in the management ranks, mostly for positive reasons of promotion to other parts of the General Foods system, was evident."

The management organization had made extensive use of the National Training Laboratories and the University of Illinois training programs, the latter for employees at the foreman and middle-management levels. But the productivity problems at Kankakee were serious enough to cause General Foods to consider a new pet-food plant.

In a sense, this was the start of a journey that Ketchum describes as having begun in a traditional management concept of the pyramidal organization but which culminated in what he now conceives as a highly participatory, almost circular, open-system organization at the Topeka plant. Walton, in the *Harvard Business Review,* speaking about worker alienation makes two points: (1) the current alienation is not merely a phase that will pass in due time; and (2) the innovations needed to correct the problem can simultaneously *enhance the quality of work life* (thereby lessening alienation) and improve productivity. [Emphasis added—RS] Because the Walton article is representative of the views of many behavioral scientists who are concerned with workplace problems, I will use it as a springboard to discuss some of the issues involved.

An underlying assumption of many people concerned with improving life at the workplace, as indicated in more detail elsewhere in this volume, is that any change or improvement must be accompanied by an increase in production. Such an assumption tends to make workers and union people suspicious that a particular change may be just another scheme to get more production out of them. All workplace changes tend to be sponsored by management, with little union or worker participation, thus reinforcing that suspicion.

Walton was involved in planning the Topeka plant. Ketchum comments: "Our enthusiasm for the practicality of behavioral science grew. We invited Dick Walton (Harvard), Don King (Purdue), and Earl Wolf (University of Illinois). The significant difference between this approach and all of our previous uses of behavioral-science knowledge and talent was application of the principles at the *level of the first-line supervisor,* rather than at the top of the organization."

What Ketchum describes as his conversion to a behavioral-science approach is further elucidated by Walton's explanation of the source of worker alienation—the six "roots of conflict":

1. Employees want challenge and personal growth, but work tends to be simplified and specialties tend to be used repeatedly in work assignments. This pattern exploits the narrow skills of a worker, while limiting his or her opportunities to broaden or develop.

2. Employees want to be included in patterns of mutual influence; they want egalitarian treatment. But organizations are characterized by tall hierarchies, status differentials, and chains of command.

3. Employee commitment to an organization is increasingly influ-

enced by the intrinsic interest of the work itself, the human dignity afforded by management, and the social responsibility reflected in the organization's products. Yet organization practices still emphasize material rewards and employment security and neglect other employee concerns.

4. What employees want from careers, they are apt to want right now. But when organizations design job hierarchies and career paths, they continue to assume that today's workers are as willing to postpone gratifications as were yesterday's workers.

5. Employees want more attention to the emotional aspects of organizational life, such as individual self-esteem, openness between people, and expressions of warmth. Yet organizations emphasize rationality and seldom legitimize the emotional part of the organizational experience.

6. Employees are becoming less driven by competitive urges, less likely to identify competition as the "American way." Nevertheless, managers continue to plan career patterns, organize work, and design reward systems as if employees valued competition as highly as they used to.

Ketchum, with consultants like Walton, planned the new facility to meet certain objectives. The main features of the Topeka design, as summarized by Walton, were: autonomous work groups; integrated support functions; challenging job assignments; job mobility and rewards for learning; facilitative leadership; "managerial" decision information for operators; self-government for the plant community; congruent physical and social contexts; learning and evolution (assessment and evaluation).

During my visit to the Topeka plant I had an opportunity to observe the operation and speak with a number of people in management and production. The plant is located on the outskirts of Topeka off a main highway, in what must have been a wheatfield not long ago. The building looks like a windowless fifteen- or twenty-story office tower. The square white structure encloses a series of huge grain-elevator-type storage bins and is lit up at night. At the base of the tower to one side is a more typical, one-story commercial-factory type of structure that covers approximately a square city block. This is a new canned-dog-food plant as well as the receiving, packing, and shipping area.

EMPLOYMENT

The entire Topeka operation is run around the clock by one hundred and twenty employees. The plant offers an interesting contrast between a continuous-process operation and the more traditional manufacturing operation in packaging and warehousing. The work is divided into three groups: (1) processing, with eight employees per shift; (2) packaging and warehousing, eighteen per shift; and (3) management, engineering, or office, twenty-four per shift.

The first employees were recruited through the Kansas Employment Service. About twelve hundred people applied for jobs, but Employment Service interviews eliminated half of those. Team leaders (once called foremen) did the interviewing, finally hiring sixty-three people. The starting rate, originally $3.40 per hour, is now $3.60. The average age of those hired is thirty. All employees are high-school graduates; one has two years of college. One is female and fifteen are members of minority groups.

Criteria for employment were based on work history, with emphasis on a high level of initiative, decision-making ability, and most important, the ability to work as part of a team. (A personal "interaction test" was used in the beginning, but dropped when found to be unreliable.)

As work groups were being assembled, prospective employees were interviewed by the team leader (part of management) to see if they would "fit in." Presently all applicants are interviewed by the work groups. If a prospective employee is not approved by the group, he or she is not hired. All new employees come through the packaging-warehousing group, which suggests that this is the lowest-status group in the plant. The team leader's job is salaried; the other employees are paid hourly. Of the six team leaders, three came from the Kankakee plant of General Foods, and three are new to the corporation.

The problems of an equitable pay scale have not been completely resolved at Topeka. The original concept was to match salary scale to the individual's knowledge of the plant operations. A new employee starts at the base rate. When the group feels he is ready, he moves from $3.60 to $3.80. The objective is to keep moving up the scale until $4.28 is reached, usually within a year. A committee of employees and management is presently trying to develop a "more equitable wage structure," but its success is uncertain. I did get a sense from some employees of an uneasiness about wages relative to responsibility. This may prove to be a greater problem than it has been during the first years of plant operation.

While the hiring of new employees seems highly participatory, it also harbors possibilities for discrimination or nepotism if individuals or groups who do not "fit in" are not hired. As one employee put it, "One of the fellas just did not fit in—he lacked initiative and could not make decisions when confronted with real problems." Unlike a situation involving a union dispute, there is no procedure for redress outside the existing institutional structure. What prevents a group from "ganging up" on an individual?

The plant has a forty-hour, five-day workweek. There are no time clocks. Benefits include nine holidays, a two-week vacation a year, five days of sick leave approved by the group team leader, and hospitalization through a major insurance concern similar to Blue Cross. Overtime averages four to eight hours a week.

Absenteeism runs about 1 percent. No record is kept of lateness, since people tend to make up time if they come in late. The work group deals with problems of habitual lateness with a warning system, as well as the authority to terminate a worker if necessary.

STARTING A NEW "TOPEKA"

The management at Gaines emphasized repeatedly that it is much easier to start up a new plant than it is to introduce the Topeka concepts into an existing plant under union contract. "When you have a union situation, you have very different problems," one management man said. "You are limited by the collective-bargaining process." He also commented on problems related to wage scales at the Topeka plant. Because the employees did not participate in establishing the wage scale, they tend to be suspicious of it, he said, adding that, if they had it to do over again, the planners would take a different approach.

The number of people in the plant is small, and employees do express the feeling that they have freedom to communicate with anyone they want to. They do not have to make appointments, nor do they have to get approval from one level of supervision to see someone at the next level. I queried management as to how large an organization could maintain this kind of openness and informality. Though I strongly disagree, they felt that the size of the plant was not the critical factor in determining the level of openness. They felt the critical variable was the size of the work group. The number seventeen seemed to be maximum. With a group that size they felt it possible to have optimum communication within the team, one of two critical elements for a successful work group. The second element is a relationship of basic trust between the employees and management. "If you can win trust, then employees will accept what you are doing." They also stressed the fact that in order to win trust there must be full participation, good communication, and an open atmosphere in the plant.

There is some evidence to suggest that the question of participation and openness is very much related to plant size. It is one thing to have an open McGregor (Type "Y") management in a plant where thirty or forty people are present at any given time. It is another thing in a plant of two thousand or ten thousand. The number of people working in a plant is a critical variable determining the level of openness. In a large organization there is an inevitable control factor. Someone must initiate the direction of the plant. Small units of operation are required to achieve a participatory atmosphere, where things function smoothly.

I tried to get some information from Topeka management people who had worked at Kankakee on how they saw the work relationships in that plant. They said that because the Kankakee plant is organized by the American Federation of Grain Millers, it has little or no flexibility. They expressed the view that the union in Kankakee was an obstacle to change, that the union sees its influence being undermined by management's efforts to improve work relationships. One person observed, "If people can go and get understanding from the employer, they don't need the union to represent them." A quick glimpse at the history of industrial management exposes this notion as fallacious. In the overwhelming majority of cases management tends to be fraught with favoritism, and employees unrepresented by a union have been subject to the capricious behavior of immediate supervisors. It is unfortunate that many behavioral scientists and industrial engineers concerned with workplace problems (Walton is an exception) fail to understand the role of the union as a form of worker participation as well as an important factor that can promote change in the workplace.

As is the case with most behavioral scientists who write on the subject, Walton (who is supportive of union participation in other things he has written) fails to mention the role of the union in the workplace in his six "roots of conflict."[2] Union people argue that such factors as Walton's "patterns of mutual influence," "self-esteem," "openness," and so forth, can be achieved only if employees feel they are not subject to the whims and fancies of management, including low-level supervisors. Trade unionists point out that people at the production level are often the victims of new production schemes that ignore their interests. Ketchum indicated that there was consultation down to the first supervisor's level in the planning for Topeka. When, then, did the workers participate in planning the new plant? Could the union have been involved in the planning for Topeka? No one I spoke to seemed to be able to consider the question lucidly. Could the reason for this be that unions are still looked upon as outside organizations?

THE TOPEKA PLANT OPERATIONS

Processing

Gaines dog food consists of corn, soya, premixed vitamins, and meat meal. The processing section is automated; percentages of the mix are predetermined. The process team consists of eight people per shift. They run the entire operation, beginning with the receipt of raw material from freight cars that dump it into floor bins, where it is then conveyed to storage. The batch man weighs the incoming material, recording the weights in order to insure maximum productivity from the raw material. The expander adds moisture to the product. The dryer takes out moisture for storage. Coating reels apply a tallow that gives the dog food a fatty, meatlike taste even though it is a vegetable. Dust is mixed in to color the Gravy Train product red to make it look like the meat for the benefit of dog owners. (Dogs do not care about the color!) It is then moved to bins for final packaging.

The whole process is monitored in the fifth-floor control room. This is a large room with a control board about eight by thirty feet divided into five or six different sections. Two or three people might be in the control room at any one time monitoring the process on a computer. The group's objective is to produce a minimum of one hundred tons of dog food per shift and to keep the packaging room continually supplied with enough processed dog food so that they never run out of material for packaging.

The process team has few, if any, routine functions. They do a small amount of maintenance, such as periodic lubrication, and they monitor the equipment to try to avoid breakdowns. They may attempt to speed up the equipment and try to surpass the one-hundred-ton-a-shift objective. A red light may go on, signaling a malfunction. The men in the control room will decide what to do. They say that sometimes dog food clogs a chute or is hung up in one of the feeder bins, and it has to be cleared. The team is a typical operations-maintenance crew, where initiative, decision making, and teamwork are essential to the smooth functioning of the process. Nothing is unusual in this type of operation. We also need to keep in mind that only one out of twelve persons interviewed was hired at Topeka precisely because of demonstrated ability in these areas. Judging from my brief visit, this group of workers has a high level of freedom at the workplace, resulting in a high level of satisfaction, a correlation that may be more general than is presently acknowedged. This was confirmed by one of the processors who had been a machinist for five years on the Santa Fe railroad. He likes the Gaines plant "three hundred percent better," he said, "because I am not stuck on a lathe, turning railroad wheels." Now a troubleshooter, he is free to roam the plant almost at will. He enjoys a number of other freedoms that I will discuss later.

The experience of the process team at Topeka supports the research of Eva Mueller at the Institute of Social Research, University of Michigan, which indicates that workers in automated operations tend to be more satisfied with their work than those in traditional production-line operations. Some of the processing men had worked on the packaging line. I asked them about that. They said they enjoyed the line experience, since they were getting the bugs out of packaging and gaining a better understanding of the line problems. They saw working on the packaging line as a part of learning the whole process, but were glad to be off it, though they were aware that they would be back on the line periodically.

I was informed that the goal of three hundred tons of dog food a day was reached quite often. Just prior to my visit, they had achieved a four-hundred-ton day. The employees described the drive for tonnage as "friendly, fierce competition which made the job more interesting." Employees also expressed the feeling that "management trusts us, and that makes this the best place I ever worked." Yet, one cannot help but wonder what the employees at the Kankakee plant of General Foods feel about what is happening at Topeka. With but sparse information at hand, I attempted some comparisons between the Kankakee and Topeka production. While Topeka reaches its average of three hundred tons a day with seventy-two people, Kankakee turns out nine hundred tons with twelve hundred people, a ratio of 4.17 tons versus .75 tons per person. We should at least parenthetically acknowledge the tremendous investment that General Foods has made in building a modern, automated plant at Topeka. After comparing wage scales, a powerful argument could be made that General Foods has not shared with their Topeka employees the fruits of the increased production. How then are the benefits of increased production divided?

Mitchell Fein, a noted industrial engineer, has argued that, allowing for the ten-million-dollar cost of the new plant, which is amortized over an extended period, the employee effort at Topeka deserves a bonus rate that would give the workers a share of the increased profit. The issue of sharing the benefits of increased productivity needs to be dealt with by people concerned with workplace problems if workers and unions are to overcome their strong reservations that improvements are simply a scheme to increase production. [For Fein's view of workplace questions, see pp. 71-77.]

Warehousing, Packaging, Shipping

While the processing part of the Topeka plant is a modern, automated operation, the warehousing and packaging is in many ways quite traditional. Workers stand all day long at filling stations, holding or feeding boxes or bags. At one station the worker takes a bag, opens it, and puts it under the machine, which automatically drops down a preweighed amount of dog food. It then goes onto a conveyor through a sewing machine, which closes the bag, and then to a pallet for warehousing. I would characterize this work as highly repetitve, boring, and monotonous, with little autonomy, no chance for worker growth and no place to go but into processing. There is a lack of freedom to walk around and socialize, so critical an element in job satisfaction.

Yet, because workers, like the rest of us, are not of one mold, one worker I spoke to said he liked the packaging line because he "did not want to think about the work anyway." The packaging line, in contrast to processing and because of the nature of the technology, hardly meets any of Walton's conditions for ending alienation. It is reminiscent of scenes from Charlie Chaplin's *Modern Times*. One of the team leaders said he did not mind the line because he did not have to stay there; he could rotate to processing. There may be a lesson in this example of two very different types of jobs in the same plant. Given the premises that jobs such as packaging and warehousing are "lousy," that some "lousy" jobs are with us to stay, and that some jobs are better than others, then maybe the "dirty work" should be rotated as they have done in this plant.

I wonder what will happen eventually in Topeka as the jobs in processing become the status positions and workers from packaging want to move up. While I was told that there would be a natural circulation in the plant and that processing workers would go back to serving in the warehousing section, I venture to predict that eventually the processing group will become the elite and few will be willing to return to packaging and warehousing.

THEORETICAL CONSIDERATIONS

In the *Harvard Business Review* Walton cites the Topeka plant as a model for decreasing worker alienation. Topeka provides an interesting case study of contrasts between two technologies occurring simultaneously in the same plant: one a continuous-process operation and the other a traditional repetitive manufacturing operation. What can be learned from the experience at General Foods' Topeka plant? What does the Topeka experience say about Walton's six "roots of conflict" as sources of alienation? How does it compare with those of other manufacturing plants?

Much of the literature dealing with workplace problems uses Abraham Maslow's concept of a needs hierarchy as their theoretical base. Maslow suggested, as did Marx and Engels, that when man has satisfied his basic needs—namely, food, shelter, and clothing—he becomes concerned with a higher order of needs. Engels suggested that culture begins with the production of surplus, meaning that surplus permits time for things other than acquiring food, shelter, and clothing. In a similar vein, Maslow suggested that when basic needs are satisfied man becomes concerned with a higher order of needs having to do with autonomy, creativity, and self-actualization.

Walton's definition of workplace problems is similar to the views of other behavioral scientists; it differs to the extent that he does not include Maslow's factors of "creativity" and "self-actualization." Walton would probably argue that his nonacceptance of these two factors makes his position considerably different from other behavioral scientists. Perhaps it does, but I would argue that a more basic issue at stake is the relationship of the individual to the institution. Can an individual worker, as Walton suggests, achieve autonomy or self-control in an institution that has as its primary or sole objective the increase of profit?

I am fearful that at least some of the definitions of workplace problems have grown out of the behavioral scientists' perceptions of people's needs, satisfactions, wishes, and wants. Some of the difficulty may be semantic, including the fact that concepts such as "needs," "autonomy," and "control" are highly relative. (But relative to what?) For instance, how does one perceive manual work from the perspective of one's value system? Intellectuals tend to view manual work as a kind of horror. They would be surprised to learn that many manual workers are horrified at the prospect of having to sit and write all day. One's perception of factories and work may be derived more from one's subjective frame of reference than from an objective test or questionnaire. Terms like "needs," "satisfaction," "autonomy," "growth," and, most importantly, "alienation" have become so all-encompassing that they may no longer have any distinct meaning.

Let us compare Marx and Maslow as two extremes, leaving Walton aside for the moment. Marx's assumptions about alienation are based on the conflict between the private ownership of the means and products of production and the social nature of the factory. He uses the term "alienation" to describe the factory workers' relation to the raw material, the process or means, and the finished product, none of which the laborer has any control over. It is a concept based on an economic and social relationship. On the other hand, Maslow's concept of alienation is based primarily on the psychological needs of some individuals.

Once again, Walton denies Maslow's influence, stating that he would not apply the terms "creativity" or "self-actualization" to factory workers because the concepts are unrealistic. Maslow himself, in *Eupsychian Management*, acknowledges that he did not think of such concepts as "self-actualization" or "peak experiences" applying to factory workers. He further pointed out that he had never tested his self-actualization material on subjects other than college students. It seems odd that many writers dealing with workers and workplace problems—Walton being an exception—seized on the Maslow schema as an explanation of worker dissatisfaction without at least questioning the basis of concepts such as autonomy, participation, creativity, or self-actualization as they apply to mass-production workplaces. I have an uneasy feeling that people who suggest that such concepts could be applied to mass-production technology either were ignorant of what goes on in manufacturing plants or vulgarized the meaning of these concepts. In the latter case, perhaps straw men were created to avoid dealing with real problems. Have inadequate pay and poor working conditions been excused by concentrating on individual psyches?

THE NATURE OF MASS PRODUCTION

Any discussion of workplace problems requires some understanding of mass-production technology, which is based on some fairly fundamental assumptions. All process and manufacture are predesigned, pre-engineered, and preplanned down to the smallest detail. "Time is money." In order to guarantee cost replication and interchangeability, every step of the production process is planned, engineered, and timed. Schedules must be strictly adhered to. No deviation from a specification is permitted. The successful completion of the final product, including its cost, depends upon everyone adhering to a master plan. Given this as the basic nature of mass production, where can there possibly be opportunities for such highly individualistic activity as autonomy, creativity, and self-actualization? I am afraid there are few—if any at all. Then why do social scientists concerned with workplace problems keep suggesting this paradigm, insisting that management can overcome boredom, monotony, and alienation among factory workers by giving them an opportunity to be creative, autonomous, and self-actualizing? Will such a paradigm bring about badly needed changes? I doubt it!

In many years of working in and around factories, I did not observe many factory workers who had much concern about autonomy, creativity, or self-actualization. There was much concern over pay, security, working conditions, and, most importantly, dignified treatment. The latter was usually achieved by unionization, since people were then no longer subject to the capricious behavior of supervisors. The level of freedom to circulate in the plant was a critical element in how workers felt about the place. Many people writing on workplace problems are not familiar with the culture of the people who inhabit factories. Social scientists tend to seek out pathologies.

Workers' lives, like most people's, are divided between work, leisure, family, chores, and so forth. Yet, there do seem to be some universals that everyone, including schoolteachers, wants—shorter work hours (probably to be more autonomous away from work), travel, a chance to pursue a creative hobby, and a choice of recreation. And, like most people, workers understand the limitations on satisfying their needs and desires *within* the factory. They are very much aware of both the magic and the curse of mass-production technology. It is "magical" to see raw stuff enter one end of a plant and come out as a working thing-amajig at the other. It may also be a curse to repeat the same little task over and over again, but they know that this is the secret of the magic. Workers understand this, and make the best of the life in the plant with humor, camaraderie, and what sometimes becomes a rich social life. When they do participate in decision making, it is mostly through collective bargaining that deals with such things as safety controls and agreements on productivity levels.

Marx suggested a collective sense of alienation as a source of worker discontent, which would create continuous problems for capitalist societies. "Countering alienation," then, could be considered from the viewpoint that worker unrest is a threat to corporate stability. Or, it might be considered from the viewpoint that the individual worker is unhappy and dissatisfied with his or her job.

However, most people concerned with workplace problems today, both in Europe and the United States, start with a psychological or pathological approach to the individual worker rather than using a socioeconomic mirror to reflect these issues. There is also a sociotechnical school that suggests that human and technological needs can be made congruent. The process department at Topeka may be a prototype for this approach.

The contemporary difficulty with Marx's concept of alienation grows out of grave doubts about whether socialist or workers' ownership and control of the means of production has given the workers on the plant floor any greater autonomy or control over the means of production or the finished product than workers in capitalist countries have. In socialist countries, factory workers find themselves in a relationship with the means of production that seems to be endemic to factories: highly repetitive work, preplanned and pre-engineered. There seems to be some exception in how Yugoslavian plants are run, to the extent that workers have some voice in who manages and how. But the organization of the work itself remains similar to all factory production techniques.[3] Marx's concept of alienation fails to note that alienation is inherent in the nature of mass-production technology, *regardless of who owns the plant*. Socialist countries, far from finding a new way to produce things, have if anything emulated the efficiency of the capitalist model to its smallest detail.

The American labor movement has traditionally dealt with "alienation" by seeking the most for its workers in pay and benefits while reducing the amount of time they spend at the job. Until we find an alternative to the factory system, history may yet reveal that this is the best and most universal response to a sometimes distasteful situation.

CRAFTSMANSHIP VERSUS MASS PRODUCTION

Some of the suggestions for improving the quality of work life reflect a nostalgia for the return to craftsmanship. In 1844, Marx expressed a sadness over the decline of the Renaissance craftsman. Concepts such as autonomy, creativity, decision making and control of one's tools are associated with handwork. While I am extremely sympathetic with that nostalgia and the joys of crafting, I am also convinced that notions of bringing back craftsmanship in any critical dimension are either based on fantasy or ignorance about mass production. There is so little traditional craftsmanship surviving that we may not even know what the term means anymore.

I spent about fifteen years of my early working life as a skilled machinist and toolmaker. Many people consider that craftsmanship. It was not craftsmanship in the traditional sense. I made no decisions about the raw material, the process, or the product. My skill, as distinguished from craftsmanship, was the ability to follow extremely detailed instruction to very fine tolerances. That requires a certain kind of skill, not craftsmanship, and above all, not creativity. I remember my old boss, to whom I was apprenticed, repeating over and over, "Follow the prints! Follow the prints!" He was referring, of course, to the blueprints.

I tried to discover the cause of the decline of craftsmanship. I found some clues in Francis Klingender's *Art and the Industrial Revolution*. He talks about the end of craftsmanship, relating how in 1830 the owners of the Wedgwood Pottery hired a salesman to find out what people were interested in buying. Queen Victoria on a horse seemed to be of popular interest. Wedgwood hired a designer to create a series of ceramics having as a motif the Queen on horseback. That act of engaging a salesman and a designer, both of whom were responding to a market, was the beginning of the end of craftsmanship in English ceramics. Klingender says that as a result of the designer's intervention the Wedgwood potter became, at best, an "inventor," who could now decide how to do it but no longer what to do.

As engineers moved into factory production, the "how to do it" step fell next. Management began to decide that. The best known of the work engineers was Frederick Taylor. He was obsessed with the idea that a man should be like a part of the machine. Thus, even the "inventor" trying to decide "how to do it" soon disappeared when equipment and machinery were designed for specific functions, and workers lost control over the method as well as the product.

The final blow came with the notion of the interchangeability of parts. The result was Taylor's phenomenally successful effort to fragment all tasks down to their smallest element so as to eliminate any possible judgment on the part of the worker—thus assuring no variation in the final product. And this worked. The factory proved to be productive beyond the engineer's wildest dreams. This success is called the Industrial Revolution. And revolution it was!

ONE FURTHER OBSERVATION

The term "Hawthorne effect" was given to the results of the psychological impact of the considerable attention paid to workers in experiments at the Hawthorne works of Western Electric in 1929. The workers in that experiment felt they were "quite special," and hence behaved so by feeling better about themselves and their work. They produced more simply because they were part of an experiment. What is the effect on workers today of an unusual amount of attention from television, newspaper, and magazine stories, and an endless stream of visitors? Topeka provides us with our first clues. Workers become celebrities. They read about themselves, see one another on television, and are continuously interviewed. This goes beyond the Hawthorne effect; this is "Topeka euphoria."

TOPEKA AND THE "ROOTS OF CONFLICT"

I would like to look at Walton's six "roots of conflict," or alienation, and apply them to Topeka, using processing and packaging as differential settings. The plant should be accepted as it is, since the product, the formula, and the process there are all established and fixed by the technology.

What happens when an employee has mastered all the functions within the plant? How does he achieve what Walton calls broadening his opportunities to assure his development? Within the Topeka plant, an employee, carefully screened as a high achiever, can master nearly everything there is to know in a few months. One can argue that after that there is no place to broaden yourself but *out* of the plant. That concept should be reflected in a high turnover rate, since the plant has limited opportunities because of its small size. (Or does one go somewhere else in General Foods? Are there opportunities for the bottom of the pyramid to move up and around?)

Applying the first "root of conflict" (challenge and growth versus simplification and repetition) to the packaging plant, it is difficult to see the development of a growth pattern. A few simple line operations, nine at most, are endlessly repeated. The line operator must keep up with the machine, filling a box or bag every few seconds. There is little opportunity for growth or challenge when one does nine movements by rote. One fellow on the line said he liked it because he "didn't have to think about dog food anymore." The machine designer in me kept saying, "Automate these jobs out." Applying my own criteria of freedom, the line operator has little or none of the freedom to move around and socialize that the processing group has. To leave his station, he or she must obtain relief, a good indicator that work is rigidly designed.

Applying "challenge and personal growth" to the processing group, one gets a different picture. Here the key factor is the computer, which actually controls the process. The process workers make corrections suggested by the computer and troubleshoot when the computer indicates a malfunction. *The process worker has no direct line function.* His work is not repetitive. There is an element of surprise that creates interest. Most important, he has total freedom to move around, socialize, disappear, talk, use the telephone, and visit other parts of the plant. Given decent wages, benefits, and working conditions, I believe that the most neglected element of work satisfaction is the *freedom to socialize at the workplace.* This means full use of the telephone to make and receive calls, to have available all the general amenities that satisfy the need for personal interaction. The freedom to interact is *real.* The notions of growth, challenge, and autonomy in a fixed, repetitive operation tend to be an illusion.

The process workers at Topeka have the freedoms indicated. We sat around in the computer control room for a couple of hours having a most enjoyable kaffeeklatsch. I repeat, for emphasis: these nonwork or what I have called the freedom aspects of the job, may be more important as job satisfiers than trying to build autonomy, creativity, and self-actualization into repetitive tasks that have been designed precisely to eliminate all those elements.

To suggest that "personal growth" results from rotating some repetitive task is fallacious. The greatest benefit of rotation may be to increase one's socializing orbit. Rotation may reduce monotony or boredom for some workers, but the reduction of a negative element does not necessarily create its opposite, a positive element. Design and tooling technology require that every step in the production process be performed according to specification. The sequence of steps may be rearranged, but I would hope that is not what is meant by "challenge" or "autonomy."

Walton's second "root of conflict" is the employees' desire to be included in "patterns of mutual influence." In the planning group for the Topeka plant, no workers were included. Management did the planning. Yet much of the writing about Topeka is about how good it is for the workers. The "mutual influence" of the employees is limited to what the computer or packaging line permits—no more, no less. If one looks for a pattern beyond Topeka in General Foods, it becomes quite vague. Lyman Ketchum acknowledges his own lack of influence in General Foods in a paper he presented to the Arden House Conference on the Quality of Working Life.

Walton says that organizations are "characterized by tall hierarchies." Within the Topeka plant there is not much of a hierarchy because of the small size of the operation. What about the tall hierarchy of General Foods? It is difficult to find any evidence that it has changed as a result of Topeka. Topeka is a small island in the sea of General Foods. Because the island is small, the hierarchy is small. But it is there. There is a hierarchical delineation of decision-making responsibility. That is the way factories are run. As suggested earlier, we do not know any other way. There is an effort in Topeka to hide the hierarchy because, I suspect, some of the local people might like to get rid of it. But do they have an alternative? In Topeka the processing jobs were homogenized and a work force was recruited with a strong capacity to handle such jobs. The status hierarchies that exist in a traditional plant like Kankakee will emerge in time, as differential capability is reflected in the wage scale and as the plant grows.

Hierarchies tend to develop and harden as organizations based on the pyramidal design become institutionalized. I predict that will happen at Topeka. We simply have not yet developed an operational model of a plant organization that is not hierarchical. What is sometimes done instead is to make the chain of command more subtle, hoping in that way to "hide" the hierarchy. In that sense Topeka's operation becomes game playing, with the foreman a "team leader." He is responsible for the team's activity. He is a "human relations" supervisor, which should make him a better team leader as long as the team wins the productivity game.

If conflict develops in Topeka, I think the team leader will become once again the foreman. Let the home office of General Foods become disenchanted with production at Topeka and the current foggy hierarchy of reponsibility will disappear. The Topeka plant, like all continuous-process plants of this nature, requires a high level of judgment from its process operators in order to keep it moving. It is unfortunate that this simple fact of technology tends to get confused with eliminating alienation through autonomy, control, and decision making.

The third Walton "conflict" states: "Employee commitment to an organization is increasingly influenced by the intrinsic interest of the work itself, the human dignity afforded by management, and the social responsibility reflected in the organization's "products." This notion is set forth by Frederick Herzberg in his writing on work enrichment, suggesting that job satisfaction must be part of the work itself. He calls benefits "hygiene factors" and suggests that they will not overcome dissatisfaction that stems from the work itself.[4]

This concept of job enrichment represents another longing to return to craftsmanship—and the good old days. In a way, it was Marx's longing too—a noble idea, but most often suggested by people more knowledgeable in philosophy or the behavioral sciences than in technology. Start with the salesman and the designer at Wedgwood, add design, tool, production, and industrial engineers, and it should be obvious that craftsmanship in the plant or factory is over. Yet, the dream and desire to return to the village smithy remains. It appears in literature quite regularly, usually under the guise of "job enlargement," "autonomy," and "skill development," all of which are antithetical to mass-production techniques. Enriching a job in manufacture means adding repetitive tasks. That does not make it creative or autonomous, nor does it stimulate growth. Some workers prefer multiple tasks, others prefer a single task, but neither should be called a "higher order of need."

Process work at Topeka is not craftsmanship. It is challenging because it requires a certain amount of troubleshooting. It can be compared to a servicing function rather than a manufacturing operation. That can be challenging because one may make decisions about what is wrong and why. On the other hand, the packaging line at Topeka is limited to a few simple, repetitive, and boring operations in front of a filling machine. Behavioral scientists underestimate workers when they suggest that by adding repetitive tasks together they have enriched a job and made it challenging. I strongly believe that the intrinsic reward given the process workers at Topeka is the freedom they enjoy in the plant. The freedom involves not only being able to roam and socialize at will but also the status of feeling that one is more like a manager than a worker—of *not* being a line operator. The satisfaction that comes from this freedom is the key factor in creating the commitment to pet food and General Foods.

The "human dignity" that Walton speaks of is a management style at Topeka. Having met Lyman Ketchum on a number of occasions, I would give him a large share of the credit for that. It is my hunch that in managing any plant Ketchum would create a McGregor (Type Y) management, which is open and humanistic. But the Ketchums may be unusual in management. I often wonder why, after all the years of human-relations talk in management, so little of it seems to have taken hold.

As for the social responsibility reflected in the organization's products, I must confess I was overwhelmed by the amount of pet food produced in this country. Topeka makes three or four hundred tons a day. The entire industry manufactures approximately two million tons of dog food a year! That tells us something about productivity, as well as about Americans and their dogs.

I am not a dog hater! When I was a kid we had a dog and he got the scraps off the table. That was a good way to recycle garbage and feed the dog. I would find it difficult to maintain any sense of social responsibility from making dog food or, for that matter, a large portion of the huge variety of other mass-produced items that factory workers make. But that judgment depends very much on one's value system. From the point of view of social responsibility, it would seem to me to be an alienating experience to make three hundred tons of dog food a day out of nature's beautiful raw materials that could feed hungry children.

TOPEKA AND THE UNIONS

The grain-handlers union has made some efforts to organize the Topeka plant but without success. They believe Topeka was set up to eliminate the union and, in time, the workers will pay for it as a result of diminished security. Mitchell Fein has argued quite vehemently that General Foods has not made an equitable distribution of the increased profits that result from increased productivity at Topeka. Union people argue that this factor gets lost in the issues of job satisfaction. Productivity is four or five times higher at Topeka than in Kankakee.

Walton says that organizational practice still emphasizes material rewards—employment security—and neglects other employee concerns. According to Maslow, when the intrinsic rewards of security, safety, food, shelter, and clothing are taken care of, a higher order of need develops. The difficulty with these concepts is deciding when the basic need for security and safety has been achieved. This is a highly relative matter, depending on education, place, expectation, and, most importantly, the relationship of rewards to the individual employee and to company profits. Sharing some of the increased profits with the Topeka employees would demonstrate the egalitarianism Walton speaks about. One of the reasons that unions are suspicious of workplace behaviorists is their failure to consider how the benefits of increased productivity are shared.

Walton's fourth "root of conflict" ("What employees want from careers, they are apt to want *right now*.") somehow suggests that today's worker is less able or willing to postpone gratification. While money is still the most important gratifier of all, it is no longer the only one. There are many others, *including* amenities and freedoms at the workplace. If however "instant gratifiers," such as participation, job enrichment, autonomous work groups, and so forth, are seen as substitutes for income, workplace problems will be exacerbated. In a consumer society it is the things that money can buy that enables workers to become status-gratified. It is what they can own that is important. Are they different from the rest of society? I think not. It is mythical to suggest that job hierarchies and career paths can be designed to give workers instant gratification. Upward mobility is always limited by less room at the top of the pyramid. To suggest otherwise creates false expectations.

The processing division of the Topeka plant satisfies what I consider the kind of gratification possible at the workplace, namely, freedom to socialize and the opportunity *not* to be stuck in one spot with one task. Similar situations exist in many process-type operations, such as chemical and food-processing plants, which are often dependent on the kind of teamwork found at Topeka.

Because process workers are on standby or monitoring a good part of the time, they can sit around, drink coffee or coke, talk, smoke, or scratch themselves—all of which I call the "schmooze factor," that is, social group interaction about a subject not particularly related to the goals or objectives of the organization. I sat with three men in the control room in Topeka having coffee, our feet up on the table. While they kept an eye on that big board, we schmoozed about whether it is better to live in the city or the country, whether girls in Topeka wear brassieres, and what unions can do for you anyhow. Once somebody suggested, "Why don't we speed the mill grinder or the conveyor a bit?" That precipitated one person into pushing a button. Then we went back to schmoozing. Schmoozing is common in offices, universities, processing plants, and many service industries. It occurs much less in manufacturing plants, but it does happen, almost surreptitiously. It would have been impossible for me to sit with three workers on any manufacturing line without permission of the management, except during a coffee break or a lunch hour. Similarly, in the packaging room at Topeka, you could not schmooze with someone on the line unless he or she was given relief.

How are the differences between processing and packaging handled in Topeka? There is a rotation. I call it sharing the lousy jobs. I have a strong hunch that this may well be the only way society can begin to deal with necessary but undesirable work.

Walton's fifth "root of conflict" is the employees' need for attention to their "emotional aspects," such as individual self-esteem, openness, and expressions of warmth. That exists in Topeka because of the smallness of the plant, the degree that one fits into the team, as well as management's style. The qualities of openness, warmth, and support are interesting because they are social qualities controlled by the institutional atmosphere. Does the institution permit employees to visit, have access to a variety of areas, support one another, and use the telephone? These qualities do not have to do with the work itself, as suggested by Herzberg and others. They are influenced by the nature of the work and how it is organized. Work can be organized in ways that permit a maximum amount of freedom on the job. The opposite seems to be the case in most manufacturing plants; unfortunately, they are designed for a maximum amount of employee time at a given spot. I consider this to be a most important source of dissatisfaction because it deprives factory workers of freedoms enjoyed by most white-collar and service workers.

A short time ago, before a Senate subcommittee on workplace problems, I testified that the first thing I would do for blue-collar workers to increase their work satisfaction is to grant them equal rights with the rest of us by permitting them free use of the telephone. Those of us who take this for granted underestimate the social role of the telephone and its value as a reliever of monotony and boredom. How many times during the day does a white-collar worker or professional pick up the phone and dial a friend? Even if the discussion is inconsequential or silly, it helps relieve tedium and makes work easier. The telephone creates a vast network for intimate contact in an unrelated world.

Walton's sixth "root of conflict" has to do with lessened competition among workers. For this, Topeka emphatically does not serve as an example. Quite the contrary. A large part of its success rests on the high motivation that comes from several fierce competitions. The first aspect of competitiveness is to beat that three hundred tons of dog food. The second is to beat the next shift and then beat packaging. The third is to know the most about the plant. That will eventually create a hierarchy based on the smartest as the "firstest." Who is the chief beneficiary of this competitiveness? The company, of course. Unions would say that this business of workers competing against each other creates speedups and will end by victimizing those who cannot compete. Elements of that appear at Topeka already. Workers say things like "If he can't cut the mustard, he'll have to go." Although the autonomous work group may seem like a highly democratic structure, I am not sure that some form of protection for individuals is not needed to guard against repression and unjust behavior. The situation is somewhat analogous to a university professor without tenure.

Unions have been a major factor in reducing competitiveness by trying to reach agreements as to what constitutes a fair day's work. I do not know that there is a fair day's work at Topeka. One management person said the men were so anxious to increase the output that on occasion they endanger the equipment by speeding it up in an attempt to break shift records.

It is unfortunate for those who are trying to improve workplaces that Topeka does not have a union. It would afford more opportunity to make comparisons since the Topeka plant is a demonstration of what a particular technology and a humane management can do. With the Kankakee plant of General Foods under contract to a union, the experiment will be seen, rightly or wrongly, as a way to get rid of the union. I do not believe that was the management group's motivation. Yet management tends to see unions in an adversary role; so, if you can avoid having them, why not? Worker participation will always be highly questionable if there is no way for workers to be assured of certain basic securities. Another new plant is being considered for Lafayette, Kansas. The union issue will come up there again. Can management consider a role for the union?

The increased productivity of Topeka over Kankakee has cost a number of workers their jobs. The issue of "security" in the face of the new model workplace is not dealt with either at Topeka or by writers about Topeka. What happens in an existing plant when production is increased with the support and help of the workers and some of them then become superfluous? The behavioral scientists' notion of group support is expressed when workers behave as a team and support each other in the face of possible layoffs. When a worker says, "I'm concerned about this man whom I've been working with and I don't want him to lose his job," this shows real commitment, involving the most nonalienated behavior.

At the plant level the union may express the best humanitarian, nonalienated impulses within the work force. People concerned with the quality of life at the workplace need to understand the role of unions. Unfortunately, many such people are employed by management, and hence tend to be less than fearless on this issue. It would be extremely helpful if business-management schools, writers, and others concerned with the institutions of work began to think about the role of the union in humanizing the workplace. The unions, too, need more understanding of the nature of work organization and how workplaces operate. If they insist on limiting their roles to traditional collective-bargaining issues, then the problems of workplace reorganization may just pass them by. The UAW has recognized this problem in recent bargaining with the auto industry. Joint committees were established to examine issues of workplace organization and operation, a giant step forward for a major union. People concerned with workplaces should understand that unions have been involved with workplace problems for a long time and that they are an important avenue for participation. Without renewed participation, suspicion will continue to grow among labor people that workplace changes are designed to counter union organization. To include the issue of workplace reorganization in anti-union charges would be most unfortunate, but the movement toward improving the quality of life will be impaired without worker inputs and union participation.

The Topeka plant is an example of what can be achieved in a small, new, continuous-process plant with a carefully selected group of employees and a highly humane, local management. The experience can be very helpful in learning more about humanizing workplaces. The people involved in planning and development should be congratulated for their efforts in spite of the shortcomings I have cited.

NOTES

1. Richard E. Walton, "How To Counter Alienation in the Plant," *Harvard Business Review*, Nov.-Dec. 1972, pp. 70-81.

2. Walton is quick to disassociate himself from behavioral scientists who would "avoid" or "get rid of" unions. In his working paper "QWL Indicators—Prospects and Problems" (Graduate School of Business Administration, Harvard University) he includes a variety of criteria for improving the quality of working life, which have long been the subject of collective bargaining and the goals of labor legislation. The existence of unions, however, is not cited. Walton does mention productivity bargaining under "Revitalization and Reform" in the *HBR* article discussed here.

3. Ichak Adizes, *Industrial Democracy: Yugoslav Style* (New York: Free Press, 1971).

4. Frederick Herzberg, *Work and the Nature of Man* (New York: World, 1966).

Search for a Better Way of Work: Lordstown, Ohio

Bennett Kreman

In some places, the lightning always seems to strike. Surely one is Lordstown, Ohio, where General Motors builds the Chevrolet Vega, its economy vehicle, now suddenly more important than ever, as anxiety persists over fuel shortages, and as auto-industry negotiations, with an unusual emphasis on work rules, speed toward an uncertain climax.

Indeed, after only an hour in this farming and industrial valley in eastern Ohio, I was cautioned by Tony Scandy, financial secretary of Lordstown's United Auto Workers Local 1112, that negotiations this year might be "a hell of a lot more complicated than you think."

This despite labor's moderate wage demands thus far in 1973 and the minimal number of strikes in recent months.

So, already I stood warned that I might see some of the same rancor and drama that erupted here in March 1972, when a strike of the Vega plant's unusually young work force drew startled attention as television cameras, for the first time, flashed images of irate longhairs, not on college campuses, but among blue-collar workers once deemed resistant to the cultural upheavals unfolding across America.

After a week of nights in barrooms in nearby Warren and Youngstown and hours at the factory gate, and after slipping into the plant on the second shift the other night, early hints of more lightning in Lordstown flashed again.

Source: *The New York Times*, September 9, 1973, Section 3, pp. 1, 4. Reprinted by permission of the *New York Times*.

For during those eight hours along the line, a rush of curses directed at the plant's managers hissed from the mouths of both assemblers and their elected committeemen as I pressed questions incessantly, determined to grasp finally what lay at the nerve and marrow of this plant. Repeatedly I was informed that more than five thousand grievances have piled up within the last six months and that hundreds more are sure to come.

And before leaving the roar of the plant with its incessant assembly line binding like a halter, forcing hours of tedious movements from thousands in its service who stand in fixed stations for blocks, I could conclude only that Lordstown's reputation as an extraordinary site in the industrial environment was not in the least larger than it warranted, but indeed, smaller. For what I'd been told there, I'd never heard before.

Eleven committeemen and standard assemblers, convinced of the need to spell out the smoldering tensions, agreed to meet me in the union hall and explain everything. Their ages range from early twenties to early thirties—an age group whose numbers will dominate the American work force within six years.

QUESTION: Why don't you introduce yourselves, fellows?
ANSWER: Al Alli, committeeman, trim department.
I'm Bill Bowers, committeeman for final line and cushion.
George Brayner, material department, committeeman.
Jim Baird, assembler, final line.
Carol Crawford, assembler, cushion.
Joe Alfona, absentee replacement operator.
Dave McGarvey, final 3, rank and file.
Gary Brainard, final assembler.
Dennis McGee, committeeman, first shift.
Dennis Lawrence, committeeman, body shop.
Robert Dickerson, committeeman.
QUESTION: When I came into this place in the strike in 1972 I was amazed at the level of anger that I heard. And now I'm hearing it again. What's the yelling about?
ALLI: The working conditions. General Motors' attitude's no damn good!
QUESTION: In what way?
ALLI: They break their agreements. You settle a grievance; then they turn right on you and break the agreement. It just tees us off!
QUESTION: I talked to some people recently who say the whole thing about the alienation of the younger workingmen is an invention of the journalists—that they made it up. Does that sound like it has any

reason to it? You must represent about three thousand men, just sitting at this table.

LAWRENCE: There's no rationale at all. The press, the news media may have coined certain phrases that are attached to the workers of today. But as far as the dissension, it's there; it's alive.

QUESTION: Is it growing or getting less?

LAWRENCE: It's growing. It's going to continue to grow until corporations realize that it's not a bunch of kids they're playing with. These guys out there—I don't give a damn if they're eighteen or fifty—they're serious, they're disgusted, they're fed up with it. And goddamn it, it's going to change, it's got to change, because if it doesn't, they just won't build the goddamned cars.

QUESTION: Is there a distinct difference between the way you people are seeing things, or feeling, or what's going on in the plant and the way your fathers saw it?

BRAINARD: Our fathers range between fifty and sixty years old, and most of them are established people. They almost have to bend to the corporation. This being a young plant, and most of the people out there being of a younger set, we don't have to take the garbage they're giving us now.

McGEE: I think we're different. Our parents were motivated to a lesser degree than we are. Maybe they didn't have the education we had. Maybe they were immigrant families that wanted to prove themselves, that their nationality was real good. They're hard workers. But we, the younger workers, have been through high school and have had advanced subjects compared to our parents. Most of us have had monetary gains, but we know that isn't all there is. We're not narrow-minded people. We know we're down here in the plant, and we know we've got to have a good time about doing it.

QUESTION: So it's not money that is bothering you. And Alli says working conditions are the main issue. Is that right?

McGEE: Yeah. Absolutely.

QUESTION: Okay, what is it about the working conditions that's creating the intensity of your anger? I've heard it for eight nights all over the place.

ALFONA: Well, like all men when they used to work, they had a specific job to do. They told them to shovel one hundred tons of coal within x amount of time, and that's what they did. And they left them alone.

But like now they tell you, "Put in ten screws," and you do it. Then a couple of weeks later they say, "Put in fifteen," and next they say, "Well, we don't need you no more, give it to the next man."

From day to day, you don't know what your job's going to be. They always either add to your job or take a man off. I mean management's word is no good. They guarantee you—they write to the union—that this is the settlement on the job, this is the way it's going to run—one hundred and three cars an hour, and we're the only ones in the world could do that pace. Know what I mean?

They agree that so many men are going to do so many things, period! Fine, the union will buy that because they negotiated it. Two weeks later management comes down and says, "Hey, listen, let's add something else to that guy." They don't even tell the union. And management says, if you don't do it, they'll throw you out, which they do. No problem. Zap! Away you go.

BRAYNER: I'd like to say something to that. What he says is correct, and we're not getting any backing from the International union in Detroit. No backing whatsoever. They came down in the strike in 1972 and sold us out, and they're selling us this year, too!

ALLI: That is right—they won't give us a strike letter [authorization] or nothing.

QUESTION: Do you people want to strike?

GENERAL: Yeah!

And the agreement in the room is noisy, intense, and total. All week I've been warned that work loads, levels of manpower, designated tasks, and the settlement of those five thousand grievances will have to be nailed down conclusively—this time with no sudden changes later on—or strike fever will gallop.

And at the moment at eighteen plants run by the corporation's hard-driving GMAD division, including Lordstown, all eyes are on the International union's GM department, which has assured these locals that mounting complaints against GMAD are being thrashed out at the big table as part of a final national agreement.

And on this promise, a fragile, impatient wait-and-see attitude barely holds along the Vega line. For there's something unique in those five thousand grievances, reflecting a fierce battle around an issue we've yet to clarify.

QUESTION: What'll happen if the International doesn't resolve things by the time these contract negotiations are finished—and at the same time you still don't get strike authorization?

ALLI: Oh Jesus, it'll be bad!

CRAWFORD: I think what you see now is the calm before the storm.

LAWRENCE: That tension in the plant now—you were in the plant; you talked to the people; you saw what was going on in there. Right now there's no tension, no pressure, compared to what it'd be if that settlement doesn't come through. Within three months the lid's going to blow off.

QUESTION: Okay, let's get to it now—to those five thousand grievances. After my research and getting the history of this plant back to the beginning, what has really come to a head is an issue we've never heard of before, which even your International is either unaware of or denies exists—and that's "doubling up."

"Relay teams" rather than "doubling up" may describe this better. On your own, without the aid of the company or the union, you're doing the same amount of work on the line, but in teams relieving each other, half an hour on, half an hour off. By doubling your speed, this method produces an equal amount of quality and productivity, but gives each person more time off the line. And this has never been done before. Am I on the track?

LAWRENCE: That's it basically.

QUESTION: How did it start?

McGEE: Well, our local union has a normal work pace out there. In other words, we don't want a guy killing himself speeding eight hours a day. I believe an individual should do his task and have a recovery time in which he can turn around and look at the car coming up next, take a breather and go on. Okay? A normal pace—not hustling, normal.

Now what happens is that the guys who have their operations side by side, they're relating together. In other words, they all worked in the same area. They started saying, "Go ahead, take off." It started like an E break—you asked for emergency bathroom call. The utility man might be tied up.

I'd say, "Go ahead, man, I think I can handle it." I'd run to the front of the car and I'd stick in the ring we used to have, and I'd run to the back then. I mean, I'm not running, really running, but I'm moving. I put the gas in, I go up to the front of the car again . . . go back again. I'm getting it done, and I'm not having any recovery time. I'm going right back again.

Well, the guys started doing this on a larger scale.

QUESTION: How far back did it start, Al?

ALLI: I'd say three years, four years ago.

QUESTION: All right. Why do people at the International say that there's no such thing as doubling up?

LAWRENCE: Goddamn it—they're just not that concerned.

DICKERSON: Yeah, they'd just as soon ignore it.

QUESTION: Why?

LAWRENCE: They don't want to take it on. They have certain set attitudes. See, you're talking there again to older people, your executive board are older, every one of them. They don't have any young people.

145

QUESTION: All right, here's another argument from the company. They say that if you double up the quality is going to go down.

DICKERSON: They're wrong.

SEVERAL: No way.

QUESTION: You have any evidence they're wrong?

ALLI: Damn right. We had better quality when they doubled up.

QUESTION: How do you know?

ALFONA: The audit tickets.

QUESTION: What are audit tickets?

ALFONA: They come down there with the corporation and they check x amount of jobs, like maybe ten out of one hundred. And they check the tickets, the repair tickets that were inspected. And they see how much repair was done to this car before it hit the end of the line.

DICKERSON: It's an inspection ticket.

ALFONA: Right, it's a rating. Like if so many repairs were on this ticket within the ten jobs per one hundred it was a good audit. But if more repairs were on it, that means that the quality was bad in certain areas. And they could detect which areas.

QUESTION: So you're saying that during the doubling up the quality, in terms of audit tickets, does not go down or does go down?

ALFONA: It goes up. I can prove it to you, because I work the line, see. And we used to double up in tail lights. It's a four-man operation— you do every other car, two people do every other car.

QUESTION: A half-hour on, a half-hour off?

ALFONA: Right. I got thrown out of the plant for a week over this issue.

QUESTION: Are the five thousand grievances related to a lot of this?

ALFONA: Absolutely. Two people would be working the job. The other two people would usually stay right there if something should happen—if the gun broke down, or if I missed a screw, I'd call my partner, who was sitting down. "Hey, catch that before it goes down to the repair station." He'd jump up, put the screw in for me. No repair. I got the next car behind me.

I'm working, working, working. If something else should happen, if I fell in the hole and missed a job, I call my sidekick again. He catches it, repairs it. It's never marked on the ticket. You get 100 percent perfect. Because we don't want no problems, you know what I mean? We're doing a good job. And I defy you to find somebody who's doubling up disciplined for bad work!

LAWRENCE: The only reason we started doubling up was to break the boredom on the damned line.

DICKERSON: I think there's a better word than "relay team"—antidehumanization team.

McGEE: I think something else should be noted about the doubling up. We had a lot of press releases concerning assembly-line work being dehumanizing. It's the hardest mental-type work in the world. Politicians have gotten on the bandwagon and started committees, they've come to the plant and rapped with people about it.

But the ones that found a way finally to beat it were the same dudes, so-called do-dos they wrote about in *Playboy*. Well, these do-dos devised the system—the workingman himself, the assembler himself devised this system.

Playboy called us long-haired hippies, spaced-out, or whatever words they used. They're a bunch of idiots; it makes no difference how long a guy's hair is. Most of the long-haired dudes in there, they're not dummies any of them. Nor are the shorthairs. It makes no difference.

QUESTION: Would you say that system was a redesign of assembly-line methods?

McGEE: Definitely. There's no question about it.

QUESTION: This is an astounding thing if it's true. It's an absolutely amazing thing. If you, by doing it your own way, produce the same quality and the same amount through your doubling, then you have redesigned the assembly line. Does that make sense?

McGARVEY: You have to double up and break the boredom to get an immediate feedback from your job, because the only gratification you get is a paycheck once a week, and that's too long to go without any kind of gratification from the job.

QUESTION: Well, management's argument is this: If you stay on the line and do a full hour's pace—a day's work for a day's pay—meaning you stand there and take the standard breaks as worked out in your negotiations, you should be able to do more work. You should be able to produce more at the end of the day.

But you were telling me the other night that in the eight-hour day, if you did it that way, the boredom would begin to affect the quality before the day was over. That, with the doubling up, you break the boredom, and when you get back to it, you work harder.

LAWRENCE: What their [management's] reasoning is against doubling up—and the only answer that I can get out of them is basic quality. But where is your quality? Where do you show me that your quality went down?

Then they come and say, "Well, it's our plant." But this idea of doubling up where you put a man on for eight hours and—after he learns that job, gets set in his ways, he no longer pays any attention to what he's doing because it's automatic—bang, bang, bang.

He's dreaming about something he's going to do tomorrow, something he did last night, whatever.

147

QUESTION: So the quality suffers?

LAWRENCE: The quality goes down. That's my experience. He don't care anymore. But at the point where you're doubling up, you've got the responsibility for two jobs. You've got to keep your mind working at all times. Because if that car, when it comes off the end of the line, if it isn't right, it goes back to the repair yard.

QUESTION: Do you have evidence that during doubling up fewer cars go to the yard?

BOWERS: The quality-index board reflected that.

QUESTION: Would that be related to resentment at working in the traditional manner or to the fact that the boredom came into it?

GENERAL: Oh, boredom.

QUESTION: So why would the company have anything against doubling up?

McGEE: This is what I just realized. Honest to God, I believe right now that they're so goddamned scared of doubling up because every job that people doubled up on the final line, they took that man away, they took him away, every single man.

QUESTION: But despite all the hassle with their clamping down and the five thousand grievances in the last six months, you manage to double up.

SEVERAL: Oh, yes.

McGARVEY: Even if they say don't double up, what you do—it's not as good as doubling up the way we normally do it—but we'll hang on the car and we'll stand there while the other guy does it. And the minute somebody comes round, we'll just put our hand in the car. We'll just play the game with them.

And they get tired of harassing us because they keep checking like bird dogs. And every time they look we're over there. Yeah, we're doing the job—but we're not really. Just to play the game.

ALFONA: You know, there were instances out there where foremen on the floor actually paid guys to double up. They paid them.

QUESTION: Why?

McGEE: Because they want the area to run smooth. That's why.

ALFONA: They turned their backs on it. You're not allowed to double up. In other words, the foreman says, "I'm going to go over to the next line for a couple of hours." Normally the guys know what they mean, and they'll do a good job for that foreman.

Then when this foreman turns to the general foreman, he tells the general foreman, "Well, my area is running perfect." Sure, because his guys are doubling up. If he had four guys working in this one spot at the normal pace eight hours, without doubling up, he's going to get less good work out of them. Even if the guys don't want to sabotage.

QUESTION: You mean the foreman knows that?

GENERAL: Right.

ALFONA: He says, "To hell with it. I'm going to walk over to the other line and get a coke," because he wants the productivity and the quality.

QUESTION: Do a lot of foremen do this?

GENERAL: Quite a few.

And now I suddenly realize that without the tacit approval of foremen on the line, efforts to double up would halt, or lead to even more explosive conflict than exists. I wonder also if the foremen might silently agree that part of the answer to the humanization of the assembly line lies in the simple antidote of doubling up. Perhaps it's not a waste of manpower.

Although GM seems convinced otherwise, even the company, like the UAW International, will not admit for the record what the Dennis McGees and Dave McGarveys are evolving on the line.

Joseph Godfrey, general manager of General Motors' assembly division has said, "Yes, workers in our plants are less willing to give maximum effort than they used to be. There is a lot of unrest in the world and we feel it on the assembly lines — war, youth rebellion, drugs, race, inflation, moral degeneration. Marriage isn't what it used to be. We feel it. Their minds are on the other things."

Yet the question remains, does doubling up lead to an equal, or even better, degree of quality because it lessens boredom? And does doubling up thus lead to less absenteeism, as some of the men have been telling me?

Could it diminish the mounting alienation of labor? Most serious, can the young, imaginative work force coming up so rapidly bear a blue-collar life-style other than the one they're developing at Lordstown?

QUESTION: So there's a philosophy behind doubling up?

GENERAL: Definitely.

McGEE: Sure, if you're on the damned line here and you've found a way to double up and you've found a way for me to shuck and jive — all day long, have a good time, help each other and get out the work. I don't have to take these pain pills no more. My ulcer's gone. Now what are you going to tell a dude? "You ain't going to do it?" My nerves was bad. I'm not kidding you.

QUESTION: Has it — your doubling up — come from laziness or inventiveness?

DICKERSON: Inventiveness. One way to explain the thing is that anytime there's a human need, there's always an invention, or a way to get around it.

McGARVEY: I'd say inventiveness definitely. I was explaining to my father what the line was like. He said, "Well, why don't you push a broom?" He doesn't understand that pushing a broom is a priority job out there.

LAWRENCE: Yeah—it gets you off that line.

QUESTION: When they eliminate the doubling up, are there more drugs? More alcohol?

McGEE: Drugs aren't necessarily connected with it. I'm saying some people on that line run out of things to think about, man. And when you get through singing that song, and telling every joke, what is there? You know, that's all there is to it.

ALFONA: And really there's no such thing as an eight-hour day. There's ten, twelve [hour days], six days a week. You have no social life. The only social life you have is in that plant, and if you're stuck on that line all that time—nothing!

But if you can get that break where you can go down and rap to your buddy or make a phone call to some chick, it's different.

QUESTION: You know, you read all these articles about humanizing the workplace, and boredom. And I was beginning to think it was an invention of journalists myself. Now, according to what you're telling me, you've gone way beyond that. It's what they're trying to do at Volvo—redesign the line. Chrysler claims it's doing this in one of its experimental plants. And here you are doing it almost unconsciously in a highly productive plant.

ALFONA: I'd explain it to the people on the outside very simply—about Lordstown and the doubling-up situation. They should think about themselves at work not at Lordstown but some other place—either in an office or in a steel mill. If they say, "Gee, I'd like to go and get a drink of water," they go. Now I might be on the line, and my break doesn't come for four hours. What am I going to do?

I'd also tell people on the outside, "Listen, if you had a job paying four dollars an hour, you and your buddy, and you're each going to carry a package"—I bring it down to very easy words so the average man can understand—"You're going to get paid four dollars an hour to each carry a package up the steps and down. Well, isn't it a little easier for you to break your back and carry two packages up and down for half an hour and your buddy resting, and then let him take over and you rest your back? If you want to go get your drink of water or go call your chick, you got the simple freedom to go, see?"

And then they understand it a little bit more. I mean, they would say, "Hey, yeah, that makes life a little easier." That's all we want.

Part-Time Employment: Ideal Work Life?

Jack Russell

The ideal work situation for most of us would be to work the number of days per week we desire, change workplaces every day, if we wished, serve in a variety of occupational categories, have ample opportunity for horizontal mobility, have transportation provided to and from work for a minimal charge, and be paid daily. Would not this enhance our knowledge and make working more enjoyable?

For many of the approximately eight hundred thousand workers who would like regular employment but are participants in the casual labor force, this is possible. These persons choose or are relegated to working on a temporary basis by (1) applying for work through industrial temporary-help services and (2) waiting on street corners where prospective employers are known to seek workers.

PART-TIME WORK THROUGH TEMPORARY-HELP SERVICES

Traditionally, temporary-help services are perceived as organizations that persons desiring sporadic work may visit voluntarily and for which they may work as many hours or days as they choose. In some instances this is true, but a great majority of workers who utilize the services of these establishments are in a somewhat different category. They are persons who try to piece together intermittent employment in an effort to be employed full time, and they are forced to do so because they lack the educational requirements, experience, specific skills, or confidence to hold down permanent jobs.

These persons—men and women of all ages, skill levels, and backgrounds—are "card-carrying" members of the casual-labor force. They are often uncounted in the U.S. Department of Labor unemployment statistics and are completely invisible in census population surveys. But to the managements of the largest corporations in the country casual laborers are a viable part of their organizations. They work alongside regular employees, perform the same tasks, are subject to the same administrative decision making, and experience the same working conditions. The social and economic distinction lies in the fact that such a worker, though an integral part of an organization, works for one-fourth to one-half the wage of his regularly employed co-worker. He or she has no union protection (if working in a union shop), no vacation, health insurance, or retirement plan—in other words, no fringe benefits and no immediate job security. All that the casual worker has is transportation to and from work. These workers are constantly treated as though they are second-class citizens who may be sent back to the parent agency if their performances are not satisfactory.

Technically the worker is an employee of the temporary-help service. The employment agencies that handle temporary clerical and professional workers are similar to regular employment agencies, but in the services that deal with unskilled laborers, the climate is demeaning. The worker may register for an assignment as early as 5:30 each morning. The establishments are usually in the worst part of town, the waiting area is unkept, and signs are posted for cheap, available rooms for the transient population. There may be a notice that checks may be picked up at "Joe's Bar and Grill" after a certain hour, if the agency is closed when the worker returns in the evening.

Many of the temporary-help offices require no formal application for prospective workers, just an abbreviated W-4 form soliciting minimum data (name, social-security number, health or physical condition). Therefore, past work history, skill level, job preference, and experience are ignored. People who are capable of performing highly skilled work are grouped with those with no skill and referred to any job or company. Many times both the worker and the company management are unaware of what they may expect from the other. Workers have no advance notice of what their duties will be; hence they often become frustrated and walk off the job when confronted with the unexpected. The manager, realizing that he has not received a person with a skill commensurate with his request, labels the temporary employee "lazy," "ignorant," or "incompetent."

To the temporary-help service the worker is a "commodity" with "a market value." The going "price" is the same regardless of the quality of the "product." The objective is to manipulate and condition the worker to accept any job offered. Companies that place profits before people quite readily purchase the "product."

SHAPE-UP—CATCH-OUT

It is conceivable that every large city in the United States has its "shape-up" corner where "catching-out" takes place.[1] There are well-known street corners in Los Angeles, New York, Atlanta, and Washington, D.C., some having been occupied since the forties and fifties. In Washington, congressmen and other governmental officials pass these corners daily, unaware of the dehumanizing transactions that are taking place within a stone's throw of their establishments.

The activity starts very early every morning. Prospective workers start to congregate at one of the many designated corners or parking lots in the metropolitan area. Persons of varying skills, ethnic backgrounds, ages, and educational levels are available for employers or labor scavengers[2] to choose from. A big day in Los Angeles, for instance, may find as many as one hundred men at Pico Boulevard and La Brea Avenue, though the average is closer to forty.[3]

Employers or small-time entrepreneurs start arriving around six o'clock; most hiring is done before nine. Most employers are familiar with the people on the corner; therefore, they are very selective in picking their man for the day. Other employers may have difficulty because prospective workers know about bad checks, low wages, authoritarian methods of supervision, short duration of a job (two or three hours work), and distance of the job from the shape-up corner.

Significant in the mechanics of how or why an employer obtains a worker is the issue of human dignity. Workers involved in this auction type of bargaining are subject to the supply and demand phenomenon of the market. But, because of their nontraditional method of working, they are "demanded" at lower wages. In essence, the supply and demand equilibrium in the casual labor market is short on full employment and operates at a wage rate that yields income below the poverty level. Naturally, people from ethnic minority groups, whose history is one of discrimination and wage slavery, most easily fall victim to this vicious system.

Low wages is just one of the injustices suffered by casual laborers. Their most basic aspirations for decent jobs and security go unmet. Employers are known to pay wages with bad checks. There are no fringe benefits such as health insurance, vacations, cost of living increases, retirement plans, and in most instances, workmen's compensation and unemployment insurance are not paid. Since workers are nonunion, dismissal is whimsical and often arbitrary, creating quite a hardship when a person is working twenty-five or thirty miles outside the metropolitan area. When this happens, workers either wait the remainder of the workday or find their own transportation back to the corner. Dissatisfaction and exploitation are in abundance, but neither sets precedents.

CONCLUSION

Theoretically, the worker participating in the casual- or temporary-job market has some advantages over members of the regular labor force. He has variety in work experience, horizontal mobility, and learning opportunities, and, being part of the internal labor market, he has access to employment information unavailable to many job seekers. Furthermore, he develops general skills that can be adapted to many enterprises.

When you take into consideration the fact that workers do not have to suffer through aptitude tests, personnel interviews, background investigations, and other criteria for getting a job, casual labor participation may seem like a "good deal." But this is far from being true. Temporary and casual workers suffer many injustices in addition to the dissatisfactions the normal work force experiences. They are nonunion, so they lack protection; they are victims of dual discrimination, from temporary agencies *and* industry; their wages are not comparable to those of regular employees, and they have no fringe benefits.

In actuality, though it satisfies the needs of industry and those who do not want a steady job, the casual-labor industry is an inefficient system that impedes permanent employment, lessens equal-employment opportunity, and virtually reduces some individuals to servitude. It may also discourage unionization and foster fly-by-night business "operators."

The recently enacted minimum-wage law will have a minimal impact on this phenomenon. Raising the wage to two dollars an hour will not reduce the long daily waiting periods prior to starting work nor compensate for travel time. Government (local and federal) intervention on behalf of the casual or temporary worker seems to be the only answer to the dilemma, since the workers lack representation by any formal organization. Thus far, lawmakers have been hesitant to take any responsible action. Senate investigations in the early 1960s and congressional hearings in 1970 scrutinized the operation of the temporary-help employers. The Illinois state government has expressed interest in improving the plight of the temporary worker, but no action has been taken. Two states require licensing of agencies but do not regulate them in any other way.

The general feeling in the bureaucracy is to "let sleeping dogs lie." The feeling appears to be that the temporary-help services cannot be regulated or that they should be exempt from regulation because workers have signed no contract with the service for permanent positions. This is the distinction between the industrial temporary-help services and temporary-employment agencies, where there is licensing and regulation.

Workers who get jobs by going to a street corner or parking lot are virtually invisible. Sociologists and anthropologists know they are there, and production output shows their contribution to the gross national product, but in unemployment statistics, union rosters, and industrial personnel files they add up to zero!

Current wage levels, working conditions, and benefits that discriminate against such part-time workers must be changed in order to increase opportunity and ease labor shortages, as new life-styles and technology emerge. Specific changes that could be implemented to reduce, if not eliminate, this pathetic situation would include licensing and regulation of temporary-help services; outreach operations by state employment services; setting aside a proportion of wages above the hourly rate for fringe benefits; paying for travel time beyond a minimum distance; establishing wage rates on the basis of experience and skills rather than position (for example, a skilled carpenter working as a porter would be paid as a skilled man); automatic permanence if a person worked for the same company for four months; and unionization or establishment of a permanent representative body for part-time workers.

Employers, management, and the temporary-help services will all argue that part-time workers are responsible for their own pathos-laden situation. They fail to see or refuse to acknowledge the fact that employers and the hiring services profit from such situations, and, more importantly, that society must take a larger view of work and examine how it relates to increased or decreased satisfaction with life, both on and off the job.

NOTES

1. Shape-up corner: a location where casual laborers go to be picked up for work, that is, a street corner or parking lot; catching-out: seeking temporary employment by waiting in specific geographical locations for an employer to come seeking workers.

2. Elliot Liebow, *Tally's Corner* (Boston: Little, Brown, 1967), p. 29.

3. Ted Sell, "The Corner—Street Agency for Job Hunters," *Los Angeles Times*, June 26, 1972.

Fifteen Years at a Defense Plant

Myra A. Peabody

From August 1956 to September 1971, I was employed by the Electric Boat Division of General Dynamics in Groton, Connecticut. During this fifteen-year period, I learned a great deal about the methods of big companies of this type and wish to share my discoveries and observations.

My first years of employment at this submarine shipyard were enjoyable. Office buildings and most yard areas were adequately equipped with soft-drink, cigarette, and candy machines. We relaxed during ten-minute breaks twice a day and at the half-hour lunch period in a cafeteria that served good food at reasonable prices.

Heating and air conditioning of EB offices, however, was a puzzling affair. Some were air-conditioned and others were not. Some systems worked well and others did not. It was not unusual to walk from an extremely warm office into an adjacent one that was frigid. Occasionally, in the winter months, typists had to wear coats and type with icy fingers. Upon occasion, I wore a nose mitten!

As time passed, EB proved to be one of the most change-oriented companies I had ever encountered. Most of the changes made, however, proved to be unwise. Changing the location of departments was very common. During my employment, we moved approximately twice a year. I was located in the main office, the shipyard office, the

Source: This article appeared in *The Humanist*, September-October 1973.

machine shop, the support building, in two dockhouses, three times in the hospital building, and finally in the new nuclear-engineering building.

On one occasion we were transferred to a dockhouse, where we occupied half the building. As we proceeded to get settled, the maintenance men brought in desks and chairs to fill the other half. For a week we waited expectantly to see who our neighbors would be! The maintenance men then returned and removed all the furniture. Each move took them an entire day. It was the most puzzling of all the moves, since maintenance received two days' pay for unnecessary work. I can say in all sincerity that I never saw a move made at EB wherein the department did not lose something in the process, often something of importance and hard to replace.

As in most large companies, humor was plentiful, although most of it did not seem to contribute to the company's efficiency. When I looked at my co-workers, I concluded that one of the requirements to gain employment at EB was to be a bit "wacky"! And, since I was an employee, I included myself in this category.

A woman co-worker in my department was nearing retirement age, having worked at EB for forty-five years. She spent her spare time *looking busy* by punching holes in blotters with her paper punch!

One particular man was a prime source of humor. He often ate stale cookies, which he kept in his desk drawer. Sometimes they were covered with ants, which he nonchalantly shook off before eating! On one occasion, he asked for my ditto knife; and, after lending it to him, I heard a swishing sound, as if someone were noisily eating soup. Glancing up, I discovered him eating raw oysters, which he was opening with my knife. Needless to say, I was obliged to replace the blade! Another of the many times we were "rearranging" and everyone was fighting to get a telephone on his desk, he was just as urgently trying to get rid of his, claiming it was a nuisance.

EB had a peculiar manner of handling problems with its personnel. It was a known fact that many alcoholics were born and bred in the EB shipyard. Many took their bottles to work with them, hidden on their person or carried in huge, innocent-appearing thermos bottles. And, while one might forgive the company's guards for not detecting these things in the morning, it was certainly obvious by day's end. Two guards had to help one worker down the front steps of the building almost every evening to keep him from falling and injuring himself as he left work. One yard worker drank so much that he had to crawl under a boat on one of the submarines each afternoon to sleep it off. He was eventually discovered, and his supervisor suspended him for a week, telling him to spend it "sobering up." I saw more than one supervisor who had been drinking at work, but for some inexplicable reason the company closed its eyes to these incidents.

Sexual activity on company property was another offense treated in an odd manner. During the night shift, a yard worker was caught making passionate love to a nurse on a cot in the hospital. The nurse was fired, but the worker was not, because he was on his lunch period. This gave the rest of us ideas about how to spend our lunch hours!

But different departments and supervisors had various methods of treating such matters. It was almost as though they had competitive standards, hardly a good procedure within a single company. Offenses were penalized or not depending upon where and for whom you worked.

Every worker doing defense work is thoroughly investigated. There are several types of security classifications: the higher the rank, the deeper the investigation.

After a few years at EB, I was granted a Department of Defense security clearance with the special badge that went with it. This allowed me access to classified information and documents. After I received this badge, I learned how lax the company was. A security lecturer said one thing, but my eyes saw another. I saw new workers, with the lowest clearances, given tasks that involved the handling of classified information. I was not surprised, because I recalled that the lecturer had said that enemy spies had been discovered in plants like ours—and some had been wearing top-secret badges!

Most employees noticed this carelessness in enforcing security rules. On one occasion in my department, an entire ledger of classified shop orders was missing, and I can vouch for the fact that the supervisors never reported this to security. Such security rules were broken daily.

Guards at the various gates were most careless in checking identification of those entering the plant. On one occasion, my own badge was missing. Unable to locate it, I entered the following morning but was not stopped by any of the guards. Since these badges were supposed to be worn constantly during working hours, such laxness was inexcusable. Not only did I go in and out of my division without a badge of any kind, but I was also allowed to enter the supervisory section of the Navy Department located across the street. I called out my badge number as I entered, and the guard recorded it without looking to see if I wore such a badge. This went on for two weeks, until I finally reported my badge missing and was issued a new one. On one occasion, some British sailors entered the plant without being stopped and were actually allowed on one of our submarines.

I was not very fortunate in getting raises during my fifteen years at EB. Again, departments and supervisors operated differently. I saw workers without my seniority passing my salary swiftly. It was not because they worked harder or turned out more work. Rather, they had more powerful supervisors. I have seen two workers, one doing all the work and the other letting him. The laggard took home the larger paycheck. As the years passed, I was shocked to see this company, where I had once enjoyed my work, going from bad to worse.

EB claimed that raises were given according to merit. Ratings were supposedly given the employees at regular intervals throughout the year. They were usually made by a senior supervisor, a man who would not even know us if he met us in the corridor! During my fifteen years, I received two merit ratings and had to *ask* for the second one. When I looked at the newest form for merit rating, I lost interest in ever receiving another rating. There were two possibilities: work satisfactory and work unsatisfactory. With the former rating, we kept our jobs; but it was not good enough to warrant a raise unless our supervisor wished to grant us one. Strikes became the only method of getting raises in most departments.

One clerical worker asked for a raise for two years without results. Joan had been working at EB for five years, but had not received a raise from her department. Eventually she found higher wages in another department, gave her notice, and left her old department. Her former supervisor filled the vacancy with a newcomer. A very wise move! Now he had a worker who had to learn the job—and at a starting pay higher than the wages Joan had received.

At one point our department was assigned a new senior supervisor. This turned out well for me, because Mr. P. took a desk in the dockhouse where we were then located and watched to see what we were doing. I normally worked hard, keeping busy with my own work as well as the work of others when necessary. It paid off. He gave me my long-awaited raise. His secretary showed me the request he sent to the office of industrial relations. It read simply, "Mrs. Peabody is underpaid for the amount of work she is turning out!"

It was five years before I received another raise, partly because Mr. P. left for a better position in the company. Meanwhile, our union went to bat for me, finally obtaining my belated raise.

Mr. M. came to the dockhouse as our new senior supervisor. Although he arrived without a secretary, he was soon allowed one. After being told to reduce overhead, Mr. M. decided that, since he now had a secretary, I was not needed by Mr. B. So I was laid off from the department where I had seven years of seniority. The new secretary, Barbara, who had just come to EB, was to have my position. She was a sweet young girl and I liked her, but Barbara did not want my position any more than I wanted to lose it, nor did she relish doing her own secretarial work and mine, too. With my own boss' encouragement, I again decided to go to the union for assistance.

The results, however, were embarrassing. Two union officials came to the dockhouse and advised Mr. M. that, in view of my seniority, it would be unwise to let me go. He refused to cooperate with them, which was extremely embarrassing for me as I sat typing nearby. Mr. M. claimed that Barbara was better qualified than I. I never could understand this since she had just graduated from high school and this was her first job. I was a business-college graduate with many years of office experience, including eight as assistant manager of a finance company.

On Friday, I was told by Mr. M. to report to another department on Monday morning, whereas the union officials instructed me to go to my regular desk. I found this situation difficult, and I failed to report for work on Monday. In fact, I decided it was time for a vacation! So I took the week off, phoning in to say that I was ill, which was not far from the truth.

I visited with out-of-town relatives, returning home the following weekend. There I found a notice to call Mr. B. immediately. When I did, he told me to report to my old position on Monday. When I reached my desk, I realized why. Both my desk and chair were filled with piles of undone work! I took the stack from the chair, arranging it with the other piles on top of the desk, then speechlessly uncovered my typewriter. I was probably more surprised than anyone to realize that I accomplished that much work in a week.

Mr. M. never again suggested that I be laid off. But he and I were never at ease with each other, finding it difficult to discard our mutual resentments.

However, there were many occasions when faithful workers did receive unfair layoffs. Those remaining on the job sometimes expressed their opinions of company tactics, but most did not dare.

While we were located at an office in the machine shop, somebody decided to remove one wall and build another to make a locker room for the men in the shop. This was done while we worked. The hammering and pounding around us was so bad that it was hopeless even to attempt to use our phones. I acquired the habit of picking up a ringing phone and giving a short speech to each unknown and unheard voice: "Can't hear a thing down here! Don't bother to call!"

But that was a minor inconvenience. Our desks were littered with broken bricks and shattered glass, and we all went home each night looking filthy. The maintenance men were even using our desks for pails of freshly mixed cement. It blended well with our paper work! But our supervisor's complaints were ignored, and we had to accept these conditions until the work was completed. When I stopped wearing the accepted office apparel and came to work in dungarees and a denim shirt, my supervisor made no comment.

I must admit that my daring in wearing dungarees to work was an act of defiance, since it was against company rules for women workers to wear anything but skirts. When we were located in the dockhouse, I often wondered why they did not allow us to wear slacks. The yard was made up mostly of men; and, though we found them courteous, we did have to get used to their stares. To enter our office, I was obliged to climb stairs on the outside of the dockhouse. Under these stairs were candy and soft-drink machines, around which men stood. I actually reached the point where my main concern was not to forget my underwear. I had accepted the fact that the yard men knew the color of my underpants each day.

Suggestion boxes in corridors invited us to win some money with worthwhile suggestions. I sent one in, but the company claimed it could not be used. Later they used this suggestion without any credit to me. I told a co-worker about it, learning that the same thing had happened to her. Our company took all from its employees and gave no more than necessary.

Many changes occurred in supervision, and any worker at EB could tell you that they were not changes for the better. There became a demand for college graduates, persons placed immediately in supervisory positions without any knowledge of what was going on! Men who had been building submarines for years were now obliged to work under men who knew less than they did. It was a sad scene.

We changed supervisors several times. Once our entire department was suddenly merged with another, undergoing a complete transformation. With this change, the work I had been accomplishing successfully for years now disappeared from my desk to be distributed among the people in the other half of our merger. I sat idly at my typewriter waiting for our new supervisor, a college graduate, to bring me an unnecessary piece of typing. The work formerly accomplished by two of us was now being distributed among twenty-five or thirty workers. New systems and procedures had been written to make simple work more complicated! I could not believe that all these people were being paid for what two once did.

I began to lose interest because of the lack of work. When the new supervisor ordered us to get busy, I learned for the first time how hard it is to look busy when you are not! I wondered: Is this being done to me because I am nearing sixty? Are they hoping I will get bored and quit? Looking around, I saw the same thing happening to others of my age.

This draining of employees continued, becoming more obvious as time passed. Hourly workers who made overtime for extra work were transferred to salary; now the company could do as they liked with them. Now they worked overtime for less money and could not belong to a union!

I became ashamed of the methods the company was using. Layoffs began, involving senior workers. These were men in their early sixties, not quite ready to retire, all getting layoff slips!

Out of four laid off in our department, one died almost immediately from a heart attack. Another managed for a year without income of any kind, until he reached his sixty-fifth birthday and could collect social security. Two others, both in their sixties, returned to the yard where they had started. One survived, but the other developed bronchial problems and died shortly thereafter of lung cancer.

Meanwhile, the company discovered many of their supervisors had been stealing. It was a disgraceful period at EB—even the general manager was fired. The FBI entered our plant, arresting some who were taken out in handcuffs for soliciting gambling bets in the yard. This had been going on for years; but, to my knowledge, it was stopped only on one other occasion.

My last years at EB were not happy ones since I had lost respect for the people I worked for and their methods of conducting business. My daily discontent and frustrations finally caught up with me. I entered the hospital for tests and was discovered to be suffering from severe hypertension. After a period of quiet and medication at home, the condition improved; but, two months after returning to work, the problem recurred. This time my doctor advised me to leave work permanently since he believed the days were too long and the atmosphere too nerve-racking.

It was a great relief to get out of the place where I had worked for fifteen years and which had become such a hell. However, I still had to eat! I had managed to save enough to keep me comfortable for a year or two. Perhaps I could also get some home typing to get by until I reached sixty-two. Also, there would be the small pension from EB to which we were entitled after fifteen years.

This proved to be a time when I wished I had read the fine print in the contract fifteen years earlier. I was in for a shocking disappointment. By deducting weekend hours, the company managed to bring my actual working time down to a total of fourteen years, eleven and one-half months. According to their calculations, I lacked two weeks of totaling fifteen years and would have to wait until the age of sixty-five to get my pension.

Today, I realize the most important thing I learned at the defense plant: It is very depressing to give all you have to an employer who ends up slapping your other cheek when you turn it! The new generation may be right when they resent working under big-corporation tyranny. Although our country is still preferable to any other in the world, the policies and principles of these fast-growing concerns are degrading us. I sincerely hope that today's young people will strive to bring back a decent though simple world where employers operate sanely and appreciate faithful workers.

There Are No Drinking Fountains Down Here

J. Davitt McAteer

There is no running water in mines, nor portable toilets; but these matters are less essential to miners than the problem of staying alive. Each year, nearly two hundred are killed and thousands are injured. So, if there is worker alienation in the coal mines, the first level is alienation resulting from injury or death. When one questions the adequacy of humane conditions in a mine, it is only after realizing that the worker's primary concern is staying alive.

Dismissing for a moment the crushed bones and funeral cars, ride the cage down six hundred feet into darkness at the shaft bottom, crawl onto a trip car, and ride swiftly through dark tunnels. You will travel miles past worked-out and abandoned areas before arriving at the end of the main entry. The tracks stop, and from here on you walk up to the face where the coal is mined. The small amounts of trapped air available for breathing at this depth are thick with coal dust, the dreaded cause of black-lung disease. The machines have been idle since the last shift went out. The foreman now spouts directions, but his words are wasted on men who know the job by rote from years of repetition. The monster machines are cranked up, their noises making talk nearly impossible.

The continuous miner, a seven-hundred-and-fifty-thousand-dollar machine, with huge rotating claws in the front and a conveyor belt

Source: This article appeared in *The Humanist*, September-October 1973.

behind, roars into action like a giant crab with an insatiable hunger. It rips the coal from the black seam and deposits it onto the conveyor belt. A shuttle car is waiting at the end of the belt to receive the coal. Coal dust is everywhere; no longer can one see the walls or the helmet lamps of the rest of the crew. It is black and dusty. The tempo is fast, and the boss *does* push. You've got to get it out.

Miners avoid the boredom and drudgery of an assembly line and the threat of a Muzak breakdown; their dangers are more real, more constant. Statistically, their profession is the most hazardous in this country. It is among the hardest physically, yet no special benefits or concessions are made to these men. They remain behind the rest of the nation in government- or management-sponsored training or social programs. There are no counseling officers in mines, nor educational projects in coal towns. Miners simply get paid; the average wage is from forty-two to forty-five dollars a day. There is no danger pay or "hot pay," as in the steel mills. It is all dangerous and all hard. But, in spite of this, "It is a good day's work for a good day's wage," and forty-five dollars is good wages in the coal fields. It might not compare favorably with the pay of steel or auto workers, government bureaucrats, or corporate executives, but in Hazard, Kentucky, it is good money.

With the money comes hardship and danger and the company man telling you what to do day in and day out. History tells us two things: miners strike, and companies demand absolute authority. But in this day of reasonable men and giant corporations, it is impossible to believe that this industrial-revolution mentality persists; yet it not only persists, it flourishes in America's mines.

National Coal Mine No. 14 is located outside the town of Delbanton in southern West Virginia. It is a small mine, only a few years old, employing about one hundred and twenty men. It is owned by the National Coal Company and operated by Island Creek Coal Company, the nation's third-largest coal producer. Island Creek is a subsidiary of Occidental Petroleum. The leaders of this giant corporation are men of much respect and renown. Dr. Armand Hammer, the oil baron who contracted with the Russian government to build a refinery and borrow priceless art works from the Hermitage Collection to be shown in the United States, is chairman of the board of Occidental. Former Senator Albert Gore from Tennessee, a southern-liberal force in the United States Senate for many years, an eloquent spokesman for the little man's rights, and a defender of the poor, is chairman of the board of Island Creek Coal Company.

Elmer Hensley and Wallace Marcum are not men of wide renown. They are, respectively, president and vice-president of union local 1748, and they both work in No. 14 mine. Elmer Hensley went to school through the fifth grade and has worked in the mines for nearly twenty years. Wallace Marcum, at thirty-one, has eight kids and has worked for nearly ten years in the mines. They have both worked at No. 14 since it opened.

Edward Simpkins is a company man. He has worked for years in coal mines all over the United States. He has done all the jobs—section foreman, mine foreman, assistant superintendent—and in 1972 he became superintendent of No. 14.

The coal seam at No. 14 is low, thirty-six to forty-eight inches high, so the mine tunnels and areas where the men work are likewise no higher than forty-eight inches. It is the hardest work when you are crouching, bending, or crawling on your hands and knees. But it is a good wage and a job, neither of which are plentiful in southern West Virginia.

On December 24, 1969, President Nixon signed into law the Federal Coal Mine Health and Safety Act of 1969. This law was the most stringent mine-safety law ever enacted in the United States. One of the less controversial provisions of this law requires mine operators to supply miners with an adequate supply of drinking water and protect this water with sanitary containers [Section 317(s)].

Miners traditionally have carried their own drinking water in their lunch buckets. But, to assure that water was under ground in the event of an emergency and to make the mine a little more on a par with other industrial working areas, Congress now requires the mine operator to provide the water.

Island Creek operates ten mines in this area in southern West Virginia, and they have a central supply shop at Holden, West Virginia, which services all these mines. It was the practice in No. 14 mine, as well as in most of the other Island Creek mines, to provide drinking water in eight-ounce plastic bottles with a tinfoil top for protection and easy opening. Superintendent Simpkins is a fastidious man; he wants to see things shipshape. When he got to No. 14 mine in October 1972, it was not very clean. According to him, there were plastic water bottles strewn everywhere; they littered the grounds on the surface of the mine and around the office, machine shop, and parking lot. Moreover, they were thrown all over the mine interior and some were even wasted. Simpkins began a cleanup campaign. He put garbage barrels around the grounds, but to no avail. His penchant for cleanliness did not, however, extend under ground to other matters.

During a three-month period, from October to December 1972, No. 14 was issued fifteen notices by the U.S. Bureau of Mines inspector for failing to comply with the law. These violations included failing to have an examination for methane gas made immediately before firing multiple explosive shots inside the mine, a violation that could easily have disastrous consequences.

But Simpkins was going to take action about the plastic bottles. One afternoon when the supply of the eight-ounce bottles was low, he ordered two five-gallon plastic jugs. The jugs had no spouts and only screw-on covers that had to be removed for each use. The men and the mine-safety committee complained almost immediately. They wanted to return to the eight-ounce bottles. Simpkins argued, but agreed to get a better jug with a spout. This time, it was metal and had a spout. The men were not satisfied with this either. The spout got dirty, and dirt got through the top of the jug. They wanted the eight-ounce bottles. Many mines in this country, as elsewhere, are rat-infested. The rats live on the water that seeps from the earth and the garbage that accumulates in a mine. They are generally big rats but they keep their distance, hiding in the worked-out area and only coming out when no men or machines are around.

The drinking water is usually kept back from the face, in the dinner hole a short distance away from the working area. The miners walk back to get a drink and to eat. But many times during the day the dinner hole is empty. The dinner hole is normally dusty so that tracks of any person or animal that has been in the area can be seen. There were, according to several miners, rat tracks around the metal water containers. No one ever saw a rat actually lick the spout but the tracks were all around the containers. The miners complained to their local union officers, who in turn complained to the management—but to no avail. A safety grievance was filed and the men refused to work. For thirteen working days they waited—losing money for themselves as well as for the company. They wanted the bottled water. But back from the company came the answer: "No! You men will never get the water in bottles because you have presented us with an ultimatum." Management could never back down in the face of an ultimatum. They would rather close the mine. The men had committed an unpardonable crime. They had challenged the company's authority. Threats of court action, firings, mine closure—whatever means necessary—must be used to maintain the company's highest right: management authority over the men. The National Bituminous Wage Agreement of 1971, between the mine operators and the United Mine Workers of America, clearly lays out the rules: management has the right to direct the work force:

Finally, the men relented, and returned to their work. The harsh economic realities of life brought them back to the pit. The company and union would take the case up through the grievance process. The company had now made a canvas-and-plastic cover for the spout to protect it against the rats. Moreover, the container was now to be placed on an eight-inch stand to keep it out of the dust and away from the rats. Also, a large chain and lock bound the top so that no one could open the containers and no dirt would be found inside as it was before.

During the work stoppage, high officials in Island Creek Company had been contacted about settling, but again to no avail. The men who had issued the ultimatum were told that they must go back to work before anything could be done. So one hundred and twenty men went back to the thirty-six-inch work space where they dig the coal. They now carry their own water and they are embittered toward Island Creek Coal Company. The case was heard at step three of the safety-grievance process under the contract, and it was not resolved. It now is in step four of the process. It is no longer only a dispute over eight-ounce bottles, but over at least seventy thousand dollars in lost pay.

Elmer Hensley and the members of local 1748 today carry their own water. They still do not have toilets in the mine and must relieve themselves in sections of the mine that have been worked out. They still spend most of their day crouching or crawling on their hands and knees, but Island Creek has not been forced to respond to an "ultimatum." According to U.S. Bureau of Mines officials, the company is in compliance with the requirements of the law.

The men are still embittered in a job that by its nature is dangerous, demanding, and brutal; but they have been taught not to issue ultimatums. They must risk their lives, work like savages, but not issue ultimatums.

The coal industry, more than most, still typifies the industrial mentality of the eighteenth century. Company officials still consider accidents inevitable or divinely inspired. They still view the workers as a threat and deal with them as though they were children. Kurt Vonnegut, Jr., wrote that all life, except for college, is high school. Miners rarely go to college. So, for them, all working life is high school. They are treated by the companies as men, for the work they can produce, but as children when it comes to human considerations.

Armand Hammer and Albert Gore drink their own water from glasses; they work in air-conditioned offices. Never do they have to spend eight hours crouched in or crawling about a forty-eight-inch-high executive board room. Finally, they have no rats in the executive dinner hole. But, on the other hand, they put in a good day's work, just like the miners, for a good day's wage.

Mines can be made humane places to work if the people running them would be more humane in their approach. The question of making mines humane is directly related to making them safe. To the miners at No. 14, these struggles are one and the same thing. They are fighting the kind of mentality that caused Kenneth Wayne Holland, age twenty-one, to lose his life in a Peabody Coal Company mine in western Kentucky, because the company had not put a guard on the conveyor-belt head. Management directs the work force, often into death or serious injury. But to make the mines more humane and safe, the union must assert its role. It must make known to the men that they have the right to a safe workplace and a decent workplace. They have the right to issue ultimatums and the right not to be treated like boys. This is the union's role, but it is also management's responsibility to see that it is done.

Worker alienation, assembly-line boredom, and mundane repetitive jobs, which most American workers face, are not the problems in the coal mines. Alienation and inhumane conditions exist as very real problems but in a way that is distinct from most other industries.

Ultimately, the question must be raised: Should mines be operated under such adverse conditions as low coal seams, dangerous methane-gas atmospheres, and work areas five hundred to three thousand feet beneath the surface of the earth? Society, at some point, must say that the social cost in terms of lives lost and crippled is too high, and it must lay out the basic standards for lowering the cost by imposing upon the coal industry requirements for safer working conditions. At some point it will be necessary to say that, if it is of sufficient importance to mine coal seams of thirty-six inches or less, then the coal company and the consumer must pay the price of mining not just the coal, but also the rock above or below the coal seam, to make the workplace safer and more humane. Society must say that the dust, darkness, and danger are unacceptable and must be eliminated from American coal mines to make them fit places for men to spend their working lives.

Our society is no longer finding it acceptable for men to spend their lives tied to a machine, placing a single screw in a single hole for eight hours a day. Yet this same society has found it acceptable to send men eight hundred feet below the surface to face dangerous physical conditions.

For the present, we must deal with the first problem of humanizing the workplace: returning to the worker his right to control his own life. The absolute authority the operators have demanded has cost over one hundred thousand men their lives and countless numbers their arms and legs during the history of mining. Until the day when a man has the right to say something about the conditions under which he works, coal mines will not be safe or humane working places.

Life-Style of the Coal Miner: America's First Hard-Hat

M. H. Ross

The coal-mine work force today consists mostly of older men shaped by the Depression, labor struggle, and bitter economic experiences, and of a growing number of young miners, about whom we know little and speculate much. One executive said that the average age of his men was forty-six. But that reminds me of the creek that had an average depth of six inches and yet was deep enough to drown a man; it can be quite deceptive. Many of the miners are fifty years and older, and a large and increasing number are thirty-five and younger. But young or old, the coal miner has been regarded by the American public as a kind of inferior, dirty, ignorant, substandard human. Who else would daily risk his life under ground and live in such drab surroundings? When a mine disaster occurs, a coal strike threatens, or union feuding erupts openly, national curiosity about the American coal miner is briefly aroused. Even that is usually directed patronizingly toward "doing something for" the miner or changing his situation or his union. Otherwise, the coal miner maintains his rural existence far from the nation's centers of decision and opinion making without being noticed or understood by his fellow citizens.

The majority of miners live and work in the heartland of the Appalachian bituminous-coal area, stretching from southwestern Pennsylvania to northern Alabama. Here, in hilly to rough terrain, with few large

Source: Reprinted with permission from *Annals of the New York Academy of Sciences*, vol. 200, pp. 186-188, 194-195; also from *Appalachia Medicine*, March 1971.

cities and little agriculture, the population is mainly rural, clustered in settlements between hills and along creeks. Far more than his urban blue-collar counterpart, the coal miner is limited by his historically isolated life, unaltered by other experiences. Large numbers of miners and their families live in small communities, formerly company towns. For the older miners, local influences are much stronger than the impact of national culture. Kinship ties are powerful, and the husband seems to be in charge, although the wife generally rules the paycheck, home, and children. Aside from the immediate family, however, it is a man's world, and the sexes usually go their separate ways socially.

As a group, miners are proud, generous, disarmingly modest about their courage and ability, hospitable, and courteous. They seem to rely on a keen intuition, a practical sense of reality, and feelings unfettered by intricate codes of etiquette. Living close together and sharing a common background, life experience, income and educational level, daily pleasure, and occupational hazard, neighbors are responsive and helpful; relationships, informal; intermarriage, common. Church membership and status are not important. Although row houses have been individualized, they are basically similar, without qualitative differences worth noting. Such housing may cost half that of a city residence, to rent or to buy. Miners tend to buy new cars, color TVs, major appliances, and modern furnishings, all of which make more sense than large home mortgages for many of them.

FROM COAL CAMP TO OCCUPATIONAL COMMUNITY

The coal miner was molded in a particular social-economic-political setting. Beginning before World War I and continuing until the mid-1930s, most of Appalachia was the arena for continual class warfare. America's last rugged frontier was not in the Far West, but here. Many older miners now working or pensioned were raised in conditions of civil conflict, brutality, starvation, terrorism, and family degradation.

Until the 1930s, mineowner dominance of the lives of coal workers and their families was complete. The owners created the mining camp or company town of necessity, because coal production began in isolated areas. The operator usually provided housing, a store, water, sanitation, police, postal service, voting "rights," medical treatment, a hospital, school, church, theater, and burial services. Absentee mine ownership resulted in lack of concern about the people and the community, their aspirations and needs. Alienation of the operators from human relationships in Appalachia, linked with fear and violence, developed a stance of snobbery toward the coal miner that became the middle-class outlook of entire counties.

In the face of wage cuts, discharge, blacklisting, labor spies, mass eviction of families, and company ownership of meeting places, streets, and roads, the miners repeatedly attempted to organize. The struggles that resulted were the bloodiest in the violent annals of American labor history.

The rough and turbulent nature of the native people may have contributed to the violent response. Many mountain counties had supported guerrilla actions against the slaveholding Confederacy during the Civil War. Indigenous coal miners were not strangers to whiskey stills, feuding, secrecy, or the marksmanship of hunters. A frequently mobile, largely uprooted or transplanted working class was thrown into strange and isolated frontier camps often carved out of the wilderness. Neither the black migrants from the South nor the southern and eastern European immigrants imported by railroad were accustomed to town-meeting democracy. The duplicity that often surrounded their importation, the wretchedness of their daily lives, and the brutality of their treatment were not conducive to a peaceful society.

The unevenness of the conflict is noteworthy. Some coal operators cared about their people and apparently made sacrifices in order to maintain jobs or improve conditions. A handful even broke with the front against the union. Basic economic facts rather than evil men generally were behind the turmoil of the 1920s and 1930s: "overproduction," price-cutting, speculation, cutthroat competition, bankruptcy. The Depression hit coal first and lasted there longest.

Miners now working were children or young men during the coal labor wars. Some bear the physical—many more, the emotional—scars of those years. For when the miners were defeated, they and their families were imprisoned. The coal camps were put behind fences topped with barbed wire, and armed guards stood at the gates to prevent anyone from entering or leaving without a company pass. Powerful searchlights assured no nighttime escape. Yellow-dog contracts, legally signed and upheld by the courts, gave the concentration camps a distinctively American touch.

The United Mine Workers have appeared to many people to be so bureaucratic or ineffective that the union's historic achievement is sometimes overlooked. But for Appalachian victims of brutality, eviction, and starvation, the "nice" people did nothing. The faculties and the students of universities were equally apathetic, as these first southern labor-organizing drives failed. The UMW conducted the war against poverty; housed, fed, and clothed its people; and fought the good fight for American civil liberties. In isolated valleys where management repeatedly pitted foreign-born against native-born, black against white, and vice versa, group hatred boiled over. But the union somehow taught the brotherhood of man, far from cultural centers and with the help of few intellectuals. It welded a work force and created a labor solidarity that bridged racial and religious boundaries during the 1920s, when much of the rural and small-town part of the nation succumbed to the Ku Klux Klan.

THE MINER AND HIS LIFE CONDITIONS

American coal miners are not a single national group like the Welsh miners. They are a wide assortment. One estimate shows twenty-seven nationalities working at Monongah, West Virginia, in the early days.[1] Considering the circumstances, the wonder is not at the initial or continuing friction but at how well people came together without serious ethnic or racial tensions. Perhaps the experience of mining develops a sense of community. Some kind of melting pot, a native and ethnic "blend," has come about among the whites. Racial discrimination has not disappeared, but in coal towns there is an easy-going dialogue and social intercourse between blacks and whites without the ugly polarization of the cities. I doubt that racially mixed married couples can live comfortably in many places in the United States, but they do in several West Virginia communities, each with a population under twenty-five hundred. Some UMW locals, with less than 20 percent black membership, regularly elect Negroes to two out of four major offices.

Small coal communities may seem so lacking in the amenities of modern life by middle-class standards that it may be easy to miss their significance in life-style. Compare bustling and growing metropolitan Charlotte, North Carolina, where Harry Golden once decried the lack of ethnic diversity: "There are no Italians, no Hungarians, no Slavs. The absence of many ethnic groups has watered down the intellectuality and culture here. Wherever he (the average white Charlotte resident) looks, he sees an image of himself—the same religion, the same ideas, the same prejudices."[2]

It is within the context of his history and background that the underground working experience of the miner becomes understandable. Because the gloomy darkness is oppressive and the work of the miner is inherently dangerous and dirty, it has seemed to some scholars that no man with an alternative would select coal mining as an occupation. Support for this point of view has come from interviews with miners about whether they would want their sons to go into the mines. Some studies took place during years when the threat to mine employment was so serious that the economics of the situation was a principal component in their replies. The American intellectual can hardly imagine today's miner thinking of himself as having a decent job. Conditioned by nineteenth-century social novels, the brutal history, or a current movie, they have little understanding of present-day coal mines or workers.

Coal miners have a proud sense of occupational identity that helps them define themselves—an identity that is often lacking in other industrial workers. Although it is difficult to prove where no blue-collar alternatives exist, I believe a large number of men select coal mining as an occupation of their own free will and choice.[3] But the miner may not express this to a strange interviewer. Remember, there is a saying: "Niggers and coal diggers." The snob society that looks down on him expects the miner to state that his decision to work in the mines was involuntary.

Today there are many affirmative reasons why some coal miners select and enjoy their occupation.

1. Most men under ground are either mechanics, electricians, or operators of large machines. Craftsmen have pride in their work; there is a sense of importance and action in being trustee of large, heavy, and expensive equipment, and men have been known to stay too long in a roof-fall situation because they did not want to "lose" their machines.

2. Compared to the firm discipline and monotony of factory assembly-line production, there is considerable freedom and little direct supervision in the mines even today (and most certainly in earlier days of independent output). The average workday at the face is six and one-half hours, but transportion bottlenecks often prevent the main machine from operating more than three hours. Foremen are somewhat limited, in the same way that combat officers are, in that it is unwise to "lean" on the men in a common setting of danger; coal management has been cognizant of their vulnerability for years by omitting foremen from grievance sessions. They may "tell it like it is."

3. The boredom of repetitive factory work can be avoided in the mines; usually job switching is allowed during the shift or during the week; men are generally permitted to develop their own job-trading arrangements so that one man may operate the continuous miner for half the shift and the buggy, the other. The union-contract rotating-lunch provision guarantees variety of work; on Saturdays and other idle days there is grading bottom, rock dusting, conveyor work, track laying, pumping, roof bolting, hanging wire. The coal miner often resembles an all-around man or general practitioner.

4. The mine-face crew usually achieves a teamwork and esprit de corps as finely honed as that of a combat squad. Company and union

appear to allow the internal adjustments necessary to achieve this, even though it may mean transferring a man by crew consensus; without it, a minimum level of production will not be reached; with it, certain implicit "rules" of team solidarity, joint decision making and worker discretion take over. Older men commonly refuse foreman jobs. The result often is an unstructured limitation on management prerogatives.

5. There is less alienation of the worker from the product in coal than in other industries. He is not a cipher divorced from the extraction process. He understands the materials, what he does, the strategy of extracting the coal, how his job fits into the overall pattern. His daily travel underground gives him an overview of the entire operation, past and present. The mine is a place of rapidly changing scenes, altering circumstances, geological pioneering. The flexible situation brings about changing rhythms in the work. He is and has been essential to the nation; what he produces is necessary for the common good.

6. Underground miners probably relate to one another in a more realistic and more supportive fashion than other industrial workers. The "regular Joe" style of coal miners can be characterized as follows: open, friendly, helping but tough; hostile to the company but not lazy; with blunt, unvarnished feelings along with tolerance, always sharing and never cheap; everyone with a nickname, indicating individual acceptance into the group; a social solidarity recognizing individualism that is quite attractive today in an impersonal and alienated world.

7. Some young miners are from families where the father was an occasional or low-wage worker, or are from broken homes, from homes where the family had been on welfare, or from rural homes in more isolated hollows with even less sophistication than mining towns.

8. Everything is relative: a coal miner today with stable employment is able to provide a decent level of family income and security in a community environment that is congenial to him and that has a below-average cost of living. In no other industry can a young man make comparable wages without a long apprenticeship.

9. The coal miner is a male in a masculine industry where others fear to tread; he is opening and developing territory never seen before. Not all men wish to be pencil pushers, and the hunting-fishing type of man may find in coal mining something like the satisfaction others get from skin diving, high-rise construction, or motorcycle riding.

Miners, although resenting the way in which they are looked down upon by others, may not articulate the sources of pride or satisfaction they have in their occupation. This is not to deny that there is an ambivalence or that elements of inertia, tradition, or habit bear on the decision to be a miner. Studies may conclude that coal miners were generally "forced" into their occupation, lacking any alternative. It is an answer true during much of the past; those who live in mining areas know it is true now for only some of the men.

If ever a distinctive occupational group existed in the nation, it is among coal miners. Their sense of job identity is so strong that it encompasses a greater community—one that goes beyond those employed in the industry—like veterans with the common experience of war. It includes ex-miners, who may be small businessmen, professionals, politicians, the disabled or retired, community-action leaders, and so forth. Almost one hundred and forty thousand men now work in coal mines. Probably there are well over one million men alive who, having worked in the mines, take on something of the trappings of this occupational community in class consciousness, pride, empathy, and outlook. Perhaps this undercurrent of pride is best implied in the opening lines of the folk song about Harlan County: "My daddy was a miner and I'm a miner's son."

THE YOUNG AND PROBLEMS OF THE FUTURE

Union loyalists, tried and true, the older men are the majority of mine workers today. The miner under thirty often appears hostile to both company and union, as well as cynical and disillusioned. Essentially an undisciplined, action-seeking person, often from a mixed ethnic or different cultural background from the older men, far more influenced by television and national norms, the young worker is unlikely to accept the older miner's relationship to the union uncritically.

The young come increasingly from outside the coal towns, from non-miner families, and they are high-school graduates. Many like horsepower—on two wheels, four wheels, or water. They love sports and fishing like their elders; they drink less. They are bright. Some are wild and try to work without much sleep. The beginning of drug usage has been noted, and this is especially dangerous in an industry requiring alertness and quick responses. With auto transportation, the miners live everywhere. At one new mine, local union officers reside in four different counties.

It is not yet clear what kind of role the young miners will play. They are part of the turmoil, the questioning, and the frustration of their generation. They have become more like industrial workers the nation over. They show signs of having adopted standard American equalitarian marriage styles. Some strive for respectability; others accept supervisory positions; still others are critical of working conditions. They read, argue, and watch television.

Large oil companies in recent years have joined steel firms in ownership of huge coal-mine properties. What they will bring to Appalachia besides a touch of Texas is still unknown. The new owners may risk confrontation with environmentalists by sharply raising strip-mine production to avoid the cost of new federal dust and safety standards underground. Or, they may utilize their vast potential for research and development to come up with technical breakthroughs that could make the mines much safer.

In the past, neglect and evasion of safety laws by the coal industry were directly connected with economics. The uneducated, untrained laborer of yesterday, with his twenty dollars worth of hand tools, was regarded as fiscally expendable. Today, the modern five-man mine-face crew, its equipment capitalized at almost one million dollars, and backup maintenance men are costly technological investments. Continuation of old attitudes will risk worker-recruitment programs and the hostility of public and congressional opinion.

Young underground miners of the future may blend something of the militancy of the older miner with that of today's public-service employee. While he makes ten thousand dollars a year, the miner often acts the way a poor man would. After all, American working-class consciousness seldom has had much to do with ideology or politics. It comes mainly from a sense of social identity that the individual gets at the work place. A dark underground mine is certainly a distinctive and alienated setting for blue-collar awareness that opposite ways of life exist in an increasingly white-collar society. The small Appalachian community in which the miner lives contrasts so sharply with status-seeking suburbia that the difference itself helps to reinforce his sense of separateness.

For the first time in American history, coal miners enjoy continuing social stability and regular employment. During the 1970s, because of the aging work force, tens of thousands of miners will retire and be replaced. The young miners are inexperienced and in need of leadership. Together, the young and the older mine workers can influence the course of events. Without their joint participation in planning for the future, the industry and union could gradually drift into a state of confusion, bordering on chaos.

NOTES

1. See F. M. Green, "Gold Mining—A Forgotten Industry of Antebellum North Carolina," *North Carolina Historical Review*, Jan.-April 1937, p. 15. Perhaps mine workers in the U.S. have always comprised a melting pot. From 1830 to 1845, there were miners speaking thirteen different languages—Jew and Gen-

tile, Latin and Nordic, native black and white, slave and free—all working the
North Carolina gold mines.

2. *Wall Street Journal,* April 2, 1970, p. 24.

3. J. E. Weller, *Yesterday's People* (Lexington, Ky.: Univ. of Ky. Press, 1966),
pp. 43, 103.

Garbage Collecting: Stigmatized Work and Self-Esteem

Edward Walsh

Some "dirty jobs" are harder and filthier than collecting garbage (for example, mining coal), but few are more stigmatized in the eyes of most Americans. In an attempt to understand the problems and coping mechanisms of garbagemen, I took a part-time job in 1969 with the Refuse unit in Ann Arbor, Michigan, and worked intermittently there for three years, until 1972. I found many aspects of the work dehumanizing, but I also discovered that the human spirit is more resourceful and resilient than many academics think. After giving the reader some idea of the less than ideal conditions under which these men work, I will present evidence suggesting that Ann Arbor's garbagemen do not have their psyches maimed or their self-esteem diminished by their work.

In the interest of privacy, I have used pseudonyms and garbled a few incidents to disguise the real crews being discussed. I carried a small notebook in my pocket as I worked on the trucks or in other situations, and whenever possible I wrote specific comments or key words from discussions on my crumpled pad (for example, as I collected trash behind a house by myself or waited in the truck's cab while the driver did the dumping at the city landfill). Most of the time, however, I wrote the field notes from memory in the evening after the day's work.

Source: This article was adapted from one chapter of the author's doctoral dissertation, "Job Stigma and Self-Esteem," Department of Sociology, University of Michigan, 1974.

THE WORK SETTING

Ann Arbor has approximately one hundred and fifteen thousand residents, a median income of slightly over twelve thousand dollars (1970 census), and a black population of only 7 percent. I was surprised therefore to discover that more than 90 percent of the garbagemen in Ann Arbor are black, and most of them said they were told only of openings in Refuse, when they came looking for work in the forties, fifties, and early sixties. Over half of these black garbagemen were raised in the South. One white veteran of the Streets Division told me that he would seriously consider doing just about any kind of municipal work except collecting garbage. "That's for uneducated southern blacks," he explained. The Streets, Sewage, and Parks units in Ann Arbor employ white workers who entered with about the same educations and skills as the blacks in Refuse, and most of the garbagemen are well aware of the fact that they have been victims of institutional racism.

Most municipal employees agree that garbagemen perform the most demanding physical labor of all, but their annual wages are at least five hundred dollars less than the wages of comparable workers in Streets, Sewage, and Parks. The garbagemen also have less opportunity for upward mobility than the other workers. There are only two job classifications in Ann Arbor's Refuse unit: one for the "pullers," who move the trash, and the other for the "drivers," who move the trucks. The Streets unit has five job classifications, the Sewage unit four, and the Parks unit seven. Thus these black garbagemen find themselves in a dead-end job where the pay and chances for mobility are lower than in other, comparable municipal jobs—and their work is harder. This combination is an adequate operational definition of "getting the short end of the stick" in the working world.

There are other indications that the interests of the men who collect Ann Arbor's garbage are at the bottom of most City Hall priority lists. When budget cuts were necessary in 1971, city officials reportedly considered laying off many garbagemen and asking others to make up for the slack by working harder and longer. (This was one of the few times I remember the predominantly white union standing up for the garbagemen and insisting that some other solution be found for balancing the budget.)

In 1972, municipal officials purchased new garbage trucks that load from the side rather than the rear. The alleged reason for the deal was that it would save the city money because fewer men would be needed to collect the trash, but some management officials said they felt that certain people received kickbacks for arranging the transaction. What disturbed most garbagemen even more than this rumored corruption at the top was the fact that the new trucks reduced the crew from four to three men and split up those remaining three into two segments, thus reducing on-the-job interaction. With the new trucks the driver does most of the actual dumping because he drives from curbside, while the other two men carry the trash from backyards. Although crews were reduced by attrition rather than layoffs, the men were bitter about the "big white fuckers." (Both trucks and officials responsible for the deal are white; hence the double entendre.)

Each crew has a daily route that requires eight hours of steady work. Because they are allowed to go home when the route is finished and are paid for a full eight hours even if finished in less time, some crews work at a hectic pace. Most, however, know that if they finish too early they will find themselves with longer routes the next week. If a holiday falls on a weekday, the garbagemen will be pressured into working for time-and-a-half on the following Saturday so that the collection service will not fall a day behind the next week.

The men are usually on their daily routes by 7:20 a.m. With the new trucks the driver often starts alone at one part of the route while the other men set out trash elsewhere. Before the new trucks arrived the four-man crew went out together, three men hauling trash from behind houses and apartment buildings while the driver helped dump. And, of course, he moved the truck along at an appropriate pace.

In the spring and autumn months the men usually wear two-piece dark-gray uniforms, consisting of a shirt and a pair of pants. In colder weather they wear their warmest coats or yellow rubberized rain suits over everything else. Most men don't like to wear them in warm rainy weather because they are so hot.

In all weather the garbageman has to contend with barking, and sometimes biting, dogs, inconveniently parked cars, and poorly packed (or unpacked) trash. My own inclination was to say "to hell with it" when I came to a residence with a menacing dog guarding the trash or a car blocking access to the rear of the house. But the men told me that in nine cases out of ten "the city don't back us up" when the citizen phones in a complaint. Since this means having to return the next day from some other route, one usually does his best to reach all trash.

When it rains, the work becomes very difficult. I wrote one evening in May 1970:

> It was a miserable day, raining and chilly. I was soaking wet by 8:00 a.m., and my fingers still ache from the wet gloves. The rain meant that besides the usual maggots and spilled garbage, we also had dirty water pouring out of the cans and down our pants. Even with my heavy boots, my feet were wet by 10:00 a.m., and before each stop of the truck, we ei-

ther had to jump off the platform or get hit in the neck with water from the roof. We had to ride the truck, though, because the houses today were far apart. It was especially hard on Bob, who is fifty-eight. The rust on the roof made the water streak everything it touched, and Bob's neck and face were lined with orange and brown because he had trouble jumping off early.

Streets, Sewage, and Parks workers get indoor assignments on such days, but the garbagemen never complained about such inequities in my presence.

It may be that when one group of men are so obviously discriminated against, they prefer not to see all that is going on. It is more probable, however, that they see things clearly but feel they can do nothing about them. A more just arrangement would find garbagemen receiving more pay for their more difficult and essential tasks. Snow and ice, as well as extreme heat, bring other problems, as my notes indicate.

> Our carts had ice frozen on the wheels, so they were really tough to pull through the snowdrifts. We had to squeeze between cars inconsiderately parked in the way of the trash, and on one occasion Jim's cart slipped away from him and down an incline into a new Buick, which was dented from the impact. Jim just finished his work and walked away, commenting: "It's a bad scratch, but it serves him right for parking the fuckin' thing there today when he knows we gotta get around it." (March 1971)

> The day was hot and sticky, and there seemed to be more than the usual number of bugs and flies around the cans. There is so little variety in the work except for the ways people think of leaving their garbage strewn to make the work more difficult! When it's completely unpacked, you can leave, by right—but Rolly told me the city usually believes the citizen complainer if it's her (or his) word against the garbageman's. The usual case is loose garbage surrounding one or two legitimately wrapped containers or cans—hence you have to wade through the rat-infested stuff to get at the other. What a drain on a man's endurance to stay at this day after day! (August 1972)

Sometimes, the "clients" become disturbed when garbagemen mistake non-trash for trash and haul it away. One day I threw a whole basket of apples into my "tub," since the basket was adjacent to the trash containers in the garage and the top ones looked rotten. The lady discovered my mistake after we were two blocks away, jumped in her car, and came to scold me publicly. After she drove away, the men laughed and told of similar incidents in which they were involved. When nature calls, the garbageman must find a place on the route to relieve himself. I was surprised the first time I saw a man go to the cab of our truck, take out the tin can next to my lunch, hold it under his coat, and proceed to urinate. I had not realized how difficult it is to find a semiprivate bush along a street of homes with children running around. On commercial routes, of which there are relatively few, the men use the washrooms of certain restaurants or other businesses. The men sometimes get lunches or beers in exchange for wrestling with defective tanks or picking up illegitimate trash behind restaurants or bars.

Victimized by institutional racism from the day of their hiring into the stigmatized Refuse unit, paid less than men in comparable units for doing dirtier, harder, and (except in the case of Sewage) more-essential work, having less opportunity for advancement than other public workers, and receiving fairly regular reminders that municipal and union officials—as well as the public—have little respect for their work, Ann Arbor's garbagemen are not ideally situated for having their feelings of self-worth enhanced, or even sustained, by their jobs. And yet, as evidence I will present will suggest, they are not the psychic cripples that some social theorists predict we will find under such circumstances.[1]

COPING WITH DEHUMANIZING WORK

I took a job as a part-time garbageman expecting to mix with demoralized men because I had no reason to doubt Everett Hughes' assertion that the kind of work a man does is "one of the more significant things by which he judges himself."[2] The job stigma attached to this work forecast low self-esteem for garbagemen, but this inference was based on the assumption that all workers attribute equal importance to job status. That assumption now appears doubtful to me.

In truth, it seems a bit presumptuous to attempt to discuss the self-esteem of a group of men when the very concept of self-esteem is so amorphous and my own knowledge of each man rather superficial. Yet, one might also question the reliability of self-reported self-esteem scores—contending that many people do not even know their true feelings—or challenge the validity of the judgments of psychiatrists or psychoanalysts, who have been known to disagree among themselves regarding the "correct" interpretation of words, symbols, and behavior. Let me admit frankly that I cannot *prove* the correctness of my interpretation; rather, I contend that many diverse indicators, including the men's comments and actions, combine to convince me that Ann Arbor's garbagemen are not walking around with maimed egos.

I understand self-esteem to refer to a liking and respect for oneself;

hence I will focus on many different individuals to illustrate various aspects of self-esteem rather than concentrate on a few men. My concern, of course, is job-related sources of self-esteem.

Ann Arbor's garbagemen give little indication that they inflate the occupational status of their jobs as a means of enhancing their feelings of self-worth, but this is not to say that they make no status claims based on their work. Most men are proud of the fact that they have a steady and relatively secure job; a number of their acquaintances are unemployed or only seasonally employed. Since many of Ann Arbor's garbagemen have advanced themselves from nearly absolute poverty, they measure their current job status with a different yardstick from that used by mainstream Americans.

I have isolated five dimensions—in addition to the mere fact of having a secure job—that are important in providing various garbagemen legitimate claims to above-average or superior ratings by their fellow workers, wives, and other acquaintances. I do not argue that a reputation for job efficiency—to take one dimension—is the main source of a garbageman's overall identity and self-esteem, but merely note that there are aspects of even this job that men use to enhance their feelings of worth and importance.

Pay

While other aspects of work may be important for any individual, none approaches money in its power to compensate men for job stigma. Goliath, a young black from Arkansas, with only three years of schooling, put it bluntly when he cut short a union president's long-winded oration about pending contract changes. "If you ain't talkin' money, you got nothin' to tell us," he bellowed from the rear of the union hall.

Curly talked about the futility of his son's accumulating years of education, then winding up with an office job paying less than a garbageman receives: "It's like a guy I know who could have taught law at the University of Michigan here, but they wanted him to be satisfied with less money because it was a higher-prestige school than some others he could've gone to. Sh-i-i-i-t, what can a man do with prestige?"

And Stick-Man told of the woman along the route who inquired intensely, "How do you ever stand all the dirt and filth, young man?" He explained the whole trick in one sentence: "The work may be dirty, but the money spends clean, Ma'am!"

The highest-paying job, among those with neither educational nor skill requirements, in Ann Arbor's Parks, Sewage, Streets, and Refuse units is that of a Parks greenskeeper; the annual wage difference between that job and laborer in Refuse is approximately fourteen hundred dollars. If one allows for the overtime the garbageman gets, but which the greenskeeper does not receive, and the average two hundred dollars in Christmas tips that come only to the garbageman, the greenskeeper cannot really pride himself on the wage difference between the two jobs. Of course, the greenskeeper will prefer to emphasize his higher status should the occasion for a comparison arise.

Only garbagemen are permitted to go home after completing their allotted work while getting paid for a full eight hours. Hence the industrious ones convert the extra time into more money. Tawny drives a cab, and Ron is a security guard. These men, and others like them, are so concerned with getting the house, car, and food money for themselves and their families—not to mention medical and other expenses—that the prestige of a particular job is a negligible variable for most of them. They are compensated for low occupational status by relatively high paychecks, and it is hard to find a sad or depressed face in the unit on payday.

> Goliath had mentioned around 11:00 a.m. that he wished they would bring his check because he had a lot of overtime coming his way. He was almost ecstatic just thinking of what he would get. He couldn't multiply very well, and it was fascinating watching this usually lethargic and rather surly individual actually yelp with joy at the approximate figures I gave him when he asked, "How much extra will I get with ten hours overtime?" He talked about nothing else all day, and when Hotshot arrived with the checks around 12:30, Goliath began to laugh, joke around, and act like a kid who'd just gotten a favorite toy for his birthday—completely beside himself with glee over the size of his check!

Efficiency

Since the garbagemen get paid for eight hours' work even if they finish in less time, there is an obvious incentive to work as quickly and efficiently as possible. This includes not spilling any trash, because cleaning it up slows everyone, and it also means taking legitimate shortcuts and developing the knack of piling as much as possible on one's cart after both barrels have been filled to capacity.

Certain men are commonly acknowledged to be the quickest, while others are tops in cleanliness. Mick told me that Joseph could collect trash on the dirtiest alley in Ann Arbor without getting a spot on himself or the ground, and "even if that fucker is old, he'll beat most of these young guys around here because he knows every shortcut possible—he taught me all I know." Wanderer and Leo are commonly acknowledged to be the fastest pullers in Ann Arbor, and Wanderer once suggested to a foreman that they arrange a race between Leo and himself on equal routes to break the tie for first.

Many of the older men regard it as foolish to rush too much because it takes so much out of a person when he's older, but men like Easy (with no reputation for speed) can "move out" when they decide they should.

On a Saturday after Labor Day, we were working to catch up so that next week's collection would be on schedule. The pay was time-and-a-half for eight hours no matter how long the route took that day (provided only that it was completed). Easy told the driver that we could finish by noon, but that it would look bad because management would surely lengthen the route. He suggested we aim for 1:00 p.m. (two hours early). Easy barked orders from the back platform as we flew around the route: "Skip that house. . . . Red house on vacation. . . . Take the truck down that alley, and I'll meet you on Huron. . . . We can get the gas station on Monday before they open." And so forth. We were the first crew in that day, and during the next week Easy had a great time ribbing Wanderer, Leo, and all the younger men. He also scolded me for my slowness and inefficiency, once remarking: "You're going to college and you can't follow my simple fuckin' advice? You must be hard to teach anything to!" Certainly Easy gave no indication of nursing a bruised ego.

A number of the younger men make each day interesting by competing to finish first; and, while this sometimes annoys the older men, who become pawns in the race, it is also a source of pride for the fast ones.

A Sharp Eye

Although most men pick up a few things from the trash daily, certain ones are proud of their ability to discern "good stuff from junk," while others brag about their knack for making money from what looks worthless to the untrained eye.

Dude had been removing shirts, trousers, and other items from the trash throughout the morning, and at one stop in the afternoon he turned to me, grinning: "Guess you know who the clothes hustler is now, huh? Wanna buy a nice suit? You know, they won't buy pants with cuffs on them now down on Navaho Street, but I'll wait a year or so and they'll be going like hotcakes again—you'll see."

Joshua was famous for his ability to repair any type of electrical appliance. Some of the men brought broken fans, radios, lamps, and other items to him to be fixed and subsequently used or sold. He did this in return for favors such as help with painting his house, fixing the roof, and putting in new cement front steps. He told me he can just look at a discard and tell if the person who threw it away "had any brains in his head."

One day I had just finished dumping my barrel into the truck and was pulling the handle to start the blade that would sweep the contents away. B.K. grabbed the emergency lever and pulled it firmly. "You never let one of these go through," he explained in an annoyed tone as he picked up a pornographic magazine and stored it in the cab. Later that day, Sammy, a puller on another truck, told me that B.K.'s truck had the best assortment of such literature in the whole unit. He said that when city mechanics were working on that truck the previous week, they stole a homosexual magazine. "That don't say much for them muthas, does it?" he laughed.

Natty laid a small doll aside, placing it on a side ledge of the truck, and smiled at me when he saw that I noticed his move. "That'll make my little one happy tonight; she always asks me, 'Whatcha bring me today, Daddy?' I like to have some little thing every night." He said he finds the best items in the trash of the poor. "The rich people got that way because they never throw stuff away with any use left in it, but the poor stay poor because they get tired of things and chuck 'em." In addition to offering a novel theory of social stratification, I wondered if Natty was not also intimating that he himself would be rich someday because of his thrifty ways.

Talk

A few crews are light on talk as they focus on speed, but most carry on interrupted conversations throughout much of the day. Some of the younger, educated garbagemen take turns commenting on current events or telling stories of personal sexual exploits, but most of the time one man dominates the conversation and the other two address comments and their own brief anecdotes to him. The driver is, more often than not, the self-appointed emcee. Sex is the most frequent topic of conversation.

Leo was complaining about a young girl who was bothering him too often at his apartment. He said he told her: "Look, I like young girls, but you're too young for me—I'm not gonna have a baby with you, 'cause next month I'll find myself doin' the payin' and somebody else doin' the fuckin'!" Albert, the older driver, listened with intense interest but was not to be outdone by this younger lover. (Albert could speak perfect English when he wanted to, but slipped into affected speech when telling a story—with the apparent intention of casting a spell over his listeners.)

Me have problem when me young man with strong worm. Young girl come to my house for grease job. Me tell her she too young and me no want baby. She cry and get real nice with me. Me pull dollar and send her for fun balloons. Me grease her and send her away, but about three weeks later she come back. Me watching TV with lights out, and me hear knock on door. Me wonder who there—me open, and it her. She hand me box, and I open. What think? More fun balloons! She say she been to three other men, but nobody make her feel as good as me do. Me say, "I do once more, but you no come back no more—if you do, I throw your ass out door, you hear?" She agree, and me grease her and say good-bye.

The incident sounded so much like the one described by Leo that I was certain Albert made it up on the spot to outshine him and give some sage advice: "Don't just send her away!"

Curly is even better than Albert when it comes to spicing up stories with vivid sexual imagery, but he prides himself most on his ability to talk people along the route into letting him fix up broken steps, repair siding, or even do gardening to improve their homes. He and some "associates" do such work "on the side," and Curly has a special talent for suggesting that something would improve the looks of one's house without annoying anyone with his subtle criticism. To one resident he remarked, "Now there's a right nice porch for sittin' and watchin' the kids play out here. I could fix up those steps in no time so you wouldn't have to jump down and climb up to relax."

Discussions often focus on management's idiocy or duplicity. Some men just gripe or enjoy hearing others do so, but there are others who pride themselves on their insights into better ways of doing the trash collecting. The men like to hear Stormy outline better ways to run the unit. He once suggested getting the attention of City Hall authorities by leaving filled garbage buggies on each floor. His best ideas focus on ways to make garbage-collection schedules more flexible, allowing men to slip behind a day without having to catch up on the weekends.

Roland does not theorize as much as Stormy, but most men regard him as one of the "gutsiest" of the garbagemen vis-à-vis management, and some of his encounters with authorities are legendary. One of the foremen insisted that he go back to a house he had skipped. Since he told the story on the way to the dump, that gave me the opportunity to scribble at some length while he was dumping.

Roland said he refused to go back because he'd filled out a slip on that house, explaining that a car was blocking the driveway. He said he told the foreman he would get it the next week and not a day before. "I was within my legal rights, ya know, and I'll be damned if I'm gonna go runnin' around for the little turd," he explained to supportive nods and smiles. "I told him if he slipped the dick to me by docking my pay, I'd get it out of his own ass sooner or later. When my paycheck came with an hour's pay short, I talked Sam and Bean into refusing any more overtime until I got my rightful pay. We screwed up two days for the little turd before he finally backed down and told them to give me back my pay. I smile real big at him now everytime we meet, and o-o-o-oh, would he like to shit on me. But just let him try!" The men seemed quite impressed at Roland's boldness, and they seemed to feel he was telling the truth.

Sometimes the conversation turned to racial matters. Mick once told me that he'd saved every newspaper account he had seen of racial strife because he's very interested in it. When the talk turns to that topic, especially in the city yard, Mick takes over. One day the men were discussing the Arab violence at the 1972 Olympics. Mick interrupted: "Look at all this sympathy the Jews are gettin' from all over the West. But who worries when Arab refugees are slaughtered and imprisoned? Why does everyone care about the Jews? I'll tell you why: they're white, and the Arabs are darkskinned people. I'll tell you who was really to blame for them deaths—it was the fuckin' Germans. They opened up on them and they weren't gonna let them leave that country no matter what." The men know Mick reads more than most of the rest of them, and they respect his opinions.

If many of the younger men emphasize the efficiency dimension, most older ones do not mind finishing a bit later for the sake of a good day of stories and philosophizing.

Dealing with the Public

The majority of Ann Arbor's garbagemen are not cowed by the bossy or pretentious public. Some men are more docile than others, especially if requested and not ordered to do something, but most will resist taking anything outside the limits of legitimate trash except when given a special tip for their labor. (Illegitimate trash includes unwrapped shrubbery, cat litter, large pieces of lumber, concrete, old bicycles.) I have often been corrected by fellow garbagemen for picking up trash lying beside a can or for starting to return empty cans to the side or back of the houses. Many men feel that the more you do for the public, the more they demand. Today's favor may be tomorrow's duty.

Some garbagemen delight in confounding irate citizens who order them around, as Hornet did when he suggested a new way of getting the old baby carriage to the dump. A woman asked him, "Well, how am I gonna get this piece of junk out of here if you won't take it? It won't fit in my car!" Hornet replied pleasantly, "You could jump in and steer it from here—it's all downhill."

Robert's succinct, if unsympathetic, response to the lady who asked him, with annoyance, how she could get rid of the maggots in her garbage cans has become legendary around the city yard. "Don't put any garbage in them," he advised.

One of the results of treating men like things is that the tactic backfires. Many women along the routes hurry out and deposit their latest additions to the trash as the garbagemen approach, but apparently they feel it would be beneath their dignity to greet these workers in a civil manner. As they nervously hasten back into their homes, without saying a word (or perhaps criticizing last week's service in a pompous tone), the men will have a few laughs at their expense.

Stray and unleashed dogs are as constant a problem for garbagemen as for milkmen and letter carriers. One day Tennessee picked up a board and swatted a menacing German shepherd across the face, causing the dog to lose its sight in one eye, according to its owner. She was furious, yelling at Tenn, "It won't bite!" He, in his usual quiet manner, replied without guile, "I know he won't bite me now, but I couldn't know that when he came at me!"

Since assertiveness is associated with high self-esteem, I have emphasized instances of garbagemen refusing to back down. I could give many more such examples, but I feel the point has been made: Most of the garbagemen are not afraid to stand up for their rights with Ann Arbor's public. The reader should not get the impression, however, that the average day has many such tension-filled encounters. Nevertheless, from what I have seen while working with these men, they are very different from the blacks who have been found to turn their aggression inward on themselves.[3]

Briefly summarizing job-related sources of self-esteem, I can say that the pay and other benefits (life and health insurance, vacations, and possible pensions) more than compensate most of these men for the stigma attached to their jobs. Since many have come from real poverty, a job that pays nine thousand dollars or more annually is nothing to be ashamed of, regardless of its prestige rating elsewhere. Of course, there are probably times when many of the men are reluctant to admit that they collect garbage for a living. For example, one told my wife during a chance conversation at a laundromat that he was a mechanic for the city; only later did we discover that he was a garbageman.

But these are not normal daily encounters for these workers. Most of their interactions are with wives, neighbors, friends, and fellow workers, who know their job and respect them for it, or with people who know their employment and may tend to despise them for it—people such as management officials, higher-status city workers, pompous home-owners. The garbagemen know what to expect from these latter sources, and, as observed, they have developed more or less successful means of coping with them. Yet even within their rather monotonous and dirty jobs, many of these men find dimensions that allow them to manifest uniqueness, compete with others, or perform in such a way as to impress others and satisfy themselves.

There are also off-the-job sources of self-esteem—families, possessions, religious organizations—that are more important to most of these men than the usual prestige ratings. I have discussed these other dimensions elsewhere.[4]

ADDITIONAL COMMENTS AND A FANTASY

Robert Merton suggests in *Social Theory and Social Structure* that the pressure to engage in deviant activity will be particularly acute in the case of garbagemen. He argues that they share the American Dream aspirations of most Americans for money and fame, but find themselves blocked from obtaining their goals through legitimate channels. Merton's theory is suspect on both empirical and theoretical grounds.

I found no data indicating that the garbagemen of Ann Arbor were more inclined toward deviance than other municipal employees, graduate students, or persons in higher-prestige occupations. Actually, the fact that they have a legitimate job is a source of pride for many garbagemen, especially blacks, because they are respected by neighbors and relatives more than are men engaged in illegal pursuits. Theoretically, the concept of relative deprivation suggests that white garbagemen will be more vulnerable to threats to their self-esteem that derive from the stigma attached to their job than will blacks. The latter have raised themselves from subsistence levels, where concern with job status was an unaffordable luxury.

In a survey reported in my larger study[5] I discovered that the white garbagemen of Minneapolis, where 90 percent are white, had more problems with job stigma than did the black garbagemen of Detroit, where 90 percent are black. A more surprising finding from that survey was that the job of the garbageman ranked higher in the black community's prestige ratings than it did in mainstream America. Such evidence suggests that American blacks, long discriminated against by being deprived of equal access to all but society's least attractive jobs, have made adaptations that protect them more than their white counterparts from self-esteem threats related to their dead-end and dirty work.

Some authors suggest that society will always have its "dirty work," and somebody has to do it. In conclusion, I should like to be permitted a fantasy. I can imagine the job of garbageman acquiring a new and higher status when residents are required by law to have their own trash cleanly packed before it qualifies for pickup. Residents will be fined when their trash is strewn about or poorly packed—the reasoning being that this is more of a threat to society's welfare and good order than double parking—and some of the "removers" (the new name for garbagemen) will be empowered to write such tickets. In addition to being neatly packed, trash must also be sorted into different categories, most of which will be recycled at the "sorting depot" (the new name for the dump). The job is no longer stigmatized because it is no longer dead-end or dirty. A man can rise from "Remover 1" all the way up the ladder to "sorting-depot supervisor," depending upon his drive and qualifications.

NOTES

1. See, for example, Robert K. Merton, *Social Theory and Social Structure* (New York: Free Press, 1968), p. 133.

2. Everett C. Hughes, *Men and Their Work* (Glencoe, Ill.: Free Press, 1958).

3. See, for example, Abram Kardiner and Lionel Ovesey, *The Mark of Oppression: Explorations in the Personality of the American Negro* (Gloucester, Mass.: Peter Smith, 1951).

4. See the author's unpublished Ph.D. dissertation, "Job Stigma and Self-Esteem," University of Michigan, 1974.

5. *Ibid.*

Humanizing Offices
by Participatory Design

Walter Kleeman, Jr.

There are offices where men and women labor to produce the written work of business, government, education, and the professions, but very little attention has been paid to the personal environmental needs and wishes of individual men and women working there.

Temperature, light, and ventilation requirements have been increasingly considered, of course, as available technology has become more nearly adequate for meeting these needs. Yet, while there have been quantum leaps in the design and complexity of electrical, electronic, and mechanical devices, the basic desk, file, table, and chair have remained relatively static. Designers and manufacturers have virtually ignored available data, the use of which could ameliorate the comfort and physical well-being of those who work in offices. Also, a wide variety of largely unspecified human social needs and wishes not only go unsatisfied but are not even addressed in office planning and design.

Data exist that could be correlated and used to meet social as well as comfort and physical needs. In fact, this information has been available for some time in the literature of psychology, psychiatry, anthropology, anthropometrics, and several other disciplines. Since this data has been scattered and uncorrelated, however, the task of designing offices humanistically has been slowed.

To advance the art of office design, a team has been formed, consisting of the team leader, Sam A. Sloan, architect and president of People

Space Architecture Company in Spokane, Washington; Dennis E. Green, architect with the Office of Construction Management, General Services Administration, Washington, D.C.; Robert Sommer, a social psychologist and chairman of the Department of Psychology, University of California, Davis; and the author, a behavior-oriented interior designer. The team's work is dedicated to the idea that the office must be designed to satisfy the wants and desires of people. We abhor the designer on an ego trip, who functions in the mode of the archetypal Scandinavian "form giver," imposing a design straitjacket on the luckless workers from a lofty position on high. Frequently this procedure results in a uniformity which, while it may be aesthetically pleasing to the designer, does not involve the workers or necessarily satisfy their needs, since they have no chance to share their views. Dennis Green has refined the philosophy of the team in a ten-point statement that he calls "User Participation: The Power of the Process."[1] In putting the team's philosophy into effect, we hope to:

1. relieve the worker's potential anxiety that results from meeting the unknown;

2. act as a self-actualizing process, in which creative activity is stressed as normal rather than abnormal;

3. produce a physical design more related to the balance of the worker's aspired values, desired values, and actual values;

4. create a setting in which a total range of values and preferences can be uncovered and in which the employee's point of view can be shown as a positive force in the design process;

5. provide a more democratic climate and an emphasis on individual responsibility as an important ethical base;

6. create an awareness of what the design process is and provide practical experience for the participant that can be applied in a wide range of activities;

7. dispel the employee's idea that "nobody cares about how I feel and therefore I'm probably not worth very much";

8. arrive at a much better relationship between artifacts and individual human beings' ergonomic fit;

9. deal realistically and openly with conflict and resolve it through positive complementarity rather than negativistic compromise;

10. provide a logical framework in which interdisciplinary actions can complement each other rather than contend for dominance.

Mr. Green also originated the "social water hole" theory of how an office actually works, and he has applied this theory to practical design. He feels that, in addition to its ultilitarian aspects:

The office is also a vital human gathering place where people congregate not only to perform a work task, but also to share their daily experiences. In today's office environment, we can find people as much concerned about their own personal problems and aspirations as they are about the routine work tasks. Discussion for the day often centers not around work itself, but about the individual accomplishments and tragedies of the worker and his family and friends. Even political and religious haggling competes with the functional activities of regular work flow.[2]

Mr. Green points out that the meeting and gathering places of the past—the marketplace, the town hall, the church, mosque, temple, or synagogue, and the village fountain or "water hole"—no longer function as they once did—if they are even still in existence. In an impersonal urban society the office now assumes the social role that these gathering places once had. He believes, as all the team members do, that unless individual social needs are satisfied by user participation in the design process, the value of design cannot rise above the merely functional, remaining largely mechanical and cosmetic.

To give some idea of what we do as a team to humanize offices, utilizing user participation in the design process, I will describe a recent project: the behavioral design and space development of an office for approximately four hundred employees of the Northwest Region of the Federal Aviation Administration in Seattle, Washington. The project tests the hypothesis that people working in an office can participate in designing their own working environments with confidence and direction. Their individual physical, social, and territorial requirements, determined by adroit questioning and observation, can be translated into design issues and requirements with the aid of a computer and can then be woven into the total design. However, the usual communications survey is not enough.

So that the contemporary needs could be accurately assessed, the design team determined that the investigation of seventy-four design issues or requirements identified by a cursory examination would provide the necessary data, not only for the meaningful development and arrangement of working spaces but also for each individual's selection of artifacts and tools as an integral part of his or her participation in the design of his or her own work station. Before specifically investigating the seventy-four items, we found it necessary to evaluate the FAA's previous facilities to identify workers' environmental concerns and also to provide the design team with a basis for comparison of workers' reactions to the new offices. After implementation, this same analysis of environmental quality could be made to ascertain the effects of carefully devised individual research and user participation in design upon the actual quality of the built environment. The initial questionnaire and its results appear in Figure 1.

From the results of the questionnaire, completed by the one hundred and eighty-five employees then working, it was possible to make certain gross physical assessments of the existing FAA offices. The facilities have poor to bad acoustics, fair to poor air temperature and comfort, good to fair lighting, fair space and furnishings, and fair to poor equipment.

After the completion and tabulation of the first questionnaire, we held interviews that included a more detailed and individualized seven-page questionnaire. It provided enough information on each individual so that acute needs could be identified and then checked through cross-analysis on a computer. These acute needs are flags that warn the designer to check out the other issues within the same category. Thus, when Mary Jones reveals an acute need for privacy, the designer can check her answers to questions on various types of privacy needs—audio, visual, security, or smoking. In this way the answers from the questionnaire and interview become design tools to enable the designer to satisfy individual human needs.

In addition to the privacy criteria, the seventy-four design issues and requirements analyzed included the following:

1. Personal proximity needs on a highly social to antisocial scale; color preferences—bright, medium, or none; territorial needs; motility or mobility characteristics; hierarchical orientation; aggressive-nonaggressive traits; need for living plants; extent of disablement, if any; acuteness of sight and hearing; sensitivity to temperature change, noise, and visual distraction; adequacy of artifacts and tools such as desks, files, chairs, tables, wall-mounted items, machines, and storage cabinets.

2. Maintenance: volume of waste and dirt; extent of interior and exterior traffic.

3. Reuse preference for specific artifacts and tools.

4. Requirements for group work and social space.

5. Comfort ratings for seating and work surfaces.

Simultaneously with this part of the study, the widest possible range of artifacts and tools was developed within space and budget limitations. In this selection process heavy emphasis was placed on the ergonomic characteristics of the artifacts offered so that, as the workers change, the artifacts or tools can be adjusted to the requirements of successive users.

In an unused section of a hangar near the new facilities each indi-

FIGURE 1: SYNTHESIS SHEET

MAJORITY RESPONSE
SECONDARY RESPONSE

This is your opportunity to help us do a better job of planning facilities. Please give us your best opinion of the following list of items in this room by making an appropriate check (✓) on the rating lines. And if you rate something on the poor side, try to tell us what you think the problem is.

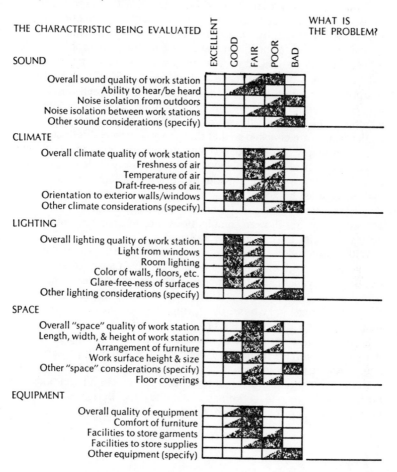

THE CHARACTERISTIC BEING EVALUATED — EXCELLENT, GOOD, FAIR, POOR, BAD

WHAT IS THE PROBLEM?

SOUND
- Overall sound quality of work station
- Ability to hear/be heard
- Noise isolation from outdoors
- Noise isolation between work stations
- Other sound considerations (specify)

CLIMATE
- Overall climate quality of work station
- Freshness of air
- Temperature of air
- Draft-free-ness of air
- Orientation to exterior walls/windows
- Other climate considerations (specify)

LIGHTING
- Overall lighting quality of work station
- Light from windows
- Room lighting
- Color of walls, floors, etc.
- Glare-free-ness of surfaces
- Other lighting considerations (specify)

SPACE
- Overall "space" quality of work station
- Length, width, & height of work station
- Arrangement of furniture
- Work surface height & size
- Other "space" considerations (specify)
- Floor coverings

EQUIPMENT
- Overall quality of equipment
- Comfort of furniture
- Facilities to store garments
- Facilities to store supplies
- Other equipment (specify)

COMMENTS: Perhaps we have missed something in the above list that you'd like to comment on. Please do so below or on the back of this questionnaire. We want to know in what ways this building "turns you on"—or off!

199

vidual designed his or her own work station with a member of the design team. Each piece of furniture offered was available so that a work station could be arranged in its actual pattern to verify its workability. The floor was carpeted and a ceiling installed to simulate that in the new building. Typical furniture combinations were developed for executive, supervisory, secretarial, and technician tasks at each work station. If our work has been successful, each work station will reflect the personal requirements of the person occupying the station.

Simultaneously, group space was developed with a proper compromise between individual and group requirements. The major design issues of group orientation are territory and traffic. Personable people can provide a fence for less sociable workmates, and people needing privacy should be placed so that they will not easily be disturbed.

In the design of group space and individual work stations, we attempt to actualize the basic needs of each worker. Each artifact and tool is run through an ergonomic or human-factors sieve to determine whether or not it meets the necessary criteria for comfort and safety. Desk surfaces are checked so that they are glarefree and reflect properly to permit the worker to concentrate without creating problems. Chair fabrics must be not only long-wearing and easily cleaned but also woven so that the surface provides necessary ventilation. Chair heights and backs must be adjustable so that they can accommodate the expected range of workers. Different sizes and shapes of work surfaces, as well as varying drawer combinations, are offered so that task requirements can be individually satisfied.

With thirteen desks, fifteen chairs, six credenzas, sixteen colors of fabric, a full range of telephone colors, and even six different in and out baskets available for each person's choice, the power of selection is real, and it is being exercised. These choices are not just the means of satisfying personal whims; by making these choices the worker participates in the design of his or her own workplace.

From the initial reactions to our work, we feel that this design activity by the workers themselves, concerned as it is with posture, storage, aesthetic preferences, and so forth, realizes partially what Maslow calls the self-actualization process, especially since mind and body are both involved in one coordinated activity—the design of the individual workplace for one human being.

NOTES

1. Unpublished manuscript.
2. *Ibid.*

New
Directions

Preface

Roy P. Fairfield

So much for past and present. What about the future? Although it is too much to expect radical shifts from present workplace practices and while it is doubtful that many of us would wish for the negative utopias of *Brave New World* or *1984*, surely there is a place for some brave new *ideas* and *acts*. Such is the case for the applications that Walter Kleeman suggests in the preceding essay and that Robert Schrank delineates in the following section of the book. We have only begun to see the possibilities of cross-cultural fertilization.

With women now constituting between 40 and 50 percent of the work force (not counting forced housework), can there be any denying the impact of women workers upon job conditions in this country? In view of the movement toward the "service society" that Gartner and Riessman depict, can there be any denying that women's influence may be enormous and vital? With the current feminist movement having generated nearly a decade of ferment and momentum, can anybody have missed this as a new direction? But there are long distances to travel. To maintain that momentum women must continue to challenge conventional male *and* female wisdom in every workplace, from the most professional to the most mundane, from the most structured to the most anarchistic, from the most hierarchical to the most participatory. To those who ask skeptical questions, "But will the cost be too great—the cost to 'female character' or the cost of such necessities as child care?" we must answer, "What price the alternatives?"

Both Louise Kapp Howe and Stevanne Auerbach-Fink sketch some of the salient features of a climate in which we need many brave ideas and much brave action. There is no place in America for second-class citizens, individually or collectively, regardless of group, creed, or sex. But our major problem is to translate that historical and traditional rhetoric into everyday living situations.

Howard Radest's critique of patchwork approaches to workplace issues is a new vision, reminding me of a debate I once heard between Leon Keyserling and Robert Theobald. The former was arguing for full employment, the latter for full unemployment! With our enormous capacity to produce, there is certainly no good reason to contend that anybody should be ill housed, ill fed or ill clad. Hence Radest's fundamental linking of work and play, scarcity and wealth, conventional wisdom and innovation surely constitutes the grist for both imaginative schemes of action and playful fantasy. (Remember my cousin's boyhood dream of two six-month vacations per year, with pay!) Radest is certainly "right on" when he observes that "the application of playfulness to work life and not a surrender to 'free time' is the doorway to industrial society's human potency." Our questions of Radest may be legion. For instance, how *should* work and play be related in a humane society? In short, is there a humanistic moral imperative? Is it feasible to claim both political and economic rights? If so, who will construct and apply an economic bill of rights? If playfulness is to serve as an organizing activity for humans, if we are going to convince any significant number of people to come to grips with the essential elements of work and leisure, can we ask any particular group to begin? So, why not ask the readers of these words, "If you believe, why don't *you* begin?"

Women in the Workplace

Louise Kapp Howe

On the wall, reports the *Wall Street Journal*, is a picture of Israeli leader Golda Meir captioned "But Can She Type?" There are other feminist posters, too. Seated around the room are forty women—all employees of Westinghouse, all invited to this "motivational" workshop because the company says it is interested in helping them to advance to higher positions within the corporation.

Actually, Westinghouse is under the gun to help them do so. Like all major corporations with a history of sex discrimination—in short, *all* major corporations—it could be declared ineligible for federal contracts if it does not comply with new regulations to show affirmative action (which now means specific goals and timetables) to recruit and promote women to all levels within its job structure.

That is, of course, why every other week or so we hear of new company plans and programs and occasionally statistical progress, such as IBM's announcement of a 35 percent increase in its female managerial staff over the previous year. Though this sounded impressive, it was never made clear exactly what *numbers* were involved. More impressive are the recent strides in opening higher-level jobs and awarding back pay to thousands of women working for Ma Bell.

In any case, the Westinghouse workshop takes place in a motel conference room in Pittsburgh. For two days the invited employees debate

Source: This article appeared in *The Humanist*, September-October 1973.

whether it has been sex discrimination or women's own inadequacies that have kept us from the nation's top ranks of management. Because of the attention given to the feminist movement in the past few years, the women respond instantly that it has been the fault of our lousy male-chauvinist occupational system—or do they?

Not here, not yet. Doubts and self-doubts instead. The women worry openly about their abilities, or rather their lack of them. They also express concern about losing their femininity or damaging their relationships with men by concentrating on careers. Although less than a quarter of the women present are married and living with their husbands, most still foresee and fear a future conflict between home and career. "Remember," one woman says, "it's more socially acceptable for a man to sacrifice his home for a career than it is for a woman."

Finally, according to *Wall Street Journal* reporter Ellen Graham, they decide to put the question of sex discrimination to a vote. At this point a woman named Janet pulls out a book of statistics showing that women college graduates earn on the average more than five thousand dollars a year less than their male counterparts. "Now won't you agree women have been discriminated against?" she asks. "Men are making more money because they're more qualified," Irene retorts. "If you're held back, it isn't because you're a woman, it's because of your own inadequacies." The vote is taken. Doubts and self-doubts. Irene wins.

Nevertheless, by the time it is over, the workshop seems to have made a difference in the way the participants feel about themselves. There was only one avowed feminist when they began but now the entire group's consciousness has been raised for the future. Bring on the promotions! The workshop is praised.

Doubts and self-doubts still chip away at the potential abilities of how many women? *What should I be? What can I do? What will I have to give up to get there?* Spurred by the feminist movement, many thousands of women are refusing to give yesterday's ritual reply: wife-and-mother, period. Many who would not have done so ten years ago are now seeking careers instead, or careers *as well,* if they can manage it.

But, as the Westinghouse workshop showed, for other women—for no doubt the vast majority of other women—the old conditioning about sex roles—that a man is your basic security, that his work always comes before your own—has not lost its power in a few short years. How could it? For most women the objective conditions that would breach the doubts have yet to arrive.

On the same day in April 1973 that the *Wall Street Journal* reported the steps Westinghouse and other corporations were taking to help women advance in work, another item tabulated the latest rate of unemployment among married men (2.5 percent). Washington experts will tell you that this is the one rate that matters the most. Although the rate is far lower than the overall jobless figure that encompasses us all, officials look at it first when unemployment starts to climb. The overall figure is not really that critical, John B. Connally announced definitively a couple of years ago. At that time it was 6 percent and he was secretary of the treasury; after all, "it includes so many women and teenagers."

Our employment policies have always been based first on the male breadwinner's needs. During depressions, recessions, recurring periods of high unemployment, his prior right to available work, the *best* available work, has never been seriously questioned. It was he about whom the government worried, to the extent it bothered to worry about its job-reduction policies to stem inflation at the beginning of this decade. And of course that was far from a frivolous concern. Nothing could have been more memorable than some of the shocked and saddened faces we saw on television at that time: white middle-aged breadwinners who had thought that they and their families were secure for life; after all, unemployment was something reserved for "lazy kids and blacks." The irony of their past bigotry, in some few instances an awakening to the inequities facing others for so long, came through on the tube as we watched them. But what the television cameras failed to show, what government officials failed to consider, in addition to the then deepening problems among the poor and the black, were the faces of the women who were also being laid off, women who needed work just as badly.

We keep hearing the statistics, but that does not mean they are taken seriously. Forty percent of all women who work are dependent on neither a husband nor a father for their support. Of the thirty-three million women now in the labor force, more than 20 percent are single; another 20 percent are widowed, divorced, or separated; and about 15 percent more have husbands who are earning less than five thousand dollars a year. Thirteen million American women who maintain their own households are responsible for the welfare of about ten million children. The rate of unemployment is consistently higher for women than it is for men—more than two times higher for female heads of households than male—and the gap has widened in the past decade. Despite the Equal Pay Act of 1964, the disparity in pay has widened. Far from working for pin money, there is evidence, as the *Washington Post* put it, that the "working woman is to some extent doing in this country what the U.S. government seems incapable of doing. Increasingly, she provides the essentials of life for the poorest of families and is pulling a very substantial number up the ladder into middle-class life."

Yet, when we hear about the plight of the unemployed, when we read about the problems of workers in general, or for that matter, when the subject of "the worker" comes up in almost any context, what picture is being drawn for us? Yes, most always it is the picture of a man—although 40 percent of the labor force is now female. Pick up a book about "sex roles" and you will spend most of your time reading about women. Pick up a book about work (the meaning of work, the alienation from work, the value of work) and you will mainly be reading about men. Workers are men. Women are, well, *sometimes,* women workers.

These attitudes obviously did not start with, nor are they confined to, the current administration we have all come to know and love so well. Paradoxically, Nixon and company appear to have done more to advance *and* to retard the cause of working women than any administration in recent history. On the one hand he giveth (through enforcement of equal-employment-opportunity codes), while on the other he taketh away (by vetoing major child-care legislation that would have made it possible or less difficult for working mothers to take advantage of the new opportunities).

Surely, politicians or men of any stripe can compete with Mr. Nixon's ability to make his position on an issue so perfectly confused. But one thing about the President, he may aid and abet you, he may benignly or malignly neglect you, he may even do worse, but he is far too politically astute to ever forget that you exist. Senator Edward Kennedy, on the other hand, conducted two full days of hearings on worker alienation in 1972. Research has shown that women are nearly twice as likely as men to express discontent with their jobs. Yet neither the Senator nor his staff remembered to call one single woman to testify at those hearings. And in a putatively more radical vein, three scholars from Cambridge and Canada edited a five-hundred-page Random House reader, *Worker's Control,* consisting of more than forty articles on current work life and how to improve it, again without a single article by or about a woman.

Of course these gentlemen could argue that, after all, the issue under discussion is not gender but work. The reasons people become dissatisfied with their jobs—the routine, the lack of autonomy, the low status and pay—have nothing to do with their sex. But if these men say this, then they have not considered why it is that women just happen to be concentrated in the lowest-level jobs. And they have not stopped saying it or tried to perceive what the women at the Westinghouse workshop knew, what all women know, that try as you will it is impossible to separate life into neat, discrete pieces that do not affect each other. The areas of family life and employment are inseparably related, and for millions of women, not only in America but throughout the world, these areas are in conflict.

To work or not to work—that is not the question. "The most important fact" to remember, in the words of the HEW report, *Work in America*, is "that almost all women are working unless they are disabled. Some work in the market for pay; others work in the home; and many do both."[1]

More and more do both. In 1900 about 20 percent of women were in the paid work force; today the figure is about 40 percent. In 1900 most job-holding women were young and single (while older, married women then generally confined their labor to the home—working in the fields, doing piecework or other kinds of in-house jobs, in addition to child care and housework). The large increase in women workers after World War II resulted mainly from the influx of older, married women into the labor force. The *new* change is due to the sharp rise in the number of working mothers with young children, including currently a third of the mothers with children under six.

There is now every sign that these percentages will grow. The main reason, it would be nice to say, is the impact of the women's movement in sparking our sisters to embark on promising careers. Envision all of us going off in the morning to fight disease in the hospitals, defend justice in the courts, wheel and deal with Henry Ford II on the executive floor—in other words, doing all the things that men in the most prestigious, high-paying, and "satisfying" occupations have largely kept as their own preserve.

And it is true that in the upper middle class more women are doing just that—invading the so-called male professions. Unhappily it is equally true that, for all the publicity when it happens, the invasion force is abysmally small. In 1970 women received 8.5 percent of all MDs awarded, 5.6 percent of the law degrees, and 3.9 percent of the master's degrees in business. Hardly a take-over. Still, low as these percentages were, in each case they represented a large increase over the previous year, hopefully indicating a trend that will continue and accelerate.

Meantime, in the so-called female professions a very different situation took place. In 1971 women received 74 percent of the BAs in education, 83 percent of the library-science degrees and 98 percent of the nursing degrees. If you want to guess the future career of a woman college graduate, your best bet is still teaching—42 percent of all professional women are teachers; more than one-third of all female students major in education. The reason for the overwhelming popularity of this choice is very important to understand. As Juanita Kreps notes in her book *Sex in the Marketplace:*

Are there monetary rewards in certain careers that more than offset the low pay? Is elementary school teaching appealing to women because they like the work itself, or because it is viewed as an extension of their feminine roles, or because it can be timed to enable women to perform their regular household duties? . . . It is not merely that their nonmarket work influences their decision as to whether to enter the labor force; the demands of home and family also influence *which* market jobs women are willing to take. Moreover the period of heaviest domestic responsibility occurs fairly early in a woman's work life, when she is likely to be forced to make some quite long-range decisions: whether to acquire further job training or additional formal education; how many children she will have; whether to continue working, at least part-time, during the child-bearing period. *In the face of demands on her time the young wife is likely to find that the scheduling of her job is the most important single consideration.*[2] [Emphasis added—LKH]

The scheduling of her job! Thus, although a man is able to enjoy the emotional benefits of a rich family life while at the same time pursuing a demanding career to its fullest, a woman who wants a family *and* a career must somehow find a way to juggle the two or else become a kind of superwoman, generally with the help of a stand-in surrogate worker in the home. The originally strong antimarriage, antifamily position of the women's movement was largely based on the realization of this bind. The sacrifice was too great.

The current debate is tempered by a further realization among some feminists that the abandonment of family life may also be too great a sacrifice for many women—in any case, why should it always have to be the woman who must sacrifice? The growing pressures for truly egalitarian marriages or cohabitational arrangements—sharing equally in both the home and work roles—grow out of this feeling. What is still obviously far away, however, is an occupational and economic structure—with shorter and more-flexible hours—that would make the model of shared roles possible for more than a relative handful of upper-middle-class professionals.

The rapid surge in the number of working women has *not* been primarily due to the women's movement. Inflation, taxes, and the rising cost of living have been far greater factors. The noble view of a job as a road to self-fulfillment and self-expression may indeed seem laughable to many working-class women forced out of their homes to take menial jobs to help ends meet. If she has a high-school education, she most likely will be involved in clerical or secretarial work. If she has less than a high-school education, clerical, factory, or service work is most probable. Only farm workers and domestic workers average less income than clerical workers.

Among these persons, work dissatisfaction is profound. It is in these kinds of jobs that the vast majority of women workers are still found. Compounding all the possible problems of boredom and routine that may face anyone involved in such work is the difficulty of coordinating family responsibilities that the upper-middle-class professional woman also faces. But while the professional woman often has surrogate child care and household help, plus a husband to some extent committed to the notion of equality in marriage, the working-class woman generally has neither. While the professional woman's husband is often pleased at his wife's status, male workers with low income and education register higher dissatisfaction with their own jobs when their wives work. This was the conclusion of Harold Sheppard and Neal Herrick in *Where Have All the Robots Gone?*

> The phenomenon of two or more earners in the working class family is not the unmixed blessing it is assumed to be. To put the above facts in a different form, only one-fourth of the single-earner Pennsylvania workers have the "blues" but among workers with additional earners in the family, discontent goes up to nearly two-fifths, 38 percent . . . Perhaps the belief that satisfaction among male workers should increase as family income is improved through the wife's employment is a projection on the part of the people who write about such problems. These people are primarily professional, upper middle class individuals. Perhaps these professional males feel no threat to themselves if their wives work. Indeed they may even feel proud and gain satisfaction if their wives are so engaged. And the wives themselves may work, not so much for the purpose of adding needed income to the family budget, but more for self-fulfillment . . .
>
> The working class context may be sharply different from the professional class situation, and the professional class individuals who write about worker discontent may . . . be making some wrong assumptions . . . It may be that these working class men don't feel that they've really succeeded if *all by themselves* they can't provide their families with the necessary income to pay for the level of living to which they aspire.[3]

Here, of course, the emphasis is on the job discontent of the man, not the woman. But the attitudes of husbands are far from unimportant. Among married, professional women, study after study has shown that the supportiveness and encouragement of their husbands have been crucial factors in their ability to succeed. Among working-class women, the impact of the husband's position toward their working is hardly less crucial. With less commitment to the idea of women's liberation generally found in working-class families, the husband's influence is bound to be even more pronounced. His dissatisfaction with his wife's working adds to her dissatisfaction—his tension adds to hers. Even if she finds she enjoys her job, even if it turns out to be a relief to have a break from the kitchen and kids, the very hassle of all that surrounds the job—rising early to get the house clean, the kids off to the sitter or school, then rushing home after work to pick them up and start dinner—may outweigh the satisfaction she derives. What to do?

The acute work discontent of so many women needs to be seen in all these terms—personal, social, economic. The meaning of a job to a woman changes as we go from class to class, primarily because of the differences in opportunities available (with motherhood being far more satisfying than many jobs), but also because of the differences in all the factors surrounding work from class to class—the availability of child care and household help, the attitude of the husband and other family members toward her working—all combine to make a woman glad or sorry to be gainfully employed.

One obvious answer to the discontent that appears to be growing is to make it possible for mothers *forced* to take jobs, including welfare mothers, to return to the home. If a woman—or a man—freely chooses to confine her labor to home and child care—and many do—it should be economically possible. In the 1950s we glorified domesticity for women; in the 1970s it is equally senseless to glorify the labor market. Whether 'tis nobler for a woman to dish out the ham-and-eggs-over-easy to her family at home or to a stranger at Schrafft's is hardly the issue women are struggling over. In either instance the content of the work is the same. In one instance the pay is low; in the other, non-existent. To make home and child care possible for those women who want to devote themselves to it full time, many people are now suggesting we find a way to pay for that work, through government subsidies, tax deductions, or other imaginative measures.

Overall, however, the trend toward two-earner families and working women does appear certain to continue and grow. So it is imperative to make sure that current efforts to open better job opportunities and to equalize pay for women do not fade away with the next economic slump, as many are predicting. The notion of eminent domain for the male breadwinner must finally be put to rest.

To make sure it happens, there is also a need to organize women in low-paying occupations into unions responsive to their needs. Although only 12 percent of women workers are currently unionized, there has recently been a flood of organizing among women working in large banks and insurance offices as well as throughout all levels of government. And it is the unions with large female memberships (teachers, service employees, and state, county, and municipal employees) that are now growing the fastest.

Indeed, slowly and unsurely something may be happening to the conservative labor movement—as well as the rest of the nation—regarding its attitudes toward women. Unions as well as corporations may now be sued under Title VII of the Civil Rights Act for discriminating against women, and several already have been. Many women union members appear to be going through their consciousness-raising period at conferences and discussion groups where women talk about the discrimination they face on the job and the double burdens they must carry as workers and as women. They are raising issues like child care and maternity leave (also paternity leave) with increased force.

Many unions now have women's caucuses. State federations of labor and county labor councils are for the first time starting to adopt resolutions that concern the rights of women. In the San Francisco Bay area a growing group of women from more than seventy unions have formed the first voluntary group of trade-union women specifically organized to "fight discrimination of women on the job, in unions, and in society." The organization is called Union WAGE (Women's Alliance to Gain Equality), and several groups modeled on it have begun to sprout in other areas of the country.

It was the women of Union WAGE who almost single-handedly made possible the first statewide women's conference of the California AFL-CIO. Indeed, it took a bitter floor fight at a state convention before the women were allowed to conduct it; the male trade-union leaders, while willing to make a few concessions to women, obviously did not want to see women seeking their rightful share of power within the male-dominated unions.

The conference, held in May 1973, was attended by nearly four hundred women from unions all over the state—an historic event. They discussed such topics as working women and the law, how to negotiate women's issues, how to organize the unemployed, how to move into leadership positions within the labor movement. Repeatedly, however, the subject of child care came to the fore. At one point a woman from the Newspaper Guild—a clerk, I believe—rose to voice her irritation about this.

"But what we've said is something else," answered a young woman with a long black braid flowing down her back. "We want women to become more active, to fight for more power. But right now women don't come to union meetings and there are concrete reasons why they don't. Most of the women I work with have to rush home and do all the work on their second jobs as housewives. If we want women to fight for the larger issues, we have to make it possible."

"Yes," said an older woman, a teacher, a mother, a wife, a trade unionist, a person, a veteran juggler of roles. "Yes to child-care centers. The time must come when we can say, 'Listen buddy, tonight it's your turn to start the dinner and take care of the house and the baby.' The first battle begins at home."

There are battles to win with unions, government, business, and education if women are ever to gain job equality; but for millions the first battle still begins at home. If the matter of work load is now an issue for negotiation on the job, then it should be no less an issue at home, where every working mother moonlights. If job rotation and restructuring are seen as answers to the endlessness and banality of so many work tasks, then the analysis applies with equal force in the nursery and kitchen. If classifying jobs by sex is no longer deemed lawful in business and government, then how can it be fitting at home if both persons also work in the labor market? If wages are still the *sine qua non* of participation in the labor market (and people with the lowest incomes have the lowest satisfaction), then the effect of not assigning an economic value to housework and child care must also be clear. If humanizing the workplace is really a vital issue on the social agenda today, then it is time to recognize that the home is also a place of work.

NOTES

1. *Work in America,* Report of a Special Task Force to the Secretary of Health, Education, and Welfare (Cambridge, Mass.: MIT Press, 1973), p. 58.
2. Juanita Kreps, *Sex in the Marketplace* (Baltimore: Johns Hopkins Univ. Press, 1971).
3. Harold L. Sheppard and Neal Q. Herrick, *Where Have All the Robots Gone?* (New York: Free Press, 1972).

Child Care at the Workplace

Stevanne Auerbach-Fink

Imagine, if you will, a company that cares very much about the employees who work for it, say a clothing manufacturer employing many female employees who have young preschool children. The company, after hearing about a few successful child-care centers, decides to launch such a program at its own facility. The employees of this plant in an industrial area in Southern California are mostly women and have been asked by the employer if they need child care. Their overwhelming response is "Yes!" The company chooses to act and creates, within a year, a beautiful and imaginative day-care center beside the factory. The new center wins immediate support and acclaim from the employees, who enthusiastically bring their children, forty of them, to the new facility. The place sparkles with toys, learning materials, bright and colorful walls, decorations, and sturdy outdoor play equipment. Each morning a well-qualified staff of teachers welcomes the children. The children go off to play happily with their new friends with a good-bye kiss from mother before she walks into the factory. Now her skills are enhanced by the security she feels about her child as well as her sense of well-being and increased motivation for the job. The employer has added caring to the workplace.

This is just one of a number of success stories about the business community's growing interest in providing for its staff in a very specific and exciting new way. Employers who have developed such programs are delighted with the results. They see an immediate return upon their investment. The turnover rate for female employees declines drastically, while motivation rises sharply. Company officials feel that such services produce dividends in excess of investment. For those employers who have decided to do a quality job with the service, the results are impressive. They find that attracting new employees is not as difficult as it may have once been. They find union grievances substantially reduced and the high cost of training and maintaining a skilled staff stabilized. The investment is costly at first, but so is any employee benefit. Few produce the remarkable results that child care can offer.

Employers have come to realize that young mothers wish to return to the labor market in rapidly growing numbers. Trained women want to maintain and improve their skills. Some want to bring economic benefits to their families. Others must work for financial reasons, due to separation or divorce and rapidly changing amounts of alimony and child support awarded to the parent maintaining custody. Still other women feel they should contribute their abilities and would be bored and restless if they stayed at home after a child is born. Whatever reason the mother may have for continuing work, child-care services are essential but hard to locate. Most communities still lack sufficient child care to meet the demand. Federal- or state-supported programs inadequately respond to economic, personal, or psychological needs. Demand exceeds the pace of government actions.

In many instances industry and business have responded instead. New York state offers a tax deduction to companies that provide child care. A growing number of businesses have seen the incentive and taken action. About two hundred across the country have established such services. Many of these are hospitals with an urgent need to maintain and recruit more nurses and aides for their operations. Their results compare favorably to those of business.

This is not the only approach, however; often employers contribute to a child-care program located at a reasonable distance from the plant and accessible to public transportation. Textile and telephone companies, hiring large numbers of female employees, often find it a problem to maintain a stable work force. One southern textile mill reported employing many hundreds of women, with a turnover rate close to 90 percent. After their child-care center opened, the rate fell to less than 5 percent. Absenteeism and lateness also declined. A nurse on duty provides care to mildly ill children, but a mother can visit her sick child periodically during the day. Without this service she and her child would have to stay home, resulting in financial loss to the family. At the center the child has quiet activities and plenty of attention and care.

Many companies that began such programs, however, did so for financial reasons, not for reasons relating to education or child development. Creating the right balance of education, play, health, and nutrition requires a sizable expenditure. Partial costs come from parents' fees, but much of the expense must be borne by the employer. The cost per child may range from six hundred to over twelve hundred dollars a year, depending upon the quality of the staff, the materials, and the equipment.

I attended the first Business and Industry Conference on Child Care, held in Chicago in 1971. This was the businessman's first opportunity to hear ideas presented systematically on the potential of child-care services. Many of them followed the examples set by the KLH company in Boston, which ran a pioneer program and an expensive one. Because of its experimental nature the federal government provided research support.

The idea of franchised child care also arose at this time, with several pioneers in this area presenting their plans and prototypes. The idea of franchising children's services like nursing homes or fried chicken appalled most professionals. A few of these programs appeared well thought out, certainly cost effective. In fact, the business aspects are certainly worth looking at more closely. Many publicly supported programs, including schools, are not always scrutinized closely or held accountable for their expenditures. These private franchisers pointed out substantial ways to save money and still produce good services. After they were initiated, however, many had little parent involvement, poorly qualified staff, and inadequate educational programs. Within two years very few of these franchised programs remained. One simply cannot profit from shoddy services to children.

Parent satisfaction is the key to the ultimate success of any educational experience. Instead of taking the franchise route, companies interested in starting child-care programs would do well to consult with specialists who know and understand how best to provide for the needs of children and their families and can at the same time establish programs of quality and repute. Several management groups have begun to work in this area to help companies plan, design, and operate child-care services. For instance, the Illinois Telephone Company consulted with the Erik Erickson Institute in Chicago. Instead of establishing one center, the Institute staff assisted the growth of day-care homes by providing a comprehensive training program. Creating this kind of service has increased the number of skilled child-care providers in the community. Also in Chicago, the Amalgamated Clothing Workers Child Care Center is a modern and well-designed facility, utilizing every inch of a long, narrow city lot; parents bring the child to the center and then go on to work. Amalgamated has also established similar programs in

Baltimore and at several Pennsylvania locations. Here too the manufacturing companies saw that the union had a good idea and were willing to support the expansion of the company-supported program. Employees without children are given other benefits.

Companies have also provided for child care by loaning money to potential child-care operators to establish new facilities and cover the costs of operation. Several companies, however, made some strategic mistakes as they ventured into child-care services; then, as a result of their losses, they decided that child care was not beneficial to them—an unfortunate conclusion. Chesapeake and Potomac Telephone Company of Washington, D.C., for instance, made a serious error by locating their center at a place inconvenient to many of the employees, and this in a city with all too few child-care programs. Unfortunately, they did not survey all of the employees to determine their residence and preference of location. The program was excellent, however, for those who were able to utilize it. The converted supermarket that housed the center was a model facility. However, from mistakes like these, management often concludes that child care will not work for them.

The cost of operating a child-care center may seriously impede the optimism of some employers at first. The location, size, qualifications of the staff, type of facility, and expenditures on materials and equipment determine overall costs. Some of the companies that have tried child-care centers have found that operating costs range from thirty to fifty dollars per week per child. Fees are usually commensurate with the parents' ability to pay, ranging from five dollars per week to thirty-seven dollars or more. For some parents these costs may be prohibitive. They must also consider the relative values of having the child near home, the transportation problems, and the kind of services offered.

Where the employer has encouraged parents to take an active role in planning and organizing the program, results have been positive. In addition to KLH, companies engaged in providing day care for their employees include several telephone companies (Ohio, Chicago, Washington, D.C.), Vanderbilt Shirt, Skyline Textiles, Joshua Tree, Mr. Apparel, Singer Sewing Machines, and Avco. The range of quality at these centers varies widely, and only time and employee satisfaction will determine the eventual effectiveness of the concept.

The employer who wants to provide a humanistic and valuable service should move cautiously, carefully surveying employee needs, as well as consulting specialists in the field to determine the most efficient and effective way to provide the service. Some may opt for company-based centers to utilize available space and ease transportation problems. Others will choose to support their employees through a voucher system, allowing a stipend for parents' choice of programs. Still others will support the establishment of a community-based program. No matter what type is planned, the company that responds to employee need through concern for their families, recognition of the value of early-childhood education, and interest in children will reap benefits well beyond the initial dollar investment. As Dr. Edward Zigler recently reported in *Day Care and Early Childhood* magazine: "Dollars alone may be critical in determining the quantity of day care, but not its quality . . . The need for day care is great, but the human resources available to deliver day care are not. What is needed in our nation, after the recognition that day care is the major problem facing American families, is a national plan in which we incrementally add day care resources at a rate commensurate with our country's ability to utilize these new resources in a manner that guarantees quality care." [1]

William L. Pierce of the Child Welfare League feels that a national licensing agency is needed to close any center that fails to meet the standards and guidelines established for quality care for children. He urges that the child come first and that the problem be solved by businessmen and educators working together. [2]

While I was a program specialist at the U.S. Office of Education, I saw the great need that hundreds of employees had for child care. That was in 1969, and I felt that in the nation's capital and at the center of the country's educational support system there should be concern for the daily plight of those employees who had young children. Since the availability of child care was meager, the idea took hold. It appeared easy at first to convince professional educators and administrators of the urgent need for child care and the benefits that could accrue from a model program, thereby humanizing the workplace, benefiting the children, setting an example for other large employers, and taking a leadership position in this growing field. A task easier said than done! Some institutions are not quite ready to practice what they preach, despite the potential benefits. For more than a year and a half we brought pressure to create such a space before the key people decided the idea was a good one and agreed to use an executive dining room and outdoor play area adjacent to the employees' cafeteria for the site. Now employees can eat their lunch and watch their children at play. The multiple levels in the interior space make much out of a relatively small area. Platforms for climbing and crawling under make the space delightful to small children.

Ronald Haase, a reporter, has asked: "What better place to set an example than in the very headquarters where the nation's policies in early education are formulated?" [3] As I reported to a congressional committee on the need for child care for federal employees, I envisioned this model being adopted by federal offices in Washington, in the other ten federal regions, by state and city governments, on Capitol Hill, and wherever else public employers might not have conceived such a service. The investment has proved itself sound where it was handled well. Benefits are great for both employers and staff. But the federal government has responded very slowly. The center established at the National Institutes of Health, following the original example of the Office of Education and the U.S. Department of Labor, has run into financial difficulty. All public employers, however, would do well to study child-care expansion carefully. Government, to be effective, must be willing to respond to all human elements, especially children. In the future, women and the nation will demand child care as a humanistic imperative.

Models for child care have spread to colleges, where married or single-parent students in housing near campus find the service essential if they are to complete their education. California universities have encouraged the development of ten such programs over the past few years, and programs in other regions have also grown. Unfortunately, college administrations often do not see the advantages of supporting such programs to benefit both employees and students. Nor have high-school officials perceived such benefits. A few pilot programs involving the care of infants of college and high-school students reveal positive results to both student mothers and infants. The findings of Jerome Bruner at Harvard and Betty Caldwell at the University of Arkansas have repeatedly shown the value of early stimulation on the mental growth and well-being of the young child.

Certainly the concept of child care at the workplace is not new. The Kaiser shipbuilding plant developed centers and programs for its employees throughout World War II. In fact, according to Dr. James Hymes, director of the Kaiser program, they also offered tired families supper at the centers or dinner to take home.

Ideas abound for humanizing the workplace. What better way to provide for the well-being of the parent-employee or student than to offer child-care services? If these programs are well conceived and not profit motivated, they can be a boon. If the company considers all of the elements needed for a successful program, involves the parents in the planning and operation, hires a well-qualified and capable staff, and makes the program accessible and advantageous to the employees, the concept will grow and flourish. If not, the point for child care will be lost. My feeling is that government at any level cannot or will not keep pace with public demand. Employers concerned about the problem may offer a good alternative to a slowly evolving public policy.

Business and industry often take the leadership in those matters where government responds so slowly.

During the White House Conference on Children I was the government consultant on all aspects of the day-care issue. Child care was a number-one issue and became the highest priority of the conference. Another concept ran a close second, namely, bringing the world of work into the lives of children and children into the world of work, a concept articulated by Urie Bronfenbrenner.

One illustration of this was reflected in the experience of the Detroit *Free Press*. A film was shown at the White House Conference that depicted young elementary schoolchildren spending a regular school week visiting the newspaper staff to learn the many facets of newspaper work. The children asked to be assigned to various jobs, and the staff responded by adopting them and sharing all they could about their work lives. The children were delighted to learn about the inner workings of the newspaper, how it is prepared, printed, and produced. Both they and the *Free Press* employees benefited from the educational experience. Workers found the children's inquiries stimulating and satisfying, finding joy in answering their many questions and in providing them with papers to read and assignments to complete. This proved to be an expansion of classroom activities beyond all imagination. The children learned firsthand the meaning of the world of work. This sort of experience is different from the typical plant tour, however educational such a field trip may be. Far better for the child to explore the inner workings of a place of work to gain skills and understanding unavailable from books. Such opportunities are plentiful in factories, public utilities, stores, and other businesses.

Child care and exploration of the world of work are but two of the ways that business can respond to human needs. Still others emerge. For example, in considering some urgent issues of family life-styles, such as having sufficient time to interact and pursue common interests together as a family constellation, employers might do well to consider *increasing* part-time-employment opportunities. If each parent could work part of the day to meet their economic obligations, they would have more time to spend with their children and each other. This plan might also alleviate stress and unemployment, and increase individual incentives. Part-time employment would be particularly effective in the fields of education, health, and many other skilled and moderately skilled jobs. Also one might *expand* the use of company facilities for adult education during lunch hours and after work to increase job-related skills and other educational opportunities for employees. Many adult educators would surely be willing to extend their programs to business places if employers and employees were willing to cooperate in expanding these frontiers.

Providing opportunities for education, direct employee service, and public service are some of the ways business can become more responsive to the society. As we look at the drudgery of so many jobs, we realize that people who maintain production output need concurrent inner refreshment. Providing music, lounge areas, places to relax and talk is another way employers can respond to psychological and social needs. The possibilities are endless for employers who care. But we should begin with children; education and care for the young are the immediate first steps on the long road toward making the United States the human-oriented society it can and should be.

NOTES

1. Edward Zigler in an article in *Day Care and Early Childhood*, 1, No. 1 (Sept. 1973), pp. 114-120.
2. William L. Pierce in an article in *Day Care and Early Childhood*, 1, No. 1 (Sept. 1973), pp. 114-120.
3. *Ibid.*

Toward a Greater Flexibility

Richard J. Schonberger

Everyone who has ever worked knows, either consciously or unconsciously, that jobs are restrictive and confining—the counterculture would say "oppressive." The great expansion in opportunities for personal choice during maturation comes to an abrupt halt when one takes his or her first job. During one's career as a jobholder the narrow availability of options on the job is in stark contrast to the wide range off the job. This situation has existed for a very long time.

In the 1920s, plentiful jobs, trade-union activity, the Hawthorne studies, and other developments led to considerable dissatisfaction with the inhumanities of the workplace and to pressures for significant changes. The changes that have arisen from these dissatisfactions have been of a predictable type. In keeping with the traditional melting-pot mentality, our lawmakers, our business and labor leaders, and our sociologists have determined what is best for all, and the results have been imposed on all.

Thus, to correct the "oppressions" of the workplace, wage-and-hour and union-shop laws have been passed. And progressive firms provide coffee breaks and clean-up time; group health, life, and accident insurance programs; recreation and retirement plans; and collective bargaining for collective needs.

This emphasis on collectiveness was directly supportive of a melting-

Source: This article appeared in The Humanist, September-October 1973.

pot value system. But, as many have recently pointed out, that value system is dying. Keith Davis, in a paper on social responsibilities, presented to the 1970 meeting of the Academy of Management, pointed out that the emergent norm is "social pluralism," which is characterized by groupism and individualism, instead of collectiveness. In popular parlance, this means "doing your own thing."

The question is: Will the nation's employers respond to the change in values by relaxing rigidities in the workplace? Or will they react negatively, thus provoking radical or revolutionary reaction in an attempt to dismantle the organizational structures that impose the oppressions? My own optimistic belief is in the former. Indeed I believe that the trend toward greater flexibility has begun and cannot be stopped. It is being fueled not only by outward social pressures—especially from feminists, young people, senior citizens, and black, Chicano, and other ethnic coalitions—but also by the promise of economic advantages for firms willing to change.

Following are ten specific kinds of change that we might expect to see increasingly in the decade ahead, along with the rationale for each.

1. *Work-hour options.* If we are interested at all in improving the lot of our working citizenry, the place to start should be in the area of working hours. It is always difficult and sometimes impossible to make the work itself palatable, but it is usually relatively easy and inexpensive to offer work-time options that can do much to improve the quality of life *off* the job. The employee who has some say about his or her working hours may better coordinate his or her work with the time schedules of family and friends, recreational outlets, place of worship, shopping and banking facilities, educational centers, and commuter traffic patterns.

Riva Poor's book, *Four Days, Forty Hours,* nearly became a best seller merely by extolling a four-day, instead of the usual five-day, forty-hour week. This is merely an exchange of one kind of oppression for another. The real need is for personal options—that is, options that meet individual rather than collective needs.

Permanent part-time jobs (as opposed to occasional part-time work) is another option. My research indicates that a large number of housewives desire but are unable to find permanent part-day employment.[1] In recognition of this problem, employment agencies specializing in placing women in permanent part-time positions have sprung up in New York, Washington, and Philadelphia. But it is not only women who are interested in less-than-full-time work.

Flexitime, which is popular in Switzerland, Germany, and some other European countries, is another option. Under flexitime an employee may vary the numbers of hours he works per day as long as he averages forty hours per week (or somewhat more in European firms). Usually there is a five- or six-hour core in the middle of the day during which all employees are expected to be present. Some initial evidence indicates higher productivity and lower turnover and absenteeism in firms on flexitime. A salutary fringe benefit of flexitime is that many employees elect to avoid rush hours, thereby decreasing peak traffic loads in their communities. (The alternative in a growing number of cities, Toronto for one, is to impose staggered working hours on major employers in order to lessen the surges in usage of public facilities.)

It is a cruel irony that compulsory overtime is most common in the types of work that are the most tedious and boring, such as in automobile assembly. It is no wonder that absenteeism in the auto industry is often highest on weekends among workers called upon for overtime, time-and-a-half wages notwithstanding. There is a need for an amendment to our Wage and Hour Law to restrict compulsory overtime to a certain number of weeks or months per year, per employee.

2. *A share of fringe benefits for part-time employees.* Part-time employees are commonly denied most of the perquisites of employment—for example, vacation and sick time, retirement, and group-insurance benefits—that are enjoyed by the full-time staff. As Kirsten Amundsen observed in *The Silenced Majority: Women and American Democracy,* astute employers have found that they can avoid costly fringe benefits by maintaining "a skeleton crew of prime full-time workers, eliminating the young, the old, and the inexperienced women, and then to hire a supplemental crew of part-time workers, . . . a floating crew of experienced workers at cheap rates." Lionel Tiger, the Rutgers anthropologist, in discussing women part-time workers, states that "habit, inertia, [and] the reluctance to face complexity" stand in the way of offering benefits in proportion to contribution. [See also Jack Russell's article on pp. 151-155.]

3. *Child care as a fringe benefit.* The Nixon administration initially favored day-care legislation, but a bill that passed in Congress proved too expensive. Perhaps a more acceptable solution, which has been advocated by Senators Percy and Javits, is the employer-furnished day-care center. Although common in several European countries, especially France, child care as a fringe benefit is rare in this country. The exception, as noted in a Department of Labor survey, is the hospital industry: ninety-eight American hospitals had their own day-care centers in 1970. The employer-furnished center has, for the parent, a great advantage over the centrally located, public center—the advantage of convenience. The evidence thus far is limited, but this advantage to the parent seems to have corollary advantages to the

employer, such as higher employee productivity and less absentee-ism. [2] [See also Stevanne Auerbach-Fink's article on pp. 215-222.]

4. *Nonlinear or "team" approaches to assembly.* The Department of Health, Education, and Welfare task force that authored *Work in America* devoted numerous pages to discussion of current experiments in redesigning assembly-line work around a team concept. In the auto industry, Volvo and Saab have taken the lead in such experimentation. But the most far-reaching attempt to make assembly work more flex-ible is in General Foods' Pet Food plant in Topeka, Kansas. [See Robert Schrank's study on pp. 119-140.]

Such work designs are long overdue and likely to increase rapidly in industrial firms. Unfortunately there is some evidence of a disturbing countertrend in the services sector. For example, the enormously suc-cessful McDonald's chain has always employed a rather flexible non-linear work design. Socially interactive teams of employees have pro-duced the eleven billion hamburgers that it has sold. Burger King burgers, on the other hand, are produced in a linear machine-paced process involving just two machine tenders. The highly efficient machine runs the workers rather than the other way around, but the profit margin appears to be considerably higher on a Burger King burger than a McDonald's burger. The authors of *Work in America* called Taylorism—the use of scientific but often depersonalized work design—anachronistic. But in the services sector the Tayloristic era appears to be just beginning.

5. *Retirement based on functional rather than chronological age.* This was the recommendation of the 1971 White House Conference on Aging. Although primarily aimed at the plight of healthy and capable elderly citizens who do not want to retire, this suggestion benefits the employer and the economy. Why have a system that retains employees who have lost their desire or ability and that retires others, somewhat older, who are still able and willing?

6. *Home work, sabbatical leave, and summer-off options.* Chris Argyris has convincingly argued that organizations hire mature adults but then discourage mature, responsible behavior. A case in point: We allow, indeed require, teen-age students to study extensively at home, but employees (except at higher managerial levels) are expected to do all their work on the premises. The working mother especially would welcome a policy that permits occasional home work. And there are plenty of engineers, draftsmen, programmers, and writers who could do a large amount of their work at home as well as at the office. Instead, we have rigid policies that encourage abuses of sick leave and sudden, unplanned absences.

Frederick W. Taylor discovered decades ago that occasional short rest breaks—today institutionalized as the coffee break—have positive effects on short-run productivity. But the coffee break is not an adequate antidote—nor is the two- or three-week vacation—for the more persistent forms of weariness that many workers experience. Expanded and longer-term options are needed: the sabbatical, perhaps, for the employee with considerable time in service; or the summer-off option for the parent (wife or husband) who might like to stay home when school-age children are at home. The latter is practical in that summer replacements—high-school and college students—are readily available.

7. *Extraordinary job-rotation options.* Progressive firms have long recognized the values of job rotation for career development and, secondarily, for establishing interpersonal ties and promoting understanding. (Regarding the latter, the Chinese have a saying: "If you know how to eat rice, learn how to grow it.") Job rotation could, additionally, serve as one more option for renewal and recovery when an employee feels unable to bear his usual workday routine. Thus, the mentally fatigued white-collar worker might elect to pack crates or run a fork lift for a while; and a bored production-line worker might work with a landscape or janitorial crew for a time. Where such temporary assignments fail to rejuvenate, policies should permit or encourage a more permanent type of job rotation, namely, a second career. As it stands today, career patterns, employment policies, and seniority systems have the negative effect of keeping dissatisfied employees in an unsuitable occupation, and both the employee and the employer are the losers.

8. *Supply and demand as a basis for pay rates.* As Kenneth Boulding has maintained, good and evil tend to occur together in economic and social systems. The good of minimum-wage laws is apparent. The evil is that they tend to keep certain kinds of people—the unskilled and inexperienced, those of the "wrong" sex or race, and those who are too young or old—from getting jobs. Our congressional leaders periodically review bills to modify the laws to permit lower pay for teen-age trainees, as is the case in Japan and certain European countries. This idea could be extended to include the elderly and the untrained and inexperienced of any age. A unique variation of this idea would be to provide special pay options for those who consider work to be a secondary pursuit in life, as do some housewives or "househusbands." Under such a plan employees could periodically be offered the opportunity to choose *career status* with high pay but commensurate high responsibilities and performance standards or *job status* with lower pay and lower responsibilities and performance standards.

9. *Relaxation of no-nepotism policies.* Widespread rules against

nepotism, like minimum-wage laws and job evaluation, are bad only in that they are overly rigid or restrictive. Some control over the hiring of relatives is desirable. But we should soften those rules that result in injustices such as that which confronted Dr. Harry F. Harlow and his talented partner, the late Mrs. Harlow, at the University of Wisconsin. A no-nepotism rule prevented them, after their marriage, from both holding professorships in the Department of Psychology. The University of Wisconsin has relaxed the rule since then.

10. *Transportation services for employees.* A study by the Stanford Research Institute indicates that inadequate transportation significantly hampers job hunting by the unemployed. Employer-furnished transportation could alleviate this problem, as well as the related problem of alleged undependability of minority-group employees. This idea relates to some of the previously mentioned options. For example, as an alternative to providing child care on the premises, an employer could help to get employees' children to and from community centers; and if an employer is firmly against hiring two or more members of the same family, perhaps that employer could help to unsnarl family transportation difficulties resulting from family members having to go in different directions to different firms.

These ten suggestions are not, for the most part, startling or radical. Rather, they are concerned with relaxing rigid practices. Conventional wisdom has become outmoded, and the business firm that resists societal trends may run into difficulties in hiring new people and difficulties in retaining and satisfying the old. Conversely, firms that are willing to become more flexible may find broader labor markets from which to choose better employees.

It is no accident that flexitime sprang up in Germany and that child care as a fringe benefit is found in this country only in the hospital industry. The reasons are the chronic labor shortage in Germany and the chronic shortage of nurses in hospitals. Employers do adopt innovative policies that are attractive to employees if there is necessity or competitve pressure to do so. Once innovations are shown to work, inertia and resistance to change wane and competitive pressures to follow the leaders grow. Some of these ten items are still experimental, but the time is ripe for all of them to be sought by prospective employees. The nation's employers will have to meet the demand.

Although flexible working conditions can be difficult to administer, there may well be compensating benefits, such as more-satisfied and perhaps more-productive employees. As a final point: In today's affluent and abundant society—some would say overabundant—we can afford to tamper with that which is traditional. Indeed, it might better be said that we can ill afford not to.

NOTES

1. See "Ten Million U.S. Housewives Want To Work," *Labor Law Journal*, June 1970.
2. See "Day Care Services: Industry's Involvement," *Women's Bureau Bulletin*, 296, p. 13.

For a Worker-Exchange Program

Robert Schrank

I have sponsored and participated in a number of conferences on work-place problems. Generally, those participating in these conferences are industrial engineers, academics, psychologists, sociologists, econo-mists, some corporation people, and a few union representatives. Dis-cussions ranged over various issues and solutions. These conferences left me with an uncomfortable feeling because we were discussing the lives of people who were never present. If we had been primarily con-cerned with the university as a workplace, then the participants would certainly have had some firsthand knowledge. But there have been a lot of papers and discussion on what is wrong with places where *others* work! While the absence of "the people we are concerned about" was often mentioned by those present at the conferences, there seemed to be a kind of hopelessness about ever hearing from the workers them-selves. This lack of representation was most dramatically demonstrated by the absence of women. Since women make up about 40 percent of the work force, their collective and individual views should be heard.

I do not want to suggest a conspiracy among these professionals, who are "expert" on some phases of workplace organization, but a rather exclusive group does show up at these meetings. However, they need support from a much wider group. Each expert is convinced that he has at least part of the solution to workplace alienation. I do not

Source: This article appeared in *The Humanist*, September-October 1973.

know whether each one does or does not. That is not the issue. The critical ingredient in consideration of workplace change is representation of *the people who work there*. I believe that no one else has enough knowledge about another's desires to decide the "best" way to organize his or her workplace.

Some remarkable generalizations have been made about people's needs at work. They include the need for autonomy, the need to participate in decision making, the need for immediate feedback, the need to self-actualize, and the need to grow. Defining some of these needs is difficult inasmuch as they tend to be relative. Also, the experience of others confirms what I learned in my factory experience: one worker's needs are not necessarily another's. Some people *like* boring, repetitive jobs. I do not know how many jobs there are in which people can be both creative and self-actualizing. I suspect very few. I hasten to add that a lot of jobs could be made more human, more interesting, and less monotonous. To achieve this, however, there should be a clear input from people doing the jobs, because one man's monotony may be another's music.

There are some real problems with the notion of the workers' participation in the reorganization of their own workplaces. Workers often see no other way of doing what they are doing; their frame of reference may be very limited. They tend to accept what exists and believe that management has some special wisdom about how to build the business and operate it. Workers are seldom, if ever, encouraged to consider alternative types of organization. The fact is that organization of the workplace is, as always, a management prerogative. Workers, therefore, consider it a management responsibility.

Workers need to be drawn into the deliberations, planning, and modifications in workplace organization. To participate intelligently, they need to come to terms with the concept of workplace organization, the possible alternatives, their own goals of accomplishment, and the method of obtaining these. In a sense, what is needed, at least for openers, is consciousness raising about workplace problems to encourage workers in the same way that women first began to ask questions about their roles in society. Without such participation and consciousness raising, there is a real danger that solving the problems of the workplace could become yet another example of manipulation of people by "experts."

ONE SOLUTION: WORKER EXCHANGE

The notion of a worker-exchange program grew out of asking the following questions: Could we begin to get some worker participation in workplace reorganization discussions if workers had an opportunity to enlarge their frame of reference? Would sending workers to see different organizations change their perspectives and thus help them to think about improving their own workplace situations? Would not the insights of the professionals working in this field be greatly enhanced by the ability to get feedback from workers as to how they perceive a variety of workplace reorganization schemes?

There have been many exchange programs, Fulbrights, Guggenheims, and so forth, mostly for academics, students, artists, and government officials. Such programs are designed to enhance both the knowledge of the individual participant and the field in which he or she practices. So why not a worker-exchange program to enlighten the individual participant as well as advance our knowledge in the field of workplace problems?

When we first began to talk about the worker-exchange idea, it occurred to me that the elitist character of the work-life issue had to be changed if workers were to develop confidence in making workplace changes. It also occurred to me that consulting the industrial engineer, psychologist, sociologist, and so forth, might recall to workers the old time-and-motion man, who was anathema to them. This might create even more suspicions. I hasten to add that most persons involved in discussions about the quality of work life represent the highest humanitarian commitment. Yet that commitment alone, without worker participation, seems to have a sterile quality. It was therefore gratifying to receive such a positive response when the worker-exchange idea was raised.

In a number of workplaces around the United States and Europe experiments in reorganization are being made. They vary in objectives, but all contain the goal of increased job satisfaction. There have been suggestions that intensive case studies of these experiments be undertaken to encourage others to do likewise. The worker-exchange program is another way of doing a case study. It permits workers within an industry to work in a plant with a new type of work structure and to record their perceptions of what the new plant experience is about. It can take place within one country or among several countries. The exchange program is an attempt to increase workers' knowledge about workplace organization.

Objections to an exchange program are based on a fear that the impact of a new environment would distort perceptions; being away from old problems may make the world appear as though seen through rose-colored glasses. There are also possible negative results from experiencing different customs in strange places. These problems may exist; yet I believe they can be taken into account, and their effects, if not sifted out, at least minimized. A key person in the exchange program is the reporter. His job is to sort out, with the members of the exchange group, their perceptions of what is going on in the workplace, how it compares with their home organization, and the various alternatives available. It is essentially an experiential learning process. The recorder simply puts down the thoughts, reactions, and behavior of the exchange group.

The exchange program must start in one or two places as an experiment. We need to learn how it can be made to work. Management may be resistant, seeing the program as an intrusion, but I doubt whether this reaction will be universal. My hunch is that there will be enough companies interested in the employees' perceptions of the workplace to make such exchanges possible.

HOW THE WORKER-EXCHANGE PROGRAM MIGHT WORK

Einar Thorsrud, of Norway, who has been a leader in workplace reorganization, suggests as a model workplace a reorganized Norwegian paper mill. A group of people from the United States recently visited the mill and learned about all the various workplace changes, responsibilities, and functions. It all sounded plausible and interesting. But making a judgment as to whether it was better or worse than some other arrangement required a paper-mill frame of reference, which no one in the group had.

A group of paper-mill workers from Maine or Louisiana would have provided such a frame of reference. A group of ten workers from a paper mill in the United States could go to work in the reorganized Norwegian paper mill for a period of two to three weeks. A group of ten Norwegian workers could go to work in an American paper mill for the same period of time. Each group would have its coordinator-recorder. Workers may not be inclined to write, but most surely can talk! (Studs Terkel in *Working* has taught us something about tape-recording people's thoughts and then transcribing, editing, and publishing them.)

The recorder's job would be to record the reactions of the group to the daily happenings in the new workplace. These reactions could then be published as pamphlets, articles, and books and distributed widely among workers to give them a sense of alternative workplace organizations. Other media could also be used, giving the exchange workers a voice in the discussion of alternatives in workplace organization. They would constitute a new input into the issues on workplace problems being debated.

Some questions have been raised about who would go. Participants from the plants should include workers in leadership positions, union officials, and others who are concerned and articulate about workplace problems. In unionized plants, cooperation of the union is essential, lest the program become a threat to union officials.

Once agreements have been obtained from companies willing to participate (some suggest this as a major problem because of fear of industrial spying) and the selection of exchange workers has been completed, there would be two or three days of orientation. This would be a period of sensitizing the workers and instructing them about where they are going, the purposes of the experiment, and the differences they will encounter in organizational structure. Meetings would continue during the exchange, culminating in a series of concluding discussions when the group returns home. Where there is a pay differential, the disadvantaged exchange worker would be reimbursed.

A number of workplace experiments are taking place in the United States and Canada. It has been suggested that exchanges between those workplaces can be as useful as the European exchange. I agree. The European exchange is suggested because the experiments there are more dramatic and widespread. There is no reason we could not try it within one country or between two similar countries. The issues do not stop at national boundaries. Furthermore, though the issues are of primary concern to the highly industrial nations, the Third World countries are quite concerned about ways to avoid or solve such thorny problems.

The program should start with a pilot group to test some of the ideas and to develop a group organizational format, and then expand to include a variety of industries. Government workers for instance, should be given an opportunity to see not only similar workplaces in other countries but also similar government bodies, such as city councils, boards of supervisors, school boards, and other institutions.

The product of the exchange should be a body of literature that sets forth the workers' views of what workplaces should be like. To accomplish this, a multimedia approach may be the best way to capture the thoughts, responses, and general reactions of the exchange groups to new workplace experiences. These reactions could be made into a series of booklets, audio cassettes, and video programs on different workplaces.

A series of conferences could be held when the exchange workers return, to give them an opportunity to talk about their experiences. Although some questions have been asked regarding "expectation raising," it is difficult to predict how workers will perceive the experiments. I am not sure that it matters. The key element is participation. We may get surprises and we may not. But, if we are committed to participation, that is the chance we take.

WHAT NEEDS TO BE DONE?

The worker-exchange program, if it "flies" well, will need a home. It needs a neutral place. That means a public institution, such as a labor institute in a public university. A place that has experience in developing materials for workers is preferable. A number of places around the country may be interested.

The next problem is: what industry and what companies? There are paper-manufacturing companies in the United States and Norway that are interested in workplace organization. There are also American and Canadian auto-parts and aluminum-ingot manufacturing companies that might be interested. Upon agreement by the companies, the problems of housing, transportation, pay scales, group recorder, and so forth become live problems.

Recruiting must be done carefully for the exchange programs. The competition at first will no doubt be keen; therefore, it is important to define the program's objectives. The recorder-coordinator should be "on board" when the recruiting is under way to make sure that everyone is vibrating on the same tone scale.

Prior to leaving for the new work area, the exchange group could spend two or three days in orientation. The object would be to learn about workplace issues, be sensitized as to what to look for, and do some role-playing about what is ahead to try to decrease culture shock. Orientation would be generally concerned with expectations, both great and small.

Let us assume the exchange is in effect. The workers meet at night to talk about how the new workplace looks to them. Questions arise. How is it organized? Who gives orders and who receives them? How are orders given? How do the physical surroundings affect the worker? How are health and safety rules enforced? Do people work harder than in the home plant?

After a time a different set of questions may emerge. Is work under this arrangement harder or easier? Why? Are there other ways to run this plant? Is the plant at home more or less efficient than this one? Which workplace is more tiring? How could the plant at home be organized differently?

These questions are only lead-ins. The exchange worker will have to be encouraged to talk both in specific terms and in the broadest general way about how he perceives the workplace. The recorder might hold group and individual sessions to assure that individuals do not get lost in the group.

Once the recorder has transcribed the notes and tapes, he would ask the group to respond to them. This type of feedback assures that what is recorded is an accurate reflection of what people have said.

When the exchange group ends its stay in the guest plant and returns home, there might be a day or two of feedback, preferably after the participants have been home for a while. These sessions would "check out" reactions from the perspective of the home environment. There might also be some sessions between workers in the home plant and exchange workers, to see what things remain strongest in the latter's recall.

Hopefully, this experience, carefully recorded and edited, would be available to all persons interested in workplace problems. It could be used as educational material in schools, labor newspapers, and seminars. The material would start a library of ideas and opinions of workers about workplaces. It could prove to be a most useful source of information for workers considering the quality of their work life.

The Virtues of Wastefulness: Possibility or Myth?

Howard B. Radest

A journey through the workplace tells us that the crisis of industrialism is moral and not technical. "Efficiency" and "quantifiability" are loaded with moral assumptions. However, these are ignored as we try to treat industrial society operationally. So, while we find ferment around the concepts of job enrichment, humanizing the workplace, and worker participation, we are still caught in the deterministic assumptions of atomism and marketing. Thereby, we are driven to hopelessness; for if these are in the nature of things, the dissatisfactions of our dissatisfied society are unavoidable.

An alternative appears when we look anew at work and play. We construct of class of "parasites" by our inhumane policies toward people in trouble, on welfare, or unemployed. Dismayed by our own uselessness, such parasites serve to relieve our anxieties. The young, the old, the black, the poor—the list of dependents grows very numerous. At the same time, those who are "free" enough to reject the obligations of society and contrary enough to dispense with industrial virtues become objects of envy. Play is thus surrounded by bitterness, and work by anger.

Under the rule of the market, the antagonism of work and play leads ultimately to a deterioration of both. When we think of work as merely instrumental, and play as its reward, we demean the former as labor and trivialize the latter. But they need not be enemies. Humanized work is really a form of playfulness; play when directed to worthy ends has all the features of workmanship. This suggestion may seem like idle foolishness, or worse, mere moralism. After all, philosophers "never have to meet payrolls," and theorists notoriously ignore the realities of earning a living, fighting with the boss, going on strike, or signing in at the unemployment office. The rule seems unchallengeable: "necessities" must be earned, and play is only an afterthought. But it is precisely the practical and moral connections among wealth, work, and play that must be challenged. What would happen if these connections were reconstructed?

We really try to avoid this radical question. Guaranteeing the "right to a job" so that everyone can "earn a living" evades it, as do most suggestions motivated by a sense of justice. Basically, these only universalize surrender to a life of labor. Still infected by market assumptions, they are rightly resented by the victims of the conscientious. Moreover, such guarantees involve us today in the processes of job creation. A make-work society results in demeaning both work and worker. It is not sufficient merely to adopt a principle of social justice. A just society could, after all, still be a society of clients. We could be politically free, economically cared for, and still be unhappy as before. If the dissatisfactions of industrial society tell us anything, it is that there is an irresistible demand for self-definition and self-determination. That being so, amelioration—radical or reformist—cannot meet the problem. We must still attend to how and what we do, not to the perquisites that attach to these improvements or to their modes of distribution.

Remove the "bribe of bread," said Bernard Shaw in *Major Barbara*. Common sense recoils: people would not work; necessities would be neglected; sloth would become epidemic; dust would fill the streets; production would grind to a halt. But this, in fact, comes very close to describing exactly what is happening today in our make-work society. Common sense, ignoring experience, uncritically echoes the doctrine of lazy and evil man. But it is blind to the facts of modern life: the failure of the bribe.

We have evidence enough to tell us that human beings are not, by preference, lotus-eaters. True, within systemic industrialism, with its policy of human redundancy, routine and slipshod performance is the rule. But, on the fringes and usually in privacy, interesting and significant work is still being done. The search for a meaningful hobby, the fascinations of research, the do-it-yourself puttering around the house, the nurture of gardens amid pitifully small specks of greenery are signals of what we are about when released from the "rule" that connects wealth and work. Play, even the isolated private play that modern society permits, is the sign of the human being *at work*.

Under industrial conditions, which convert the worker into an adjunct mechanism, we *labor* but we do not really *work*. The difference is not just semantic. A mean and error-filled view of human beings narrows motivation to the paycheck. And truly, industrial labor needs the bribe. But, we *work* because we enjoy it. We like making things; we want to be useful; we want to come in touch with others; we want to test our capacities. When we examine energetic people under conditions of freedom, we find them very busy indeed and not only with trivia or in momentary bursts of attention. The corruption of our natural propensity for productivity—in which play and work come very close to each other—is the curse of industrial labor and, we suspect, the reason for industrialism's contradiction: its potency and its evident inadequacy. Yet, even under industrial conditions, we can find people at work—but not in the work space at all.

Is the idea of separating work and wealth only a pipe dream? Their connection was a response to a situation of scarcity. With too little to go around, there was a certain crude wisdom in leaving it to individual and tribal energies to determine distribution. If many fell by the wayside, at least this process provided a rough mechanism for parceling out the goods that existed. Even the first stage of communism was to be guided by the motto: from each according to his ability, to each according to his *work*. Capitalistic competition was not, therefore, the only villain of the piece.

The promise of systemic industrialism, however, is that neither a mood of scarcity nor the competitiveness that it evokes is needed any longer. We perpetuate the habits of the past, but we live under a different human condition that makes them irrelevant and, when perpetuated, morally obnoxious. Starvation in the presence of farm surplus is not only stupid but evil. And when overproduction is seen as a recurring problem, then only in the most elliptical fashion can we claim that we are living under traditional scarcities. In short, principle and possibility could at last come together under systemic industrialism, although we have not yet grasped that fact.

II

We must attend to what a history of poverty has done to us. A psychology of scarcity permeates our lives despite brave talk of affluence. Futurists settle for extending current practices, with correction of manifest mistakes, envisioning a technologized utopia suitable to ideal machinery but not to human beings. Managers and engineers become reformers, to be sure, but within a marketing frame of reference. Poets turn from epic and social themes to intimacy. We tend—beyond redress of obvious past injustices—to put before ourselves a compulsive and shared voraciousness as our ideal vision of the future.

It seems almost impossible to break free of history's burden after conditions of scarcity began to vanish. Our imaginations remain impoverished long after our bodies are fed. Often, the best we can do is to dream of an era when free time outweighs coerced time, as when "working" hours are reduced. But the content and quality of that free time is ignored. Our vision of the future is restricted, pathetically, to an ever expanding availability of goodies. And, when the realization hits us that these are finite, pessimism about the human future is the only logical outcome.

The correction of a psychology of scarcity can be found by reconceiving work and play. Common sense demands that work be attached to necessity and play to freedom. Only as our needs are taken care of can we afford to play. Ironically, this puts play and morality both into the same never-never land. When life was a brute struggle for survival, there was some justification for this division. To the human being, hungry, cold, and exhausted, a life of play was an idle and insulting dream. He did find time, however, to adorn his hut or cave, sing songs, and dance dances—but such activities were generally restricted to the ceremonial. Looking toward a privileged few, or to the gods, he might find hints of a life of leisure forever denied him. His own play, in periodic holidays, had the intensity of orgy. Compressed into his brief release was all the energy held in check during long days and months of drudgery. Unlike the leisured few, the play of most men was not so much a rich experience as a form of explosion. The ills of play—narcosis, drunkenness, and violence—were its norms. The contest was a refined form of battle; the Saturday night binge, a form of escape. At its best, when organized as religious ritual, play served to deny daily life here and now.

A pattern of drudgery and release is perpetuated long after the situation has changed. So we have a society where wealth is confined by the usages of poverty. Habituated to a demeaning labor and an equally demeaning recreation by generations of scarcity, we extend the pattern. Systemic industrialism does not realize its possibilities at all. Instead, the capacities it affords—economic, technical, and political—are crippled by the weight of a presumed necessity. Luxury becomes consumerism and free time becomes only an extended break from coercion. Since the real situation has changed, however, drudgery becomes an affront and recreation a dissatisfying escapism.

Society is still caught in restrictions that go by the traditional name of necessity. We tend to think of it as a natural law. Of course, there remain certain organic minimums with respect to food, shelter, and clothing. By moving beyond these to the need to be loved, the need for sensate experience, or the need to participate, modern man really extends choice and minimizes necessity without realizing it. "Need" becomes a misleading term. And when we move from social and generational definitions of "need" to what people say about themselves, the variety of needs ("necessities") becomes almost inexhaustible. The alleged coercions of life—beyond some tiny fixed minimum—are really not embedded in nature at all.

Even when most people were impoverished, necessity was a category of choice. It was the name given to alternate social institutions, such as slavery and monarchy, under conditions of deprivation. But human beings were in charge of necessity even then. Systemic industrialism makes this clear—which accounts, perhaps, for the political ferment of our age. "Need" is redefined in the context of freedom. Yes, there will always be a very few necessities, but most of these are set before us directly as choices or covertly as social policies.

We move from natural necessities—such as in the fearful life of rural and hunting cultures, where each moment was a life and death struggle—toward self-consciousness about personally and culturally chosen necessities. Survival seems hardly a matter of choice. Institutions gained legitimacy by providing for it, but today, this is only a tiny fraction of their total functions—for example, as we move from the defensive to the welfare or communal state. Our lives are spent in making choices well beyond the issue of survival. It is a far different matter, having chosen a career, to be required to learn its disciplines. This is necessity, but of a decidedly different sort from natural necessities. The city dweller must pay attention to garbage and traffic if he wants to survive. But the city itself is a function of explicit choices. The instrumental necessities that follow choice are different in kind from those that confronted the shepherd, farmer, or hunter, who inherited his place and destiny. Modern necessity follows upon personal choices; traditional necessity was rooted in their absence. But in both cases, necessity is really a political idea.

We know we are free, yet we still feel trapped. Released from the institutions of necessity, we still find ourselves hedged in by inescapable demands. We resent those who enforce them and yet are afraid of our freedom. Our anger therefore seldom breaks out into open revolt, for to succeed in revolution is to accept the burdens of being free. That is perhaps more frightening than coercion itself. We detest and love our jailers; modern politics becomes peculiarly totalitarian, not because some people want authority—they always did—but because most of us really beg them to take it.[1] The populist dictatorship and the corporation are norms of modern sociality. Finally, since we do not want to admit that we have surrendered our freedom, we adopt an ideology of industrial inevitability in order to provide ourselves with an alibi.

It is characteristic of industrial societies, however, for self-definition to be the primary category of biography. Even modern theories of determinism leave open, paradoxically, the possibility for change by the action of the newly "awakened" person. That, after all, is the intention both of revolutionary ideologies and psychoanalytic therapies. For traditional cultures, as it was with one's father, so it will be with one's self and one's children. This "natural" dictation is in striking contrast to the variability of industrial societies even when perceived as inevitable. Yet, "I want" becomes "I need." The assertion of personality is distorted by a lack of ability to be self-critical. A sign of our inexperience with self-definition, the assimilation of wants to needs converts choice into necessity again—this time a psychological necessity. Wants, being nearly insatiable, drive us where we have to go. In that way, the very center of freedom—self-definition—is surrendered thankfully to necessity again.

The confusion of wants with needs also shows up as social pathology. The forces that produce the manipulated market of mass societies produce the "demanding" child. Our ambivalent need for necessity is thereby collectivized. Again, however, we do it by disguising it as freedom. By clogging the market, we find safety in large numbers of goods, messages, and people. Choice is thereby converted into random action and becomes invisible. So we have the strange situation of avoiding responsibility and being "oppressed" by vast ranges of choices. Under traditional necessity we really did not have much to choose among. Freedom was then a dream and revolution a function of slavery. The case is different with us; but, like the prisoners in Plato's cave, we prefer the safety of the shadow world of coercion to the rigors of the sunlight.

The shift from necessity to freedom is latent in systemic industrialism. Its present coercive character and its tendency to foster dependent human beings are in large measure results of the distortions worked upon us by traditional scarcity. If systemic industrialism promises anything, it is the transformation of rigidity into variety, of natural demand into self-chosen career. This message is getting through the noise. A renaissance of activity already appears in the experimentalism of our young, in the emergence of multicareer biographies, in our students moving away from the regular course of things for a time. We have even begun to normalize bohemianism. Bank clerks and bureaucrats, still afflicted by expectations of regularity and order, now wear their hair long, don new and colorful costumes, find themselves far more tolerant of sexual "deviance," and even smoke pot and collect modern art. No doubt, much of this is superficial, a ready victim of commercialization. Yet, these straws of change remain elusive enough so that the market never quite captures them. They open a gap for the possibilities of freedom. What we lack, however, is an education in taste, which is something industrial society needs more urgently than "training." Ironically, the liberal arts, which do just this, are today in greater danger than ever before—one more symptom perhaps of an "escape from freedom."

III

Once upon a time everything had its place and everyone knew what was required of him or her. Neatness, busyness, and calculations expressed the moral preferences of that coherent world. The virtues of hard work, the "bourgeois virtues," were embedded in a metaphysical anthropology. But only as long as we believed society and industry to be instrumental to otherworldly ends could we perpetuate the myth of operationalism here on earth. But means are never neutral and are formed by and help to form the ends of which they are extensions.

Hence, it takes no special insight to understand "efficiency" as a term of valuation. Our language and our practice are filled with its moralistic derivatives. "Wasteful" and "lazy" are judgments posing as descriptions. Efficiency, to be sure, has a peculiar relevance to the functioning of machinery, but even there it is a way of prizing and appraising. Thus, we applaud a combination of wires and gears that does its job with the least possible expenditure of energy. Moral geometry infects us with the notion that the shortest distance is also the best distance. These are images of sparseness with few prizes for many claimants. Our fascination with speed, our horror at "wasted" time, our anxiety to be bustling and to look busy reflect a perception of reality as a race or contest.

But there are various efficiencies, just as there are different kinds of waste. A machine may be judged by its design under a rule of economy of means and by its employment of appropriate materials. This is both economic and aesthetic. Lowest cost is clearly desirable. And it is appropriate to speak of a "beautiful piece of engineering" or to express pleasure at the facile solution of a problem. Yet, there are times that, with a certain contrariness, we enjoy doing something with more rather than less. And a bird watcher's "stroll" would be inefficient at fifty miles per hour, even if less energy were used to accomplish it. In other words, criteria for a good machine tell us only about one kind of efficiency.

It becomes a problem when we extend efficiency beyond the

machine to societies. Yes, the machine provides a partial and useful mode. With energy and material in short supply, there is virtue in using it economically. To get the best result from the least effort is not only practical but good. But, if traditional and rigid categories of scarcity vanish, then machinelike efficiencies are no longer believable. In the face of technical facility, which must meet limits of time, resources, and energy, we can afford a society that permits a more complete response to aesthetic sensibilities as to the notion of "results" more generally. Continuing our appreciation of classic simplicity and of functionalism, we know that we do not thereby exhaust the possibilities of taste. We do enjoy adornment, even if it *does* nothing. We want to try out unsuitable materials even if other materials would do the job better. Above all, we want to put our own stamp on an object even if more competent object-makers are around. It may be more efficient to settle for communal kitchens or to swallow tablets that help us meet our nutritional requirements. Still, the joys of eating good food really find no surrogate in chemistry.

As we take account of these human responses, we depart from the common sense of efficiency. For example, without quite knowing why, we resent building public structures according to narrow economic criteria only. It is instructive that the Great Depression, surely a time of "scarcity," gave us public works that were not merely useful. Murals and libraries, public parks and poems, oils and watercolors—strange how these became affordable when we had to put people to work under threat of social dissolution. Stranger still that under conditions of "affluence," public buildings like the Pentagon, U.S. post offices, or modern schools (especially without windows and adornment) are impoverished and impoverishing to the human senses.

Traditional efficiency, still holding our loyalty, is revealed as a function of narrowed perspective and not of the situation's resources. Nor are aesthetic considerations the only ones that challenge it. Of course, we do not want an incompetent surgeon because he has a good "bedside manner." But we need the relatively inefficient "mother" in preference to the public creche. Tender loving care—TLC—tells us to fondle, croon to, and hold babies for the sake of their human survival. The pleasure that attends making something for one's own use is a commonplace. Even our marketing society recognizes this, when, for example, it touts the personal contribution of the homemaker in preparing premixed cakes and pies.

Ignoring all of this in a burst of rationalist enthusiasm, traditional efficiency in fact leads to our wasteful society. For example, anyone who has tried to eat in a restaurant that uses mass-produced food products must be appalled at the amount of nourishment that fills its garbage pails. So-called convenience foods, such as TV dinners, are characterized more by the efficiency of their production than by their edibility. Our behavior is really quite revealing. Efficiency can provide for an adequate diet—chemically. However, except under emergency conditions—for example, for the very poor or for "C" rations on a battlefield—supplying adequate diets is rejected. Thus the very efficiency we boast of becomes the source of the pollution that chokes industrial societies.

Food waste is only an illustrative and obvious case in point. Facing increasing environmental decay, we still fall back on traditional efficiency to avoid waste. But our indigestible heap of discarded goods is a consequence of our "economies" in production. Hence, to increase efficiency is to increase waste! Consider, by contrast, how carefully we guard a personal object, a gift, our child's crude handicraft. We cherish them in recognition of the fact that something went into them that is precious in itself. Mere products, lacking aesthetic and loving qualities, are partially used and then thrown away without care. The heaps of discarded automobiles that meet the eye when one travels across the country are symbolic of the waste to which efficiency leads. Mechanism, in short, is quite effective as long as the inhabitants of society are machines. Since we are not, mechanism turns out to be a disaster.

Consumer discards are only one part of our wasteful efficiency. We are, in more serious ways, a wasteful society. We rationalize a vast production of weapons, planes, tanks, submarines, and rockets as necessary for "defense." Simultaneously, we agree that their use could signal our defeat—that is, a failure of "defense." They serve, we say, as "deterrence" and are effective only as long as they sit quietly in stockpiles and are not used. Even where we achieve peace agreements, military production still continues. The so-called peace dividend resulting from the Vietnam "truce" simply vanished in an enlarged military budget. As Mr. Nixon talked of a "generation of peace," his military staff was already testifying about the next generation of armaments. There was only a touch of political dishonesty and irony in the rhetoric. Rather, it indicated how we all fail to comprehend modern social economy. It is inconceivable to us that a society would not have to find ways to throw away part of its productive capacity. Its release for other social uses would, we fear, result in a society that could not be controlled or in a population of spoiled clients who got what they did not earn. Ironically, this is precisely what we have—a society where efficiency produces pollution and where make-work practices produce dependents. Rather than face that fact, we attempt to solve problems that appear by doing the things that create the problems themselves. Thus, military production is an almost classic symbol of institutionalized wastefulness,

which, when justified as "defense," becomes acceptable to our efficient society.

Traditional efficiency and modern waste are not antagonists at all
but are related to each other almost as cause and effect. While criticizing them, however, we cannot dismiss entirely the values that they
preserve. It is a far different matter to recognize the need to discover a
modern concept of efficiency. In it, economy of means retains its virtue. The preciousness of finite resources and time demand, however, a
more careful selection of relevant efficiencies. As we shall see, that
leads us directly to playfulness. In the shift from necessity to freedom,
efficiencies, too, become functions of human autonomy.

IV

The iron laws of industrialism turn out to be imperatives of human
policy. The rule that connects work and wealth is everywhere and sec-
retly eroded. The worker goes through the motions to qualify for a paycheck, knowing all the while that he is not really needed. His place on
the assembly line, in the service industry, or in the office is a type of
social therapy, survival politics, and continuing habit. But he is re-
placeable almost at will, and not necessarily by other human beings.
He thus receives payments but not wages. Necessity turns out to be a
function of social decision, and efficiency, misreading the human
being as a machine, ends in waste. The upshot is a society whose root
assumptions no longer apply. It is this that identifies our moral crisis.
When the values of a society no longer hold the allegiance of its members, then we call that society incoherent. When those values are empty, then that society becomes hollow. That, and not just inadequate adjustment of this or that social arrangement, is what is going on. We
have not merely lost God; we did that many decades ago. We have not
just moved away from classical moral values; these vanished along
with the elites that carried them. We are losing, instead, the very
values that formed industrial society itself.

The experience of people in a society undergoing this loss is one of
anguish, despair, and bitterness. And insofar as it is publicly denied,
people also experience a frightening puzzlement. The so-called lazy
worker only reflects this valuelessness. The demoralized citizen is not
disloyal but in a desperate search for disappearing loyalties. The sabotage of modern society is not a testimony to man's obtuseness but is a
symptom of the felt absence of anything worth preserving. Because
this is becoming increasingly evident, even worthwhile reforms cannot really succeed. Presuming the continued existence of values that
are disappearing, the reformers can only temporarily ameliorate con-

ditions. Job enrichment and the humanization of the workplace, like
political reform and efforts to secure economic justice, are born under
a dark cloud. They count on the persistence of traditional industrial
values like saving, and on the just connection of work and wealth. Under the conditions produced in systemic industrialism they fail, or they
become subversive of the very structure they must shore up. This tells
us why current reform is so shaky. As soon as its import becomes evident, we must retreat from it, for we need systemic industrialism. It
tells us why political and social élan is found these days among the
outsiders. Insiders, such as the liberals and the children of the middle
class, flock toward the fringe, adopting its language, style, and values. Thus, for a moment they turn back the clock to a tradition that
once worked.

The erosion of work, necessity, and efficiency point to playfulness as
a fit replacement for the sober rationalism of industrial life. Unfortunately, play comes to us shadowed by scarcity. We are biased against
the playful; we also envy those free enough to play. The rich man, the
child, the hobo, and the retiree are objects of scorn and desire. We ele-
vate childhood, sacrificing for it, or proclaiming inanely, as in com-
mencement addresses, that it is the "future." On the other hand, we
limit the experience of children through schools that hedge them in,
train them for "maturity," and force them to leave playfulness behind.
Despite more than a century of reform and decades of turmoil, our
schools by and large retain their rigidity. Public policy channels
schooling into a narrow vocationalism. School architecture is still impoverished. The accusation of "waste" or "coddling" is guaranteed to
send any school board into retreat. Taxpayer revolts are more and more
frequent. The hobo is also a folk hero. But we keep him locked up, too,
in slums like the Bowery in New York or the West Side in Chicago.
We are avid for gossip about the rich, while sneering at the "jet set."
And we exalt retirement, while we cripple the retiree economically and
exile him socially.

There is, to be sure, warrant for the derogation of playfulness, for we
make it impossible to be playful about anything important. Childhood
is reduced to childishness, which is not so much playful as trivial. The
hobo sinks into social limbo; he is not the wandering singer of earlier
ages but today's "bum." The jet set plays its social and sexual games in
public and for public amusement. The senior citizen is certainly senior
but is scarely a citizen. So we can justify our dismissal of play as recreation, escapism, or irresponsibility. Respectable adults are allowed to
play, too, but only under severe restrictions of time and as a self-con-
scious break from the real world.

Play, however, is too important a matter to be resigned to triviality.

As an alternative to efficiency it has its source in human nature and history. In the sober world of industrialism, play is set aside. But the root of play is *poesis,* the ability to make things, to have experiences, and to share joy with others in song, dance, poem, and gesture.[2] As children, we express play's genius when we build our sand castles. We carry it with us into maturity when we exhibit that curiosity that drives us to the stars, to climb mountains, or to probe the fascinations of molecular structure. The teen-ager demonstrates playful erudition in his interests. Simultaneously, he is learning to devalue his play. His schooling is radically ignorant of him. The very erudition he shows on his own vanishes when he is being "educated." So we complain that the student won't learn when in fact he is quite learned about matters of his own choosing. Adults, too, are fascinated by hobbies and sports. They still retain a play impulse, but in weakened form and kept severely in check. Something in human beings will not be coerced. Clearly, it is a functionalism ignorant of humanism that condemns playfulness to mere silliness or to moral disaster.

"Playing truant" is greeted with uncomfortable laughter. Since we know—or think we do—that the absence is only temporary, we can accept it. When, however, as increasingly happens, the absentee tries to make it permanent, our laughter ceases. Then we start to worry about "dropouts" and complain of betrayal. Then, too, we invoke the guilt that surrounds playfulness in our society. The youngster who takes a year off to "find himself" is acting on an implicit principle of integrity, which our culture pretends to admire. Even those who, tragically, vanish into the half-world of drugs are making a judgment about the inhumanity of our society, with which most of us agree. It was the respectable adult, after all, who first complained of the "rat race," was cynical about politics, and was convinced that money could buy just about anything or anyone. To drop out of such a situation is a sign of moral sanity, if not of practical wisdom.

Artists who become models of playfulness are also objects of dismay. To be sure, we can be comfortable in the artist's presence when he enters the marketplace and becomes "successful" or takes a teaching job. For those of us who are neither dropouts nor artists, play is a limited and limiting situation. Thus, we do not know play at all. And, by returning to the "real" world of seriousness as we must, we atone for enjoying our release.

Playfulness is everywhere sacrificed to "reality." Unfortunately, the sacrifice is pointless, for the real world to which we return is trivial too. Under industrial conditions, the work we do is unimportant, just as our play is unimportant. Condemning playfulness for the sake of more important matters, we find that both work and play are alike in their deterioration. Habit still separates them, and the connection of work and wealth sets up a barrier between them. But essentially they are more alike than unalike in their unimportance.

Once upon a time, play and work were significant because they were part of each other. In an earlier world, play was the arena of the arts, of philosophy, of the gods themselves. Play was the work of leisure. Then, neither work nor play had the connotations of triviality so poignant today. The outcomes of the life of art are still described as "works." Industrial society, which separated work and play and tried to democratize both, ends by nearly destroying them. Hopefully, that same industrial society opens possibilities for playfulness and work never before imaginable.

Seriousness, in other words, is not the enemy of playfulness. Instead, we contrast work with drudgery [3] and playfulness with dullness. Our society apparently finds room for neither work nor play but for their opposites. Yet, it is inherently roomy when contrasted with scarcity-based societies and traditional aristocracies. To propose playfulness as the source of reconstruction is to seize on qualities of industrialism we have nearly lost—its potency, variability, inclusiveness, and above all the inventiveness that attends its continual rebirth. Despite these promising features, industrial society under the rule of traditional efficiency forces human beings into a shadow world and produces wastefulness of the most disastrous sort. Perhaps under the rule of playfulness, its other virtues can appear.

Utility cannot be the only measure of the significant. True, industrial society is naturally biased toward the instrumental. Functionalism, the "pay-off," and the "bottom line" are guides to what is worthwhile and what isn't. But only as we make choices can we really assess the value of an instrument or measure its effectiveness. And the choices are neither in the universe nor self-evident. Paradoxically, while pushing us in the direction of instrumentalism, industrial society opens up possibilities of freedom and variety. Such a society, in other words, may also be approached from the side of taste and style.

It is not a little ironic that the battle cry of the 1960s, "Do your own thing," comes back to us now. Arising in a crusade against systemic industrialism, it turns out to be the imperative of an alternate industrialism. The realistic preconditions for playfulness are well established in our technology and in our economy. But we still think we are caught in the demands of drudgery. It is this illusion that fosters our descent into triviality. The application of playfulness to work life is the clue to industrial society's humanization.

V

Efficient industrialism produces a wasteful society, generating ever growing piles of garbage. A shift to playfulness is not, therefore, the surrender of an effective society for its opposite. In fact, the reverse is likely. After all, it is under systemic industrialism that we have learned to live by the morality of the discard. So careless are we of things that we cannot escape the dung heap. It is not only objects that are matters of indifference to us. Human beings are put out of the way in schools, the military services, or retirement communities. And even our offices, shops, and factories look like storage facilities. In them, while we are allegedly productive, we are really underemployed and redundant.

Contrast this general wastefulness with our experiences of play. How often do we discard the meaningless object after the initial thrill of possession wears off? The shiny but impersonal toy gathers dust. Meanwhile, the child plays with the wrappings or makes an imaginary house out of the cardboard carton in which the gift was packaged. Occasionally, a new doll moves in. More often, it is the old, worn, torn, and damaged bit of rag that keeps our loyalty. Each of us lights on objects that are peculiarly our own, that we make into our own. Unlike the things that overfill our lives, it is these items that we protect. It is their loss that we mourn, their acquisition that we remember. And it is these things, interacting with our lives, that are *not* wasted at all.

Playfulness, you see, leads to preciousness. The icon is carefully taken from its place at festival time and used in sacred ritual. By contrast, the public building of our society is more abused than used. We care for our homes and are indifferent to the motel room or public lobby. When we erect a monument, we respect it to be sure, but only by alienating it from both use and love. Even here, however, the trend is toward disdain. Museums keep on adding guards; city halls are defaced; churches are robbed. The epidemic of graffiti on walls and subways in cities like New York is a pathetic attempt to personalize the impersonal.

Houses built efficiently, as in public programs, get the same treatment as other consumer goods. The user cannot be convinced that it is really his home. He knows better, for he experiences the carelessness with which it was built. He is oppressed, too, by a bureaucracy that intrudes into his life space with empty rules that disregard him as a person.

The message of our indifferent consumerism, of the abuse of the object, has not been received. Rather than pay attention to it, we indulge our prejudices against vulgar humanity. "If only people would disappear," we seem to be saying, "what a fine, clean, and lovely place this earth would be." Chemicals are set to work to clean up the disasters of past chemistry and lay up new disasters for tomorrow. Rules grow more rigid and penalties for their violation increase, but to no avail. In an indifferent society, indifference remains the rule.

Traditional efficiency leads directly to a concept of "success" defined by amounts of expenditure and acquisition. Playfulness, on the other hand, demands choices of both means and ends. We can easily believe that a laborer discards his shovel, is careless of a machine, or is inattentive to his part of the job. We cannot imagine an artist as cavalier with his canvas, paints, or brushes. For the toolmaker, tools are extensions of his own being. The hobbyist babies his equipment. The homeowner cares for his furnishings. The worshiper treads softly and respectfully into his church. The feel of my own bat or tennis racket is real enough to me, even if invisible to anyone else. In the experiences of playfulness there are no *mere* things. They take their imprint from their users, have histories, and so enter into an organic continuity and are identifiable.

Above all, playfulness is not wild abandon. It has its own standards and norms. These depend, however, on the exercise of choice and the possibility of participation. Organization is an imperative of any human situation and playfulness is no exception. True, bureaucratic organization is said to flow from the needs of very large numbers. But, just as the so-called economies of scale reach a point of diminishing returns, so the benefits of bureaucracy approach limits too. Playfulness poses the issues of size, quantity, and growth in qualitative terms, informing us that these cannot be ends in themselves any longer. Thus, while organization in some form is inevitable, bureaucracy is not.

Industrial society pretended to instrumentalism by presuming fixed natural or transcendent ends. A blind expansionism followed. Territory was acquired; populations expanded; and the market appeared everywhere and in all things. A vast distributive mechanism evolved, justified as efficient by criteria that reduced to blind counting. Incomprehensible state and private bureaucracies appeared that now are falling of their own weight. Few of us, however, are prepared to take the risks of decentralization and growth limitation in their most radical form. Surely these are dangerous, even sloppy. But the upshot of continuing the errors of traditional efficiency is the unchecked rise of manipulative policies that cannot even claim to protect us against nature or society. Our goals disappear even if our rhetoric persists.

When, for example, industrial sabotage becomes epidemic, we turn to gimmicks that reduce it and improve morale temporarily. But we continue to work on the worthless. Our so-called humanizing devices work only for a short time, and we must always keep looking for newer ways of easing the situation. The need to make work worth doing and to work at something worth making is hardly attended to. After all, it does not take genius to figure out that making junk, even as a participatory worker, is still making junk. So, after the fascinations of the latest innovation die down, the situation remains pretty much as before. Perhaps it is even worse, for we cannot escape the uneasy feeling that we may have been tricked.

Bad as efficiency is, it seems to be the "only game in town." We need to be reassured, in other words, that playfulness will not throw us into chaos or a new scarcity. After all, playfulness asks each of us to be about his favorite things, and thus seems to propose a serendipitous and individualistic life just when social needs have become very great. But the radical individual is a creature of mechanistic perceptions and not a human reality. Playfulness and personality emerge from sociality and grow as they are shared. The fear of chaos also ignores the fact that human beings respond to a realistic sense of duty. A playful society would not then be a chaotic society at all, for it would not have to be insanely individualistic in order to protect sanity; nor would it have to be ignorant of emergencies.

We know that the choices of play lead us to accept the most difficult and demanding disciplines. Our sports and hobbies demonstrate this almost to a fault. The agreement to play leads those who agree, to create the possibilities of play. They adopt common and public rules, clear the playing field, find room for spectators, appoint umpires, establish training regimens. In short, a playful society might well be the "contract" society envisioned in democratic political theory but betrayed by traditional efficiency and the economics of greed. Playfulness is not as neat as efficiency perhaps, but it is clearly not the same as anarchy. The presupposition of playfulness is human participation and that, above all, is what mechanism cannot take account of. The rule of efficiency, lacking confidence in human beings, substituted the goad of guilt, the threat of punishment, and the inventiveness of technology for the less obvious but really more effective ordering of autonomy.

Let us admit that in a society built on playfulness rules can only be partial and the participants can never be fully accounted for. An interest, a curiosity, an attractive possibility may lead the player off the field, sometimes when we most need him. But that is the risk of all human encounter, and it is an illusion to think that in a world of human beings such risks can be avoided. To put this differently, a perfect contract does not and cannot exist.

Organization can be seen to emerge from choice and need. Biology is more helpful here than mechanics. After all, it is beings and not parts that inhabit our environment. Garret Hardin, for example, commented:

... It is not necessary that there exist in some mind the idea of a beautifully adapted machine in order that this machine may come into existence. It is enough if nature be permitted to try countless experiments—"mutations" we now call them—among which a tiny percentage produces good results. Each such successful experiment is saved by natural selection and used as a base for further experimentation and natural selection. Mutation occurs at random and entails enormous waste, but natural selection acts like a ratchet to preserve each tiny element of progress; thus do nature's beautifully adapted machines come into being. There need be no blueprint for design to emerge; trials and error suffice. Something of this sort must have been meant by the poet William Blake, who said, "To be in error and to be cast out is a part of God's design." Design, can emerge from blind waste . . .[4]

Admittedly, this guarantees continuing harshness in experience and points out that playfulness may be enjoyable but is not necessarily kind. As an alternative to the demoralization of industrial society's failing attempt to protect against risk, the pain of evolutionary error is preferable. At any rate, we need not choose between organization and chaos in the move from efficiency to playfulness. Both will be organized, but in radically different ways. The difference is crucial. Traditional efficiency seeks protection at the cost of impoverishing life's quality. Essentially it takes the emergency as normal. But permanent crisis is unbelievable and industrial organization finally comes to rely on social myths and blind authority.

The risks of playfulness are great. Play always carries with it the chance of failure, of the dangerous choice, of the dead end. But play can be an organizing value for a society where the energies are available for moving beyond mere survival. Risky though it may be, at least play does not demand the surrender of our human capacities. Significantly, playfulness is a term of autonomy and participation, the very qualities whose absence identifies the dissatisfactions of our dissatisfied society and the failures of man at work. And that is why playfulness is, paradoxically, a very serious matter indeed.

1. For a classic discussion of this point, see Erich Fromm, *Escape from Freedom* (New York: Holt, Rinehart, 1941).

2. In a brief autobiographical comment, Albert Einstein spoke of "holy curiosity," and traced it, and his work, to childhood experience. Jacques Barzun rightly called science the "glorious entertainment."

3. We tend to make work and labor synonymous in current usage. Yet we do

not speak of the "labors" of Da Vinci; we do speak of the "labors" of Hercules. The former are properly called "works." Similarly, we would not really think of a ditch as the "works" of the men who dug it, though we might think of a canal as the "work" of its designer. The issue is not really semantic, however. We need to make a useful distinction that our language has blurred. Marx tried to make it as well, identifying man as a "worker," corrupted by exploitation into doing mere "wage labor."

4. "In Praise of Waste," by Garret Hardin, an occasional paper on the meaning of biological thought in human affairs (National Institute of Public Affairs), p. 1.

Epilogue

Roy P. Fairfield

Recently one of my students sent me some notes from his log, in which he recounted the story of his nine-year-old son, Andy. He observed that the child felt lonely when he saw the bus driver go home from work in an empty bus. Somehow or other I identified with the boy's poignant loneliness, scribbled a poem, and sent it to him through his father, Pete.

SOLITUDE?

He drives.
the bus home
empty ev'ry nite
wrapped in the warmth
of people memories
populating street corners
with loving faces
he welcomed
each new tomorrow . . .

Pete reports that Andy has my poem stuck to his bedroom wall.

Maybe we are rearing a generation who can more quickly identify with workers at their workplaces, whether such places are at a fixed point in a factory or rolling through the streets. I have great hope that the Andys of this land will imagine brave new ways to extend human imagination and improve the human condition.

Contributors

STEVANNE AUERBACH-FINK

A consultant in child care and education, Ms. Auerbach-Fink is the author of *Parents and Child Care,* a study of parental expectations for child-care services, published in 1974 in cooperation with the Far West Laboratory for Educational Research and Development. She is a graduate of Queens College and George Washington University, and received a Ph.D. from Union Graduate School, Yellow Springs, Ohio, in 1973. Ms. Auerbach-Fink served as the child-development specialist of the National Research and Demonstration Program at the Office of Economic Opportunity. She was responsible for establishing the first child-care centers for the children of federal employees at the Office of Education, HEW, and OEO. She is the mother of four children.

IVAR BERG

Dr. Berg is George E. Warren professor of sociology and business at Columbia University Graduate School of Business. Awarded a Ph.D. in sociology from Harvard University, he has been a Woodrow Wilson fellow and Fulbright scholar at the University of Oslo, and a Guggenheim fellow. Professor Berg was associate dean of the faculties at Columbia, 1969-1971, and consultant to the President's Crime Commission, 1966-

1967. He is the author of *Education and Jobs: The Great Training Robbery* (1970) and *Human Resources and Economic Welfare* (1972) and joint author of *Democratic Values and the Rights of Management* (1963, with Eli Ginzberg), *Life Styles of Educated Women* (1966, with Ginzberg, *et al.*), and *Guidance, U.S.A* (1971, with Ginzberg, *et al.*). Professor Berg is a fellow of the American Sociological Association and a member of the American Association for the Advancement of Science.

IRVING BLUESTONE

Mr. Bluestone is the vice-president and director of the General Motors Department of the United Automobile Workers. Since 1945 he has held a variety of positions in the UAW, and has participated in all UAW-GM national contract negotiations since 1948. He received his education at City College of the City University of New York and the University of Bern, Switzerland. Mr. Bluestone is a member of the National Trade Union Council for Human Rights, the board of directors of Martin Luther King Homes, the Citizens Advisory Committee of the University of Michigan, Dearborn, and is cochairman of the American Trade Union Council of the National Committee for Labor, Israel.

ROY P. FAIRFIELD

Coordinator of the Union Graduate School, Yellow Springs, Ohio, Dr. Fairfield has taught social sciences at Antioch, Bates, Hofstra, and Athens Colleges, and at Ohio University. His writing includes *Sands, Spindles and Steeples,* a history of his home town, Saco, Maine, and the editorship of the *Federalist Papers* and *Humanistic Frontiers in American Education*. A graduate of Harvard University, Dr. Fairfield is on the editorial board of *The Humanist* magazine.

MITCHELL FEIN

Mr. Fein is a consulting industrial engineer. Since 1937 he has served more than three hundred companies in a broad range of industries, concentrating on developing ways to increase productivity. He has written numerous articles for technical and trade journals and sections in the *Industrial Engineering Handbook* (3rd ed.) and the *Handbook of Business Administration*. Active in the American Institute of Industrial Engineers, he is adjunct associate professor of industrial engineering at New York University and serves on the arbitration panels of the American Arbitration Association and the State Mediation Boards of New York and New Jersey.

ALAN GARTNER

Codirector of the New Human Services Institute in New York and professor of education at Queens College, City University of New York, Mr. Gartner is the publisher of the periodical *Social Policy.* He is the author, with Frank Riessman, of *The Service Society and the Consumer Vanguard* (1974) and *Public Service Employment: An Analysis of Its History, Problems, and Prospects* (1973), and he has also written *Paraprofessionals and Their Performance* (1971).

LOUISE KAPP HOWE

Ms. Howe, a writer and editor, is the editor of *The Future of the Family* (1973) and *The White Majority* (1970). She received a Ford Foundation Travel and Study Award in 1974 to study women workers and is at work on a book about them, which will be published in 1975.

WALTER KLEEMAN, JR.

Dr. Kleeman is an associate professor in the department of home economics and family living at Western Kentucky University, the design editor of *Furniture News,* and a consultant at Union Graduate School, Yellow Springs, Ohio. He is a fellow of the National Society of Interior Designers and a member of the Human Factors Society, the Ergonomics Research Society (England), and the International Ergonomics Association. Dr. Kleeman is the author of a bibliography, "Interior Ergonomics: Significant Dimensions in Interior Design and Planning."

BENNETT KREMAN

Mr. Kreman is a free-lance writer.

MICHAEL MACCOBY

A fellow of the Institute for Policy Studies, Washington, D.C., director of the Harvard Project on Technology, Work, and Character, and a practicing psychoanalyst, Mr. Maccoby is currently directing the Bolivar Project, sponsored by Harman International Industries and the United Automobile Workers. The goal is to restructure work in the Harman factory according to principles of security, equity, individuation, and democracy. He is the author, with Erich Fromm, of *Social Character in a Mexican Village* (1970).

J. DAVITT MCATEER

Solicitor for Safety Affairs with the United Mine Workers of America, Mr. McAteer teaches courses on coal-mine health and safety at West Virginia College of Law. He is the author of *Coal Mine Health and Safety in West Virginia* (1973), and he worked for two years for Ralph Nader's Center for the Study of Responsive Law.

MYRA A. PEABODY

Ms. Peabody was for fifteen years a secretary at the Electric Boat Division of General Dynamics Corporation, about which she has written. She is now a free-lance writer, author of articles in the *National Retired Teachers Association Journal, The Humanist,* and *The Marian.*

HOWARD B. RADEST

Dr. Radest received his Ph.D. in philosophy from Columbia University, where he was a Phi Beta Kappa. He is director of the School of American Studies and professor of philosophy at Ramapo College in New Jersey. Author of *On Life and Meaning* (1964) and *Toward Common Ground* (1969) and editor of *To Seek a Humane World* (1971), Dr. Radest is a consultant to the New Jersey Public Broadcasting authority for a film on work. He is a member of the American Philosophical Association and the International Humanist and Ethical Union.

MARCUS RASKIN

Codirector of the Institute for Policy Studies in Washington, D.C., Mr. Raskin is the author of *Being and Doing* (1971), and has coauthored *After Twenty Years: Alternatives to the Cold War in Europe* (1965, with Richard J. Barnet) and *American Manifesto: What's Wrong with Amer-*

ica and What We Can Do About It (1970, with Barnet). With Barnard Fall, he edited *Viet-Nam Reader* (1965).

FRANK RIESSMAN

Mr. Riessman is the editor of *Social Policy,* a professor of education at Queens College of the City University of New York, and, with Alan Gartner, is codirector of the New Human Services Institute in New York City. With Mr. Gartner, he is the author of *The Service Society and the Consumer Vanguard* (1974) and *Public Service Employment: An Analysis of Its History, Problems, and Prospects.* He has also written *New Careers for the Poor: The Nonprofessional in Human Services* (1965).

M. H. ROSS

Mr. Ross is the administrator of the Fairmont Clinic, Fairmont, West Virginia. He is a fellow of the American Public Health Association and a director of the Group Health Association of America, and was formerly a union organizer for the Congress of Industrial Organizations' southern campaign in coal and metal mining.

JACK RUSSELL

Mr. Russell is a senior research assistant at ACRA, Inc., in Washington, D.C., and a graduate student at the Union Graduate School, Yellow Springs, Ohio. For the past three years he has been doing research on casual laborers, industrial temporary-help agencies, and the participation of street-corner workers in the labor force.

RICHARD J. SCHONBERGER

Associate professor of management at the University of Nebraska, Mr. Schonberger's interest in the inflexibility of the workplace began when he was a civil servant at the U.S. Naval Base at Guantánamo Bay, Cuba. There he discovered that many American housewives wanted to work as teachers, nurses, and clerks, but were prevented from doing so because they could only work part-time. He wrote a master's thesis, "The Relationship Between Part-Day Employment and the Role of the Woman in the Home," at the University of Iowa in 1968. Mr. Schonberger is a member of the Academy of Management, Social Issues Division.

ROBERT SCHRANK

Mr. Schrank is a project specialist for the Ford Foundation. A former factory worker, union official, and plant manager, he specializes in problems concerning humanizing the workplace.

GEORGE STRAUSS

Dr. Strauss is a professor in the School of Business Administration and acting director of the Institute of Industrial Relations, University of California, Berkeley. He has been an associate and acting dean of the School of Business Administration at Berkeley and also managing editor of the journal *Industrial Relations*. He is coauthor of three books, *The Local Union, Personnel,* and *Human Behavior in Organizations,* as well as the author of articles in the fields of labor relations and organizational behavior.

FRANKLIN WALLICK

Mr. Wallick is the editor of the United Auto Workers' weekly newsletter, *UAW Washington Report*. He is the author of *The American Worker: An Endangered Species* (1972), and is a councilor to the Society for Occupational and Environmental Health. After World War II Mr. Wallick was a United Nations famine-relief worker in China and taught at Yenching University and the Peking American School. He worked in Wisconsin to build a rejuvenated, progressive Democratic Party, and during 1969 and 1970 he was deeply involved in the campaign to pass a national worker health and safety law.

EDWARD WALSH

Assistant research scientist at the University of Michigan, Mr. Walsh is on a leave of absence to study the conflict among the Teamsters, the United Farm Workers, and the growers in California, on a grant from the Ford Foundation. He worked as a part-time garbageman for three years in Ann Arbor to gather material for his dissertation, "Job Stigma and Self-Esteem," and also studied garbagemen in Detroit and Minneapolis. He is a member of the American Garbagemen's Association.